PRAYING WITH AUTHORITY AND POWER

Taking Dominion Through Scriptural Prayers and Prophetic Decrees

Barbara L. Potts

Scripture quotations in this book are taken from the New King James Version, unless otherwise noted in the text. Any emphasis in Scripture quotes is the author's own. The following Bible translations were used: *The Open Bible*, New King James Version, copyright © 1997, 1990, 1985, 1983 by Thomas Nelson Publishers, Inc., *The Holy Bible*, New International Version (NIV), copyright © 1978 by New York International Bible Society, *The Amplified Bible*, Expanded Edition (AMP, TAB), copyright © 1987 by The Zondervan Corporation and The Lockman Foundation, *The First Scofield Reference Bible*, King James Version (KJV), copyright © 1986 by Barbour and Company, Inc., *The Message* , New Testament, Psalms, and Proverbs in Contemporary Language (MES), copyright © 1993,1994,1995 by Eugene H. Peterson, NavPress Publishing Group.

The editor has taken the liberty to respectfully acknowledge the Lord by capitalizing specific words relating to His Kingdom. These are: (the) Covenant, (the) Church, (the) Body (of Christ), Believers, the Blood (of the Lamb); and any pronouns referring to the Deity. McDougal Publishing also has chosen to *not* respectfully acknowledge satan by *not* capitalizing names relating to his kingdom, such as satan, allah, devil, and (the) enemy.

McDougal Publishing is a ministry of The McDougal Foundation, Inc., a Maryland nonprofit corporation dedicated to spreading the Gospel of the Lord Jesus Christ to as many people as possible in the shortest time possible.

Published by:

McDougal Publishing
P.O. Box 3595
Hagerstown, MD 21742-3595
www.mcdougalpublishing.com

ISBN 1-58158-081-9

Printed in the United States of America
For Worldwide Distribution

ACKNOWLEDGMENTS

I give praise and thanksgiving to the *Holy Spirit* for teaching me how to pray and for guiding me in the writing of this manuscript.

I thank all the *intercessors* who prayed for me to realize this dream and bring it to fruition.

TABLE OF CONTENTS

"CALL TO ME, AND I WILL ANSWER YOU, AND SHOW YOU GREAT AND MIGHTY THINGS, WHICH YOU DO NOT KNOW."

Jeremiah 33:3

INTRODUCTION

GOD'S PROMISE TO ISRAEL

The Lord gave the children of Israel a wonderful promise in Jeremiah 29:10-13:

> *For thus says the LORD: After seventy years are completed at Babylon,* I will **perform My good word** toward you, *and cause you to return to this place. For I know the thoughts I think toward you, says the LORD, thoughts of peace and not of evil, to give you a* future and a hope. *Then you will* call upon Me and go and pray to Me, and **I will listen to you.** *And* you will seek Me and find Me, *when you search for Me with all your heart.*

God was saying to Israel that after the appointed time of judgment in Babylon was complete (God had exiled them to Babylon because of their rebellion and wickedness), He would then come and fulfill His promises to them ("perform My word"). He said He would cause them to return to "this place" (Jerusalem), which was not only their homeland but the place that represented God's covenant promises. He said that He would come to them as they sought Him "with all their heart." He would hear their prayers once again ("I will listen to you") and restore them to a place of covenant blessing.

PRESENT-DAY APPLICATION

This has an application for us as intercessors today. In Scripture, Babylon prophetically represents the "World Order," or the kingdom of this world. God is the One who initiates intercession. And as He draws us to call upon Him (verse 12), in accordance with His perfect timetable (seventy represents perfection and completeness) and in accordance with His Word, He says He will visit us and *perform His good word* (verse 10). This then fulfills our future of hope (verse 11). During this time of visitation, we will see a manifestation of His presence and demonstration of His Word in our midst. The result will be the reemergence of His covenant blessings within the Body of Christ. This will usher in, not only revival and Harvest, but the end-times Church. Christ's pure, spotless Bride (Ephesians 5:27) will arise and shine as the true Light of the World (Matthew 5:14) as the glory of the Lord rises upon her! (Isaiah 60:1).

MY CALL

In my twenty-five years as an intercessor, my most challenging assignment came about three years ago when the Lord called me to a daily 2 to 3 AM prayer watch over the Church. About this same time I had a vivid dream which impressed me as sort of an "exclamation point" to what God was calling me to. And it continues to propel me forward in this call.

My dream...

In my dream I was at a seaside town with people I didn't know. There were signs that a terrible storm was approaching. The rough waves were battering the coastal houses, and the sky was very dark and ominous. The wind was blowing fiercely. The fearful people looked to me for guidance, and so I proposed a plan for safety. I told everyone to get up to the higher ground away from the threatening winds and flooding sea. At that point, I heard a loud, authoritative voice from above say: "TAKE DOMINION!"

Upon awakening, as I meditated on this dream, I was reminded of the Lord Jesus on the Sea of Galilee in a boat with the disciples. When a storm came up, the Scripture says He "rebuked the winds and the sea, and there was a great calm." But first He rebuked *the disciples* and said, "Why are you fearful, O you of little faith?" (Matthew 8:26). The picture I had concerning my dream was that the Lord was calling me (and all intercessors) to not relinquish territory, but to *stand the ground, in faith,* and rebuke the enemy in the same authority that He exercised while on earth. Indeed, Jesus said:

> *"He who believes in Me, the works that I do he will do also; and greater works than these will he do."*   John 14:12

EQUIPPING THE BODY

My prayer watch continues, but has expanded to a longer watch (5-7 AM), which now encompasses the nations as well. During this sequestered time before the Throne, the Lord continues to teach me about spiritual warfare, taking dominion, and praying with authority and power. My passion is to inspire and equip Believers with solid biblical principles and strategies of intercession, so that they can move forward in the authority that they have been given by God to fulfill their commission to take dominion in their lives and in the earth.

What most impressed the people when Jesus began His earthly ministry was the authority with which He cast out demons and healed the sick and oppressed…

> *Then they were all amazed and spoke among themselves, saying, "**What a word this is! For with AUTHORITY AND POWER He commands** the unclean spirits, and they come out.*   Luke 4:36

This is the Word of *Dominion—of Authority and Power—*which we have been given by God to establish His Kingdom in the earth and to cast out the kingdom of darkness.

TAKING DOMINION WITH THE SWORD OF THE SPIRIT

In spite of what the media would have us think, the world's future is not in the hands of Islamic terrorists, the United Nations, America's military might, or any other institution of men. God has a plan for world judgment and redemption that He will implement *through the prayers of His people.* As the Body of Christ activates the Sword of the Spirit by agreeing with and declaring the Word of God in prophetic prayers and decrees, we will fulfill God's command to take dominion, and we will see God's Kingdom come and His will be done on earth as it is in Heaven (Matthew 6:10). Amen !

Author's note: *This compilation of prayer strategies, principles, prophetic decrees and scriptural prayers is by no means an exhaustive study. Rather, it is an outflow of my personal spiritual journey in the area of intercession, undergirded by the Word of God, and amplified by quotes from men and women of faith who have inspired me on my way. My prayer is that it will in turn inspire the reader in the purpose and power of prayer, and motivate him or her to a deeper passion for and commitment to the discipline of intercession.*

PART ONE

❖ ❖ ❖

PREPARATION FOR SPIRITUAL WARFARE

Basic principles of prevailing in prayer.

Chapter One

THE CALL TO PRAY

"Pray without ceasing." 1 Thessalonians 5:17

WHAT IS PRAYER?

The great preacher A.B. Simpson once said, "Prayer is the link that connects us with God. It is the bridge that spans every gulf and bears us over every abyss of danger or need." This wondrous link with our Creator is the high privilege and earnest duty of every child of God. We could say that prayer is that petition from the heart of His people that touches the heart of God and moves His hand.

Intercession is a specific kind of prayer where the one praying takes a stance in between a person (or need/situation) and God, and petitions God on their behalf. Rick Joyner has said, "Intercession is no longer just an option for the Church. The basic calling of the Church is to be a 'house of prayer for all nations (Mark 11:17).' "[1] Indeed, the Lord admonishes us through the apostle Paul to "pray without ceasing" (1 Thessalonians 5:17). Paul instructed the Ephesians to gird themselves with the "whole armor of God," and take "the sword of the Spirit, which is the word of God; *praying always* with all prayer and supplication in the Spirit… *with all perseverance*" (Ephesians 6:13-18, emphasis added). We see from this passage that, whatever else prayer may embrace, first and foremost, it involves engaging in spiritual warfare. When writing to his protégé, Timothy, Paul put prayer first in ministry priority: "I exhort *first of all* that supplications, prayers, intercessions, and giving of thanks be made for all men…. For this is good and acceptable in the sight of God…I desire therefore that men pray everywhere, lifting up holy hands" (1 Timothy 2:1, 3 and 8). The apostle James admonished the brethren that "the effective, fervent prayer of a righteous man avails much" (James 5:16). It is clear from Scripture that prayer is a high-priority issue with God. We were saved not merely to get to Heaven, but to *bring Heaven to earth* through our love and compassion for others, love and obedience to God, and "effective, fervent prayer."

SCRIPTURAL MODELS

The Scriptures are replete with examples of intercessors from whom we can learn about effective intercession. For example...

MOSES

Moses had the very challenging job of leading a rebellious and faltering people to their destiny in God. He reached this place of leadership after many years of training: crucifying his flesh and edifying his spirit through intimacy with God. Scripture reveals Moses as a man who communed with God. God not only spoke to Moses out of a burning bush, but Exodus 32:11 records that "the Lord spoke to Moses face to face, as a man speaks to his friend." This intimate friendship put him in a place of favor and credibility before God, where his words carried the weight of authority and power.

In Exodus 32 we find the nation of Israel in a critical situation. When Moses ascended Mount Sinai to commune with God and receive the Ten Commandments, the Israelites got impatient waiting for him to return and made their own "god" in the form of a golden calf. God's wrath then "burned hot against them" and He sought to destroy this "stiff-necked people" (verses 9 and 10). Enter Moses, the intercessor (verses 12 and 13):

> *Then Moses pleaded with the LORD his God, and said, "LORD, why does Your wrath burn hot against Your people whom You have brought out of the land of Egypt with great power and with a mighty hand? Why should the Egyptians speak, and say, 'He brought them out to harm them, to kill them in the mountains, and to consume them from the face of the earth'? Turn from Your fierce wrath, and relent from this harm to Your people. Remember Abraham, Isaac, and Israel, Your servants, to whom You swore by Your own self, and said to them, 'I will multiply our descendants as the stars of heaven; and all this land that I have spoken of I give to your descendants, and they shall inherit it forever.' "*

The efficacy of Moses' passionate intercession can be seen in God's response in verse 14:

So the LORD relented from the harm which He said He would do to His people.

In Moses' prayer we can see some key elements of intercession. First of all, he pleaded with God to *honor His Name* before the heathen. For what would the heathen say if this Great God of Israel rescued His people from bondage in Egypt only to destroy them later on? Frequently in the Bible we see people beseeching God to forgive or restore them for *His name's sake*, or for the honor of His name. (We will talk more about this in Chapter Seventeen.) Secondly, Moses *put the Lord in remembrance* of the "everlasting" Covenant (Genesis 17:7) He had made with Abraham, Isaac and Jacob. As we pray God's Word (and covenant promises) back to Him, we are putting Him in remembrance of the veracity of it. For He has said concerning the fulfillment of His own Word:

"So shall My word be that goes forth from My mouth; it shall not return to Me void, but it shall accomplish what I please, and it shall prosper in the thing for which I sent it."   Isaiah 55:11

JEREMIAH

Jeremiah was an Old Testament prophet of God who was probably best remembered for his passionate intercession. In Jeremiah 9:1 he cried out to God, "O that my head were waters, and my eyes a fountain of tears, that I might weep day and night for the slain of the daughter of my people!" Jeremiah's passion for prayer was no doubt fueled in part by the prophetic calling that God placed on his life (see Jeremiah 1:5-10), but also significant was (like Moses') his intimate relationship with the Lord. For he was a man who also spoke with God, as it were, "face to face."

For instance, in Jeremiah 12 we see the prophet grieving over Israel's rebellion and sin. The apparent prosperity of the wicked and their blindness to their imminent judgment were deeply troubling to this man of God. And so Jeremiah boldly questioned God's dealings with these wayward people, while reminding God of his own faithfulness, as though he was speaking to God freely, in His presence:

Righteous are You, O LORD, when I plead with You; You let me talk with You about Your judgments. Why does the way of the wicked prosper? Why are those happy who deal so treacherously?... You are near in their mouth but far from their mind. But You, O LORD, know me; You have seen me, and You have tested my heart toward You. Pull them out like sheep for the slaughter.... How long will the land mourn...for the wickedness of those who dwell there, because they said, "He will not see our final end." Jeremiah 12:1-4

Passion fueled by intimacy and confidence are key elements of effective intercession. Jeremiah was bold before God, and, as New Covenant Believers, we are exhorted to "come *boldly* to the throne of grace, that we may obtain mercy and find grace to help in time of need" (Hebrews 4:16).

JESUS CHRIST

The greatest scriptural model of an intercessor is our Lord and Savior, Jesus Christ. He is the Great High Priest of the New Covenant, now seated at the right hand of God, who always lives to make intercession for us (see Hebrews 4:14; 10:12 and 7:25 and Romans 8:34). While living on earth, the Scriptures tell us, He spent much time in communion with His Father, as He frequently departed alone to the mountains to pray, and even spent all night in prayer at times (see Luke 6:12). No doubt much of His praying involved interceding for His "sheep." John 17 is perhaps the greatest prayer of intercession in the whole Bible. Here, in the dark hours before His crucifixion, Jesus first interceded for Himself, then for His disciples, and finally for all Believers throughout history. Even as He hung from the cross at Calvary, Jesus was interceding for men with His dying breath: "Father, forgive them; for they know not what they do" (Luke 23:34, KJV).

Jesus remains our Intercessor in Heaven, and He has sent His Holy Spirit to augment our prayers on earth: "For we do not know what we should pray for as we ought, but the *Spirit Himself makes intercession for us* with groanings which cannot be uttered.... He makes intercession for the saints *according to the will of God*" (Romans 8:26-27). Jesus prayed to His Father during His Passion in the Garden of Gethsemane: "Father, if it is Your will, take this cup away from Me; nevertheless *not My will, but Yours, be done*" (Luke 22:42). Praying according to God's will is of paramount importance for effective intercession.

KNOWING THE WILL OF GOD

HIS WILL IS HIS WORD

So how do we *know* what God's will is? His will is expressed in and through His Word: "All Scripture is given by inspiration of God" (2 Timothy 3:16). Further, Scripture contains "all things that pertain to life and godliness" (2 Peter 1:3). Therefore, every situation of life has an applicable scripture (or scriptures) to focus our prayer. Having said this, we must understand that there are general principles which govern our lives as Kingdom children. For instance, the Bible doesn't tell us specifically which person we should marry. But it does say that we should not be "unequally yoked together" (2 Corinthians 6:14). When concerned about things of the future, the Scripture says that we are to not lean on our own understanding, but to trust in the Lord with all our heart. Trusting in the Lord involves believing in, and obeying, His Word. Then as we acknowledge Him (and seek His direction through His Word) in all our ways, *He shall direct our paths* (see Proverbs 3:5 and 6).

When we invoke God's Word in prayer, we can avoid soulish, self-centered prayers that seek to control things according to *our* will. But when our will lines up with His, we can be sure that we are praying prayers that will be answered:

> *Now this is the confidence that we have in Him, that if we ask anything according to His will, he hears us. And if we know that He hears us, whatever we ask, we know that we have the petitions that we have asked of Him.*   1 John 5:14

Jesus said that if we abide in Him and *His words abide in us*, we will ask what we desire and it will be done for us (see John 15:7).

FOUNDATIONAL TRUTH

Some general truths of Scripture (the Will of God) which can provide foundation for intercession are:

- *It is God's desire that ALL men should be saved and live a holy life following His commandments.* His eye is on the Harvest. (See 1 Timothy 2:4; 2 Peter 3:9; Philippians 2:13; Luke 19:10; and Luke 10:2-3.)

- *God's love and mercy overshadow all His dealings with men.* (See John 3:16; Psalm 145:8-9; Lamentations 3:22, 23, 31-33; and James 2:13.)
- *God's covenant promises (which include health and wholeness of mind, body and spirit) are provided through Christ's Atonement, and belong to every born-again child of God.* (See Isaiah 53; 1 Peter 2:24; and Matthew 8:16-17.)
- *God provides for all His children in all stages of need.* (See Philippians 4:13 and19; 1 Corinthians 10:13; and 2 Peter 1:3-4.)
- *All governments and nations will one day be under the sovereign rule of Jesus Christ.* (See Isaiah 9:6-7; Isaiah 33:22; Revelation 11:15; Philippians 2:10-11; and Psalm 2.)
- *The biblical covenant land of Israel will be restored in the Middle East.* God has an everlasting Covenant with Israel, through which He will reveal His glory and His government. (See 1 Chronicles 17:11-27; Amos 9:13-15; Isaiah 9:6-7; and Genesis 17:7-8.)
- *God will be glorified through His Church for all the world to see.* (See John 17:20-23; Philippians 2:9-11; and Matthew 16:18.)
- *The Church and Israel share the same destiny to embody the Kingdom of God in the earth.* God is shaping all history for two groups of covenanted people, Israel and the Church, to come together as "one new man" under the Messiah, Jesus. (See Romans 11 and Ephesians 2:11-16.)

[1] Rick Joyner, "The Perfect Storm," *The Morning Star Prophetic Bulletin* (Wilkesboro, NC: Morning Star Publications, Inc., March 2000), p. 5.

Chapter Two

THE ARMOR OF GOD

"Be strong in the Lord and in the power of His might. Put on the whole armor of God, that you may be able to stand against the wiles of the devil."
Ephesians 6:10-11

ALL PRAYER IS WARFARE

Perhaps you are wondering, "Why all this hype about warfare; can't I just pray?" Well, if you are praying at all, you are already engaging in warfare. For just talking to God makes you the devil's enemy and, thus, his target. The reality is, as soon as you were born again, the devil declared war against you. Rick Warren describes it this way: "The moment you became God's child, Satan, like a mobster hit man, put a contract out on you. You are his enemy, and he's plotting your downfall."[1] So you had better prepare yourself for the battle! All prayer is warfare in that it is working to establish God's will and Kingdom in the earth. And all such work is an aggression against the enemy's kingdom, or the kingdom of this world. The apostle Paul instructed young Timothy, concerning his pastoral duties, to *"wage the good warfare,* having faith and a good (clear) conscience" (1 Timothy 1:18-19). He further admonished Timothy in his second epistle to "endure hardship as a *good soldier of Jesus Christ."* He said, "No one engaged in warfare entangles himself with the affairs of this life (or "worldly" life), that he may please him who enlisted him as a soldier" (2 Timothy 2:3-4).

A good soldier must be focused on his mission and know where and who his enemy is, and how to use the weapons at his disposal. The Bible teaches that, though we live in the world…

- **Our enemy is *unseen*:** "For we do not wrestle against flesh and blood, but against principalities, against powers, against the rulers of the darkness of this age, against *spiritual hosts of wickedness* in the heavenly places." This must be emphasized: *People are not our enemies.* (Ephesians 6:12). Spiritual powers which control and manipulate people are our enemies. We must pray God's grace and mercy and salvation to all people.
- **Our weapons are *spiritual*:** "For though we walk in the flesh, we do not war after the flesh: for *the weapons of our warfare are* not carnal, but *mighty through God to the pulling down of strongholds*" (2 Corinthians 10:3-4, KJV).

THE ARMOR OF GOD

Spiritual warfare which "pulls down strongholds" requires securing our armor, taking up our sword, and going on the offensive against the enemy. The Word of God says in Ephesians 6:10 to "be strong in the Lord and in the power of His might." To do this we must gird ourselves with spiritual armor...

> *Put on the whole armor of God, that you may be able to* **stand** *against the wiles of the devil... [and] that you may be able to* **withstand** *in the evil day, and having done all, to* **stand.** **Stand** *therefore, having girded your waist with truth, having put on the breastplate of righteousness, and having shod your feet with the preparation of the gospel of peace; above all, taking the shield of faith with which you will be able to quench all the fiery darts of the wicked one. And take the helmet of salvation and the sword of the Spirit, which is the word of God, praying always with all prayer and supplication in the Spirit."*
> Ephesians 6:11-18a

The Importance of FAITH
This scripture says, "**above all,** taking the *shield of faith.*" This is of utmost importance because without faith we are unable to appropriate any of the rest of the armor. For all of it is done *by faith.* We must believe God at His Word, or we have no authority or strength to stand against the enemy. But *with* faith, all the power and authority of Almighty God rests on and

with us. This is what enables us to stand. You can see the importance of *standing* in the passage above because it is repeated four times. In Peter's first Epistle he admonished the brethren: "Be well-balanced, be vigilant and cautious at all times; for that enemy of yours, the devil, roams around like a lion roaring [in fierce hunger], seeking someone to seize upon and devour. *Withstand him: be firm in faith* [against his onset — rooted, established, strong, immovable, and determined]" (1 Peter 5:8-9, TAB). Paul exhorted the Colossians to "continue in the faith *grounded and settled,* and be not moved away from the hope of the gospel" (Colossians 1:23, KJV). 1 John 5:4 tells us that well-grounded faith is our foundation for victory:

> *Whatever is born of God overcomes the world. And* this is the victory that has overcome the world — our faith.

Very simply, faith is what enables us to grow as a Christian, and thus, to pray effectively. Taking God at His Word honors Him and empowers our prayer life. For instance, thanking God for an answer before we see it, is a prayer of faith that pleases Him. The Bible tells us that without faith it is impossible to please God (see Hebrews 11:6), and also that even good preaching and teaching, without faith, will not produce fruit:

> *For indeed, the gospel was preached to us as well as to them; but the word which they heard did not profit them,* not being mixed with faith in those who heard it.   Hebrews 4:2

Faith undergirds all that we do for, and in, God's name. This *shield of faith* protects us, surely, but it also gives us spiritual authority and victory over all the works and power of the enemy, as we shall see.

The Helmet of SALVATION

The helmet of salvation is another essential part of our armor. Through salvation, Jesus said, we are "born again" into a new Kingdom (John 3:3). We become a "new creation" in Christ (2 Corinthians 5:17), and with that comes a new mindset. The mind can be viewed as the "window to the soul." In other words, what comes into the mind directs our thinking and, ultimately, our actions. Hence, the mind needs to be protected and built up in the things of God. At the time of salvation our spirit is reborn (see John

3:3, above), but our mind still retains the old, worldly mindset *and must be renewed.* As Paul explained it to the Ephesians: "Be renewed in the spirit of your mind" (Ephesians 4:23). To the Corinthians he said: "We have the mind of Christ" (1 Corinthians 2:16). In other words, all that Christ knows from the Father He imparts to us through His Word (John 15:15) and by His Spirit (John 16:13). Our mind is a battleground between old and new, good and evil, truth and deception. We must "feed" our minds with the truth of God's Word (see Hebrews 5:13-14), while our spiritual helmet protects us from the lies and deceptions of the enemy.

The Breastplate of RIGHTEOUSNESS

The *breastplate of righteousness* protects us against demonic accusation. For as the Redeemed of the Lord, Christ has imputed His righteousness to us:

> *For He made Him who knew no sin to be sin for us, that* we might become the righteousness of God in Him.　　2 Corinthians 5:21

Therefore, it is not in our own righteousness that we stand against the *accuser of the brethren* (see Revelation 12:10), but in the very righteousness of God, Himself. The breastplate works with the helmet of salvation, for as we are made new in the attitude of our minds, we "put on the new self, created to be like God in true righteousness and holiness" (Ephesians 4:23). The outworking of this in our lives is that we must *choose to walk* ("put on") in the holiness to which we have been called, and in the righteousness which has been imputed to us:

> *Just as he who called you is holy, so* be holy in all you do; *for it is written: "Be holy, because I am holy."*　　1 Peter 1:15-16

The Girdle of TRUTH

Just as the *breastplate of righteousness* protects us against accusation, the *girdle of truth* protects us against deception. For the truth of God's Word stands against all deception of "the father of lies" (John 8:44). The devil will try to steal our hope, joy and peace that we have in Christ by sowing seeds of doubt, fear and intimidation. His lies can hold us in bondage. In order to be set free from these bondages, we must immerse ourselves in

THE ARMOR OF GOD

God's positives and refuse to listen to the devil's negatives:

> *"If you hold to my teaching, you are really my disciples. Then you will know the truth, and the truth will set you free."*
> John 8:31-32, NIV

We must not only *think* truth, but *speak* it to walk as victorious overcomers:

> *And they overcame him [the devil] by the blood of the Lamb and by the* word of their testimony...
> Revelation 12:11

The Gospel of PEACE

The *Gospel of peace* upon our feet guides us as we walk through life:

> *God has called us to peace.... As much as depends on you, live peaceably with all men.*
> 1 Corinthians 7:15 and Romans 12:18

This *Gospel of peace* that we walk in is a message of love — love that covers a multitude of sin (1 Peter 4:8). Love is one of the most powerful spiritual weapons that we have at our disposal. For it utterly disarms the powers of darkness, and everything associated with it, and brings healing and restoration. To walk in love is to walk in the power of God:

> *Love has been perfected among us in this: that we may have boldness in the day of judgment; because as He is, so are we in this world.*
> 1 John 4:17

The Scriptures tell us that God is love (see 1 John 4:16). And it was *love* that compelled Father God to send His Son into the world (see John 3:16), and *love* that compelled Jesus to come and "give His life a ransom for many" (Mark 10:45). Thus it the *power of love* that defeated the power of sin and death in this world.

Yes, love is powerful. But love's opposite, unforgiveness, is also powerful in negating and preventing the flow of life and blessings into our lives. This is why the Bible instructs us to not have aught against anyone (Matthew 5:23-24, KJV). Jesus commanded us, in Matthew 6:14-15, to forgive others and our heavenly Father will forgive us. For if we don't forgive others, He said our heavenly Father *will not forgive us*.

The Scriptures have much to say about our speech. Indeed, we are told, "Death and life are in the power of the tongue" (Proverbs 18:21). Speaking peace in love brings life and ministers healing and blessing:

> *Do not let any unwholesome talk come out of your mouths, but only what is helpful for building others up according to their needs, that it may benefit those who listen.* Ephesians 2:29

As we walk in love, we are demonstrating the Gospel of peace which we profess, and we will bring blessing wherever we go. For indeed, "How beautiful... are the feet of him that bringeth good tidings, that publisheth peace" (Isaiah 52:7, KJV; see Romans 10:15).

The Power of the WORD

The *sword of the Spirit,* which is the Word of God, is the only offensive weapon in our armor. This is what we raise against the enemy in our warfare prayers. Hebrews 4:12 says that the Word of God is "living and powerful, and sharper than any two-edged sword, piercing even to the division of soul and spirit, and of joints and marrow, and is a discerner of the thoughts and intents of the heart." First of all, this mighty sword cuts us to the quick as we read and assimilate it, bringing repentance and healing by paring away all that is unprofitable to our own spiritual growth and health:

> *All Scripture is... profitable for doctrine, for reproof, for correction, for instruction in righteousness.* 2 Timothy 3:16

Secondly, this weapon cuts down the enemy in his tracks. When Jesus faced the devil in the wilderness, He responded to the devil's enticements with, "It is written..." (see Matthew 4:1-11) He overcame the devil with the Word of God, and we can also (see Revelation12:11). The proclamation of the Word of God – the Truth – nullifies the lies and declarations of the enemy, and defeats his wicked plans and schemes. Rick Joyner reported the following prophetic message given in a vision: "The sword that is being given to My messengers in the last days can break any yoke, and cut through any chain." [2]Bill Burns, of Faith Tabernacle in Kremmling, Colorado, gave the following prophecy concerning the power of the Word spoken in intercession:

I am bringing the power of My word in intercession. I am bringing the power of prayer…as lightning bolts against all the works of the enemy. I say, pray [and] believe that when you speak the words of authority and the words that challenge the enemy that the enemy is indeed challenged and exposed and defeated. Pray and watch the enemy fall as lightning from Heaven. Your prayers will not be ineffective.[3]

In John's vision in the book of Revelation, Jesus, whose name is the Word of God (19:13), is depicted as having "a sharp two-edged sword" coming out of His mouth (1:16). In chapter 19 we lean that He uses this sword to bring judgment upon the nations. Striking the wicked nations with the sword of His mouth, is a vivid picture of the power of *prophetic intercession*. (We will be talking more about this in Chapter Five.)

The Power of Love and Righteous Living: THE ARMOR OF LIGHT
This "armor" is not recorded in Ephesians 6, but in Romans 13:8-14:

Owe no one anything except to love one another, *for he who loves another has fulfilled the law…. And do this knowing the time, that now it is high time to awake out of sleep…. The night is far spent, the day is at hand. Therefore let us cast off the works of darkness, and let us* put on the armor of light. *Let us walk properly, …not in revelry and drunkenness, not in lewdness and lust, not in strife and envy. But* put on the Lord Jesus Christ, and make no provision for the flesh….

Jesus said, "*This is My commandment, that you love one another as I have loved you*" (John 15:12). Love and righteousness are powerful weapons to counter the works of darkness in our own heart and in the world around us. As we "put on" love and walk in the character of Jesus, we will live in the victory of the Kingdom of Light and we will have great favor with God:

"He who has My commandments and keeps them, it is he who loves Me. And he who loves Me will be loved by My Father, and I will love him and manifest Myself to him."   John 14:21

Purpose of the Armor

The concluding verse in the passage in Ephesians 6 about our spiritual armor tells us the reason we are given the armor: to PRAY:

> ...*praying always with all prayer and supplication in the Spirit, being watchful to this end with all perseverance and supplication for all the saints....*
> verse 18

Thus girded with the full armor of God we stand strong in the power of HIS might and, therefore, there is NO weapon formed against us that will prosper (see Isaiah 54:17). The "accuser of our brethren" (Revelation 12:10) is continually accusing us in our own hearts and before the throne of God to try to undermine our faith and our authority. But we are told in Romans 8:33, 35 and 37:

> *Who shall bring a charge against God's elect?...[and] Who shall separate us from the love of Christ? Shall tribulation, or distress, or persecution, or famine, or nakedness, or peril, or sword?... Yet in all these things we are* more than conquerors *through Him who loved us.*

More than conquerors, indeed! "Thanks be to God, who gives us the victory through our Lord Jesus Christ" (1 Corinthians 15:57).

[1] Rick Warren, *The Purpose-Driven Life* (Grand Rapids, Michigan: Zondervan, 2002), pp. 205-206.
[2] Rick Joyner, "The Sword," *The Morning Star Journal* (Wilkesboro, NC: Morning Star Publications, Inc., Vol. 13, No. 3), p.82.
[3] Bill Burns, Faith Tabernacle, Kremmling, CO, Internet article, October 2000.

Chapter Three

THE BELIEVER'S STANDING IN CHRIST: TAKING DOMINION

"But God...made us alive together with Christ...and raised us up together, and made us sit together in the heavenly places in Christ Jesus."
Ephesians 2:4-6

CREATED FOR DOMINION

Jesus instructed His followers in Matthew 6:10, KJV to pray to the Father: "Thy kingdom come. Thy will be done on earth, as it is in heaven." This is the ultimate goal of all prayer: *to establish God's Kingdom on earth through the lives of His people, His Body, the Church.* Chuck Pierce has said, "You are a part of God's covenant plan to see His kingdom advance."[1] But before we can effectively pray this prayer, "Thy kingdom come...," we must first understand "What *is* the Kingdom of God?" and "Where is my place in it?"

Psalm 8:4-6 clearly states man's position within the created realm:

> *What is man that You are mindful of him, and the son of man that You visit him? For You have made him a little lower than* ELOHIM [often incorrectly translated *"the angels"*], *and You have crowned him with glory and honor. You have made him to* **have dominion over the works of Your hands; You have put all things under his feet."**

The phrase "the angels" would place man in an inferior position with regard to taking dominion. The Hebrew word here is, literally, *ELOHIM,* which is a covenant name of God, referring to God as the mighty or supreme Creator. What the psalmist is saying is that man was created *a little lower than GOD, and that God has given him a place of glory and honor and dominion over all of His creation.*

Man's place of dominion over the earth is also established in the book of Genesis:

> *"Let Us make man in Our image, according to Our likeness;* let them have dominion *over the fish of the sea, over the birds of the air, and over the cattle,* over all the earth *and over every creeping thing that creeps on the earth."*
> Genesis 1:26

We see here that God created the physical realm to be a reflection of Heaven, with man created in God's likeness to rule in God's stead on earth as God rules in Heaven. Man was to have *dominion, or ruling authority.* This was the functional result of bearing God's image. Psalm 115:16 tells us that the heavens belong to the Lord, "but the earth He has given to the sons of men." But what happened? Man fell through sin, and lost dominion over the earth to the "prince of the power of the air." Ephesians 2:1-6 gives us a picture of this scenario:

> *And you He made alive, who were dead in trespasses and sins, in which you once walked according to the course of this world, according to the* prince of the power of the air, *the spirit who now works sin the* sons of disobedience, *among whom also we all once conducted ourselves in the* lusts of our flesh, *fulfilling the desires of the flesh and of the mind, and were by nature* children of wrath, *just as the others.*
> *BUT GOD, who is rich in mercy, because of His great love with which He loved us, even when we were dead in trespasses,* made us alive together with Christ *(by grace you have been saved), and raised us up together, and* made us sit together in the heavenly places in Christ Jesus.

Two Opposing Kingdoms

So here we see depicted two opposing kingdoms: heavenly and worldly. In verses 1 and 2, we are told the kingdom of this world is ruled by "the prince of the power of the air." These citizens are by nature depraved: children of wrath, given over to lusts of the flesh, and disobedient to God. Filled with darkness, these people are spiritually dead. In verses 4 and 5 we see the intervention of God, because of His great mercy and love, making us spiritually alive together with Christ. Saved by grace, we are raised up to sit with Him in heavenly places. This Kingdom, ruled by God, is filled with light and life.

THE KINGDOM OF GOD

Of this heavenly Kingdom, the Bible teaches there are two dimensions. First there is a sense of the Kingdom being *within*. Jesus said, "The kingdom of God is *within* you" (Luke 17:21). And yet, Jesus also said, "My kingdom is *not of this world*" (John 18:36). He said much about how to *enter* His Kingdom:

- *"Not everyone who says to Me, 'Lord, Lord,' shall* enter *the kingdom of heaven, but* he who does the will of My Father...." (Matthew 7:21)
- *"Assuredly,* ...unless you are converted, *and become as little children, you will by no means* enter *the kingdom of heaven."* (Matthew 18:3)

We see from these two scriptures that there are qualifications for entering into and being a part of the Kingdom of God. For instance, Matthew 7:21 says that we must do the will of the Father: we must be obedient. In Matthew 18:3 we see that we must become as little children, humble and teachable. The apostle Peter exhorted the brethren that God's "divine power has given to us all things that pertain to life and godliness...by which have been given to us exceedingly great and precious promises, that *through these you may be partakers of the divine nature, having escaped the corruption that is in the world through lust"* (2 Peter 1:3-4). We enter into God's Kingdom by *denying* the lusts and corruption in this world and by *embracing* Kingdom principles found in the Word of God ("exceedingly great and precious promises"). As we do this, denying the flesh and allowing God's truth to renew our minds, God's Kingdom is formed *within* us.

So we see that God's Kingdom is not so much a *place* as it is a *state of being*. It is that state where God has absolute authority: *wherever His will is done as it is in Heaven.* The Kingdom of God exists in our individual hearts, as born-again Believers, as we are surrendered to the will of the Father. The Kingdom of God is established in the earth as God's people walk out Kingdom living in their daily lives.

REINSTATED DOMINION: HEIRS WITH CHRIST

Adam lost his God-given authority and dominion in the earth when he sinned. Jesus, the "last Adam" (see 1 Corinthians 15:45), came to restore what God had originally intended for mankind: that is, bringing dominion and authority back to the human level. This reinstated dominion is described in Paul's prayer for the Ephesians in Ephesians 1:19-22. He prayed that they would know:

> ...*what is the exceeding greatness of His power toward us who believe,...which He worked in Christ when He raised Him from the dead and* seated him at His right hand in the heavenly places, far above all principality and power and might and dominion, *and every name that is named, not only in this age but also in that which is to come. And He put* all things under His feet, *and gave Him to be* head over all things *to the church.*

Now, here is the picture of the Believer's standing, or position of authority, in Christ: We are told above that Christ is at the right hand of God (verse 20) and all things are under His feet (verse 22). So where is the Believer in this scene? Ephesians 2:6, which we quoted earlier, states that Believers are seated *with Christ in heavenly places.* Now, of course, we are not yet *physically* seated in Heaven. But this statement expresses our position of *reinstated dominion.* According to the Scriptures, through our union with Christ, we have died to sin, been buried, resurrected to new life, and are now seated with Him in heavenly places. Through this process, we have been delivered from the power of darkness and *translated* into the Kingdom of God (see Colossians 1:12-14, KJV). We literally become a "new creature" (2 Corinthians 5:17, KJV) in a new Kingdom, with a new mindset and a new inheritance. We are now "heirs of God and joint heirs with Christ" (Romans 8:17). All that Christ is and has is now ours. We are seated with Christ in authority, and all things – including all powers and principalities — are under our feet!

Authority to Command Demons

A good example of the Kingdom authority Believers have can be seen in Matthew 8:28-34. This passage records the account of Jesus' encounter with the two demon-possessed men who came out of the tombs in the region of the Gadarenes. They said to Jesus:

"What have we to do with You, Jesus, You Son of God? Have you come
here to torment us before the time?"… "If You cast us out, permit us to
go away into the herd of swine."   verses 29 and 31

In these questions the demons revealed several important and strategic
things. First of all, *they knew who Jesus was*: the "Son of God." They also
revealed that they knew *their ultimate fate was sealed:* "Have You come here
to torment us before **the** time?" And they knew, because of who He was,
that *He had authority over them.* And *they knew that they had to do whatever*
He commanded them to do: "If You cast us out, will You *permit* us to go into
the swine?"

Now here is the key for the Believer: That same Spirit that the demons
recognized in Jesus resides in YOU. When you walk by, the demons tremble
— not because of who you are, but because of *Who is in you.* You have
authority to command demons, just like Jesus did. In this entire passage, all
Jesus said was one word: "GO!" (verse 32) and they went immediately into
the herd of swine. When believers speak in faith, and in the authority of
the Holy Spirit, demons must obey. Jesus confirmed this reality to His disciples in Luke 10:19 by saying, "I give you the authority…over all the power
of the enemy, and nothing shall by any means hurt you."

If we appropriate the truth of our God-given ruling authority by faith
(just like the spiritual armor), it will change the character of our lives. For
we will no longer be "earthbound," suffering "under circumstances," but
we will see, and live, life from Heaven's perspective as victorious *overcomers:*

And they overcame him [the devil] *by the blood of the Lamb and by*
the word of their testimony, and they did not love their lives to the
death.   Revelation 12:11

THE DEVIL IS A DEFEATED FOE

The previous verse describes how Believers can learn to walk in victory
over the kingdom of darkness. First of all, it says that we overcome the devil
(and his kingdom) by the *Blood of the Lamb.* Colossians 2:15 describes the
devil's defeat by the Blood of Jesus:

Having disarmed principalities and powers, He made a public specta-
cle of them, triumphing over them in [the cross].

The devil IS a defeated foe. He works through deception and counter-feits to appear to have power and authority. The fact is, he has only as much authority as we give him by relinquishing our own place of domin-ion, and not standing in faith in the place God has called us to as *overcom-ers*. Dr. Lloyd Ogilvie, the now-retired United States Senate chaplain, once said, "The world we have, we have because man has not taken dominion as he should."

TAKING DOMINION THROUGH THE BLOOD AND BY FAITH

As children of God, we have been bought with a price (see 1 Corinthians 6:20), and are bound to God through an everlasting Blood Covenant. Through Christ's atonement we have been raised to sit in victory in the heavenly places. The power and authority we have in prayer has nothing to do with us, and everything to do with the Blood Covenant we have with Almighty God.

All the promises and benefits provided in this Covenant are accessed by faith. Faith involves *making a conscious, progressive decision to take God at His Word regardless of circumstances*. The "word of our testimony" is the declaration of our faith based on the Word of God. This is the "sword of the Spirit," talked about earlier, and is the focus of this book. Standing in the authority of Christ, with the power of His shed Blood and the word of our testimony (the Word of God) on our lips, we are well-armed to fight any spiritual enemy.

Looking back at Revelation 12:11, the phrase about not loving their lives to the death refers to the fact that we overcome, not because we love life, but because we love Him who IS life. And it is through our love for Him that we are drawn deeper into Him, forsaking our flesh – dying to self – and becoming one with Him, so that His Kingdom authority may rule in and through us.

The atoning work of Christ has brought dominion (ruling authority) back to man. As Francis Frangipane has said, the Atonement "has provided *legal* protection for the Church against the devil." Jesus is our King, Judge and Lawgiver (see Isaiah 33:22). "Because of Jesus, we have a legal right not only to be protected from our enemy but to triumph over him."[2]

THE BRIDE OF CHRIST

As we consider the Believer's standing in Christ in relation to authority in prayer and in our triumph over the enemy, we must also look at the "Bride" relationship. Revelation 19:7-8 gives us a picture of the **Bride of Christ:**

> *"Let us be glad and rejoice and give Him glory, for the* marriage of the Lamb has come, and His wife has made herself ready." *And to her it was granted to be arrayed in fine linen, clean and bright, for the fine linen is the righteous acts of the saints.*

Jesus identified Himself as the *Bridegroom* in Matthew 9:15, when teaching the disciples about fasting:

> *"Can the friends of the bridegroom mourn as long as the bridegroom is with them? But the days will come when the bridegroom will be taken away from them, and then they will fast."*

VICTORIOUS BRIDE: OVERCOMERS

So Jesus is the Bridegroom, but who, exactly, is the *Bride of Christ?* First of all, the above Revelation passage says that the Bride is one who is "arrayed" in "righteous acts." One who is betrothed to God would certainly have to be holy. Additionally, Matthew 22:14 makes the statement: "Many are called, but few are chosen." In a nutshell, the "many" who are called represents the Church; that is, all the Christians down through the centuries that make up the Body of Christ. The "few" represents the Bride, chosen from among the Church. These "few" will distinguish themselves as *Overcomers,* or those who have pressed in to victorious faith, as mentioned previously. The book of Revelation identifies at least nine rewards of *Overcomers* (see Revelation 2:7,11,17,26 and 28; 3:5,12 and 21; and 21:7). Revelation 3:21 says specifically that he who overcomes will *sit with Christ on His throne*. This will be a different group from the "great multitude" who will be "standing *before* the throne and *before* the Lamb, clothed with white robes, with palm branches in their hands" (Revelation 7:9).

PASSIONATE BRIDE: DEVOTED ONES

Overcomers will also be characterized by their *passion* for the Bridegroom. They will be those who have pressed in to know the Lord more intimately, through actively seeking a love relationship with Him as their *Beloved,* not merely their Savior. For Jesus seeks such to love Him. In fact, He *commands* it:

> *"You shall love the LORD your God with **all** your heart, with **all** your soul, and with **all** your mind.* This is the first and great commandment." Matthew 22:37-38

One day as I was meditating on this commandment during my devotional-worship time, I was deeply convicted of the deficiency and imperfection of my love for the Lord. I wrote in my journal that with this conviction came the awareness of the transcending importance of such love from the Bride to the Bridegroom. My heart cry was that, though He had supplied all my needs, there was one need I still had: that I would love Him more. I wrote from my contrite heart:

My heart calls to You in the early morn;
My soul is longing to meet Thee.
Thirsty and hungry I sit at Your feet.
Lord, fill me again, I beseech Thee —
...For I need to love Thee more...

My soul is forgiven, cleansed and renewed,
As on wings of an eagle I soar.
With power from Heaven is my spirit endued;
My sins condemn me no more —
...Yet I would love Thee more...

Lifted into the heavenly realm,
By Your Spirit I draw near,
Into Your presence. Embraced by Your love,
I have no need nor fear —
...But only to love Thee more...

Lovingly, gently You guide my steps
As I trust You with all my heart;
Strengthening me at every turn,
and though faith You do impart —
...I yearn to love Thee more...

As I lay down in peace at the close of the day,
Knowing the angels their vigil do keep,
I pray to my God who comforts me,
And gives His beloved sleep —
Lord, help me to love Thee more.

INTIMACY WITH THE BELOVED

The Song of Solomon pictures this bridal relationship in very poetic imagery. In chapter two the beloved speaks to his bride, "Rise up, my love, my fair one, and come away [with me]" (verse 10). And later, in verse 14: "O my dove,...let me see your face, let me hear your voice; for your voice is sweet, and your face is lovely." (The bride is described in several places in the Song as having "dove's eyes." The dove has no peripheral vision, but can only see what is directly in front of her.) This describes the yearning of our Lord's heart for intimacy with His Beloved. Revelation 3:20 pictures the Lord knocking on the door of our heart seeking intimate fellowship: "If any man hear my voice, and open the door, I will come in to him, and will sup (denoting intimate fellowship) with him, and he with me" (KJV). He is knocking, but will we slow down enough to take the time to answer, and then to spend the time with Him that He desires? Or will we just be satisfied with knowing *about* the Lord and enjoying the benefits of salvation? The Bride will be marked by her *love for* the Bridegroom rather than her *knowledge of* Him.

ABANDONMENT TO THE BELOVED

Jeanne Guyon was, among other things, a spiritual mentor whose writings have influenced and inspired countless seeking Christians in the three-hundred-plus years since their publication. In her classic book *Experiencing the Depths of Jesus Christ*,[3] Madame Guyon spoke about what she called *abandonment* to bring one into deeper intimacy with the Lord. This is a picture of the passionate, self-sacrificing love of the Bride who has abandoned her ALL to Him:

> *To penetrate deeper into the experience of Jesus Christ, it is required*
> *that you begin to abandon your whole existence, giving it up to God....*
> *You must utterly believe that the circumstances of your life — every*
> *minute of your life...anything, yes, anything that happens — have all*

come to you by His will and by His permission. You must believe that everything that has happened to you is from God and is exactly what you need.... There must be an abandonment in your life concerning all outward practical things...[and] all inward, spiritual things.... All your concerns go into the hand of God. You forget yourself...and think only of Him.

THE FAVOR OF THE BRIDE

The intimacy of the Bride with her Lord puts her in a very influential position with respect to petitioning God in prayer. King Ahasuerus extended to Esther the royal scepter when she approached him to present her petition on behalf of the Jews. Esther came in boldness, for she said resolutely: "If I perish, I perish" (Esther 4:16). We come in boldness also (see Hebrews 10:19), for we can enter freely into His courts with praise! (Psalm 100:4). Our King delights in our presence at His "court" and graciously extends His "scepter;" that is, the answers to our petitions. For, as Overcomers, we have learned the intimacy of *abiding*. As we mentioned in Chapter Three, Jesus calls us to *abide* in Him. This is the intimacy of the Bride. And as we abide in Him and His words abide in us, we will ask what we desire, and it shall be done for us (John 15:7).

The instruction of our Lord in Matthew 6:10 is to pray His Kingdom into the earth. His Kingdom comes initially as we submit to the Lord's sovereign rule in our own lives, and secondly, as we take dominion in the earth through prayer and prophetic intercession. As the Bride of Christ, this should be our passion. But it is most certainly our privilege, our right and our responsibility.

[1]Chuck Pierce, Internet article.
[2]Francis Frangipane, Internet article.
[3]Jeanne Guyon, *Experiencing the Depths of Jesus Christ* (Beaumont, TX: Seed Sowers Christian Books Publishing House, 1975), pp. 32-34.

Chapter Four

PREVAILING IN PRAYER

"The effective, fervent prayer of a righteous man avails much."
James 5:16

CONDITIONS OF PREVAILING PRAYER

PREPARING YOUR HEART

We need to be aware that there are things which can hinder our prayers from being heard by God. So, before we bring our intercession before the Throne, we must first prepare our hearts:

- *"If I regard iniquity in my* heart, *the Lord will not hear me."* (Psalm 66:18)
- *"Who shall ascend to the hill of the Lord? He who has clean hands and a* pure heart." (Psalm 24:3-4)
- *"Search me, O God, and know my* heart;... *and see if there is any wicked way in me...."* (Psalm 139:23-24)

We must seek the Holy Spirit, and submit to conviction in our own heart, for any unconfessed sin we may be harboring. Our conscience must be clear. In the words of Charles Finney, in order to prevail in prayer, we must have "a conscience void of offense toward man and God."[1] We must let go of grudges, unforgiveness, bitterness, envy and every other thing that would bring offense into our heart. For this will not only hinder our prayers, but will put holes in our spiritual armor, making us more vulnerable to enemy attack. However, once our sins are confessed and repented of, we can then be assured that God is "faithful and just to forgive us our sins and to cleanse us from all unrighteousness" (1 John 1:9). Confession is the first step toward God in prayer:

> *Create in me a clean heart, O God, and renew a steadfast spirit within me… [that] the words of my mouth and the meditation of my heart [would] be acceptable [to You], O LORD, my strength and my Redeemer.*
> Psalms 51:10 and 19:14

Once sin is confessed, we must accept God's forgiveness, for:

- *"There is no condemnation to those who are in Christ Jesus…."* (Romans 8:1)
- *"As far as the east is from the west, so far has He removed our transgressions from us."* (Psalm 103:12)

We are now free to "come boldly before the throne of grace, that we may obtain mercy and find grace to help in time of need" (Hebrews 4:16). Our confidence in approaching God is based on the atoning work of Christ on the cross. The author of Hebrews tells us that Christ, *"with His own blood,* entered the Most Holy Place once for all, having obtained eternal redemption…. Therefore,…having boldness to enter the Holiest *by the blood of Jesus,* by a new and living *way which He consecrated for us,* through the veil, that is, His flesh,…let us draw near with a true heart in *full assurance of faith,* having our hearts sprinkled from an evil conscience and our bodies washed with pure water" (Hebrews 9:12 and 10:19-22). Redeemed and cleansed mankind now has full access to the Throne of grace through the Blood of Jesus, the Lamb of God. And it is to this Throne that we bring our intercession.

THE ATTITUDE OF HUMILITY

We must remember, as we approach God in prayer, that it is the precious Blood of Jesus that has opened the access to His Throne (see Hebrews 10:19). And it is because of God's love and through His grace that we are invited to enter His presence with our petitions. So, as we do so, our attitude needs to be one of **humility**. The Bible instructs us to "let this mind be in you which was also in Christ Jesus, who…*humbled Himself* and became obedient [unto] death" (Philippians 2:5-8, selected) The apostle Peter admonished the brethren to *"be clothed with humility,* for "God resists the proud, but gives grace to the humble." Therefore, humble yourselves under the mighty hand of God,...casting all your care upon Him, for He cares for you" (1 Peter 5:5-7). The picture here is that our loving Father is waiting for us to come to Him with humble, trusting hearts and throw every care into His lap!

THE IMPORTANCE OF FAITH

After preparing our heart there are other conditions that Scripture tells us are necessary to prevail in prayer. Herbert Lockyer, author of the classic book, *All the Prayers of the Bible*, said, "Answer to prayer begins with the assurance that God hears and answers prayer."[2] Most importantly, we must pray in faith, believing God for the answer. We are told in James 1:6-7:

But let him ask in faith, with no doubting, *for he who doubts is like a wave of the sea driven and tossed by the wind. For let not that man suppose that he will receive anything from the Lord.*

...and in Hebrews 10:23:

Let us hold fast the confession of our hope without wavering, *for He who promised is faithful.*

Jesus instructed His disciples concerning prayer, that "whatever things you ask when you pray, *believe that you receive them,* and you will have them" (Mark 11:24). In Mark 9, Jesus told the father of the possessed boy:

If you can believe, all things are possible to him who believes.
Mark 9:23

Jesus went past the power of prayer to say that even *His works* would be accomplished by those who believed in Him:

"He who believes in Me, *the works that I do he will do also; and greater works...will he do."*
John 14:12

...A scriptural testimony

Faith is fundamental to praying prayers that get answers. Acts 3 records the account of the disciples Peter and John healing a lame man by the Beautiful Gate at the Temple. The man was begging alms, to which Peter replied, "Silver and gold I do not have, but what I do have I give you: In the name of Jesus Christ of Nazareth, rise up and walk." Peter's faith was so strong that his prayer was a *declaration of faith* rather than a petition: "Rise up and walk!" The narrative goes on to say, "He took him by the right hand and lifted him up, and immediately his feet and ankle bones received strength. So he, leaping up, stood and walked and entered the temple with them – walking, leaping and praising God" (Acts 3:6-8). The people were "filled with wonder and amazement at what had happened" to the man, as they knew the man had been lame from birth (verse 10). Peter then responded to the people:

> *"Men of Israel, why do you marvel at this? Or why look so intently at us, as though by our own power or godliness we had made this man walk?... [Jesus'] name, through* faith in His name, *has made this man strong.... Yes, the* faith which comes through Him *has given him this perfect soundness in the presence of you all."*
>
> verses 12 and 16

...A common pitfall

Faith is so essential to prayer we must mention a common prayer pitfall: *negative confession.* For instance, you are on your way home from church where you have just agreed in prayer that sister so-and-so is being healed of cancer. Then you meet a friend in the grocery store and tell her that sister so-and-so just received a shocking report and is dying of cancer. The negative confession (curse) at the store just canceled out the positive prayer (blessing) prayed earlier. We must watch what we say with our mouths: Death and life are in the power of the tongue (Proverbs 18:21). James instructed the brethren:

> *Out of the same mouth proceed blessing and cursing. My brethren, these things ought not to be so. Does a spring send forth fresh water and bitter from the same opening?* James 3:10-11

We need to keep in mind that *faith* looks at the *truth* (God's report: the Covenant promises of the Word of God) and not at the *facts* (man's report: the way things appear in the natural). For instance, it may be a *fact* that someone has been diagnosed with an incurable disease. But God's *Truth* says:" By [Jesus'] stripes we are healed" (Isaiah 53:5). It may be a *fact* that you lost your job and have no income. But God's *Truth* says: "My God shall supply *all your need* according to His riches in glory by Christ Jesus" (Philippians 4:19). It may be a *fact* that you were passed over for a promotion. But God's *Truth* says: "The steps of a good man are ordered by the LORD" (Psalm 37:23). These are *Kingdom* promises of God's Word. We need to learn to think and to speak out of a *Kingdom* mindset.

THE STRENGTH OF ABIDING

A Kingdom mindset comes from a close abiding relationship with the Lord. The word *abiding* means, literally, "to live with." Jesus said in John 15:7, "If you *abide* in Me, and My words *abide* in you, you will ask what you desire, and it shall be done for you." To put it another way, "If you *live in and partake of* Me, and My words *live in and become a part of* you, you will know how to pray according to My will, and therefore you will get what you ask for." Through abiding in God, and believing in His Word, all things are possible through prayer (Mark 9:23), but without Him we can accomplish nothing (see John 15:5).

This "abiding" is the intimacy with God that we saw in our examples of intercessors (Moses, Jeremiah and Jesus) in Chapter One. David is another good example of one who knew the discipline and joy of abiding. In fact, the Lord described David as a "man after His own heart" (1 Samuel 13:14). An example of David's passionate devotion to the Lord can be seen as "David danced before the LORD with all his might" at the return of the Ark of the Covenant to the house of Israel (2 Samuel 6:14). The importance of developing and maintaining an intimate relationship with the Lord cannot be over-emphasized. Marsha Burns, of Faith Tabernacle in Kremmling, Colorado, had this prophetic picture of the relationship between intimacy and spiritual authority and power:

> I had a vision of a dance floor and people dancing. The music was ethereal and the rhythm was distinct. Those who were moving in step with the music were crowned and carried scepters. There were others dancing, but they were out of step as though they could not hear the music. They were neither crowned nor did they have scepters. And the Lord said: *"I am looking for those who will listen carefully and move in precision with the rhythm of My heart, for I will cause your every step to be carefully choreographed to fulfill My ulti-*

mate design and purpose. You will flow with those who also move by the power of My Spirit and display a distinct poise and grace as you progress. Those who are out of step are those who are doing their own thing apart from My Spirit, and they will disrupt the flow by drawing attention to themselves. They will lack the power and authority that belong to My heirs. Be still. *Quiet your soul and attune your heart to hear and respond to the move of My Spirit.* **Therein lies the secret of power and authority**" (emphasis added).

THE CALL TO OBEDIENCE

Obedience also brings answers to prayers. As we have said, obedience to the Lord's commands keeps our heart pure and without offense, and "if our hearts do not condemn us, we have confidence before God and *receive from him anything we ask, because we obey his commands* and do what pleases him" (1 John 3:21-22, NIV). Jesus taught further, in John 15, that as we learn to abide in Him and pray prayers that get answers, we bless the Father by bearing fruit that brings Him glory (see verse 8). He said that He appointed us to go and bear fruit that would remain, so that *whatever we ask the Father in His name He may give us* (verse 16). Obedience brings fruit that honors God and brings answers to prayer.

THE NEED TO PERSEVERE

Perseverance is another condition necessary to prevail in prayer. Paul admonished the brethren in Thessalonica to "pray without ceasing" (1 Thessalonians 5:17). Prayer, simply stated, is communication with God, involving both speaking and listening. We are exhorted here to keep our heart attentive toward God at all times, speaking to Him, yes, but also listening for His voice. This is how we maintain a vital relationship with the Lord, through which we can then know His will and receive His favor.
...Parables of perseverance

In Luke 18:1-8 Jesus taught a parable "that men always ought to *pray and not lose heart.*" In the story, a woman went before an unjust judge and demanded justice from her adversary. The judge resisted her demands initially, until she persisted in asking. Then he said, "Because this widow troubles me I will avenge her, lest by her continual coming she weary me" (verse 5). "Then the Lord said, 'Hear what the unjust judge said. And shall God not avenge His own elect who cry out day and night to Him, though He bears long with them? I tell you that *He will avenge them speedily*'" (verses 6-8).

Jesus also taught about persisting in prayer, in Matthew 7:7-8, when He said, "Ask, and it will be given to you; seek, and you will find; knock, and it will be opened to you. For everyone who asks receives, and he who seeks finds, and to him who knocks it will be opened." The verb tenses in this last verse in the Greek suggest the active progression of "*continuing* to ask, *continuing* to seek, and *continuing* to knock." He who *continues* to ask, seek and knock receives answers to prayer. Or, as Paul instructed the Colossians, "Continue *earnestly* in prayer, *being vigilant* in it with thanksgiving" (Colossians 4:2).

...Persevere in faith

James tells us that the prayer of a righteous man avails much, and that the prayer of faith saves the sick (see James 5:15-16). To persevere in prayer is to persevere in faith. Hebrews chapter 10:35-38 speaks of the importance of persevering in faith:

Therefore, do not cast away your confidence, which has great reward. For you have need of endurance, *so that after you have done the will of God, you may receive the promise: "For yet a little while, and He who is coming will come and will not tarry. Now* the just shall live by **faith**; *but if anyone draws back, My soul has no pleasure in him."*

...Persevere because of spiritual resistance

Perseverance in prayer is necessary because, as we have said, God hears and answers according to His will and timing. Additionally, we need to persevere because of resistance in the spirit realm. In Daniel 10 we see an account where Daniel had been praying and fasting for twenty-one days when he had a visitation from an angel:

"Do not fear, Daniel, for from the first day that you set your heart to understand, and to humble yourself before your God, your words were heard; and I have come because of your words. But the prince of the kingdom of Persia withstood me twenty-one days; *and behold, Michael, one of the chief princes, came to help me, for I had been left alone there with the kings of Persia."*   verses 12-13

This scripture gives us a picture of the situation in the heavenly realm. There is a war going on at all times between the angels of God and demonic forces. Ephesians 6:12 (quoted in Chapter Two) gives us further revelation on this:

> *We do not wrestle against flesh and blood, but against principalities, against powers, against the rulers of the darkness of this age, against spiritual hosts of wickedness in the heavenly places.*

We must have faith and endurance to persevere in our prayers until we get the victory!

THE IMPORTANCE OF RIGHT MOTIVES

Right motives is another condition necessary to answered prayer. The apostle James said of prayer, "You ask and do not receive, *because you ask amiss*, that you may spend it on your pleasures" (James 4:3). The prayer for a silver BMW with leather interior and…will not likely be answered. So how about the promise that the Lord will give us the desires of our heart? The Lord does bless us with the desires of our heart, Psalm 37:4 says, *as we delight in Him*, because in the "delighting" (abiding) we come into such intimacy with Him that the desires of His heart become ours.

THE POWER OF PRAISE

Lastly, we should come into God's presence to pray with a thankful heart. Gratitude opens the door to answered prayer, as Philippians 4:6 tells us:

> *Be anxious for nothing, but in everything by prayer and supplication,* with thanksgiving, *let your requests be made known to God.*

Scripture commands us to live a *lifestyle of praise*: "Rejoice *evermore….* **In every thing** give thanks: for this is the will of God in Christ Jesus concerning you" (1 Thessalonians 5:16 and 18, KJV). — It is God's will for us to be thankful — not only IN all things, but FOR all things: "Be filled with the Spirit… *giving thanks always for all* things unto God" (Ephesians 5:18-20).

Robin McMillan explained the dynamics of gratitude this way:

> Thanksgiving refocuses our affections upon the Lord, resets our minds on His goodness, and prepares our hearts for what He wants to do in our lives…. Thanksgiving changes us. It is the *attitude of advancement.*[3]

Giving thanks to God for, and in, all situations honors God, opens the door to answered prayer, and releases the blessings of Heaven into our lives.

PRAYER: MORE THAN ANSWERS

PERSONAL SPIRITUAL BENEFITS
The ninth chapter of Daniel records one of the most passionate prayers of intercession in the Bible. In this passage, God sent the angel Gabriel to bring the response to Daniel's petition. Then, in chapter 10, we see Daniel interacting with another heavenly messenger in response to his prayer to receive understanding of the vision recorded in chapter 9. Through examination of chapter 10, we see that prayer offers more than just "answers." For one thing, prayer, as touching God, brings down from Heaven a strengthening in our inner man. Herbert Lockyer calls the response to Daniel's prayer in chapter 10 a "soul-absorbing vision of the glory of God." In this vision he sees five spiritual benefits of prayer.[4]

1. Prayer results in **inspired vision**. In verses 7-11 there is a description of the heavenly messenger sent to bring Daniel revelation from God. We are told that Daniel's vision was expanded to see the angel, while the others with him did not see, though apparently they heard the voice, because they fled in terror. This suggests a progression in vision. First there is a "hearing" and then a "seeing." Daniel had pressed into the heart of God with fasting and prayer for three weeks. So he not only heard the thunderous voice, but saw — and spoke to — the angel. His vision was complete and interactive. *Desperate prayer brings increased vision and revelation from God.* Though we may not actually see an angel, we will receive inspired vision as we press into God in prayer.

2. Prayer secures an **instant audience with God.** In verse 12 the angel said to Daniel, "Do not fear,...for from the first day that you set your heart to understand,...*your words were heard.*" God may not always give us the answer right away, but we can be sure that He always *hears* our prayers. Intercession brings us into the immediate presence of God.

3. Prayer results in **inspired wisdom.** In 10:14 the angel said to Daniel: "Now I have come *to make you understand* what will happen to your people in the latter days...." Again, we may not actually see

an angel when we pray, but God does impart spiritual understanding to us through the Holy Spirit. For "apart from unbroken communion with God, spiritual insight into His Word and ways is not possible."[5]

4. Prayer provides us with necessary strength. In verse 8 we are told that when Daniel saw the vision of the angel, "no strength remained in me; for my vigor was turned to frailty." Later, in verse 17, Daniel said to the angel, "How can [I] talk with you?… No strength remains in me now, nor is any breath left in me." Then the angel "touched me and strengthened me" (verse 18). Isaiah tells us that as we wait upon God, our strength is renewed like the eagle's: "He gives power to the weak, and to those who have no might He increases strength" (Isaiah 40:31 and 29). Waiting in God's presence can be both spiritually and physically renewing.

5. Prayer drives away all fear. Twice in Daniel 10 the angel told Daniel not to fear. In verse 19 he said: "O man greatly beloved, *fear not!* Peace be to you; *be strong, yes, be strong!*" He was admonishing Daniel to stand strong in faith — and not in fear. For, as Mr. Lockyer says, "Faith and fear cannot exist together: the one destroys the other."[6] Prayer strengthens our spiritual "immunity" against fear.

KINGDOM BENEFITS: THE ACTIVITY OF ANGELS

Prayer not only has personal benefits, but Kingdom benefits as well. As we have seen in our study of Daniel, prayer activates angels and stirs up heavenly places. We need to take a more in-depth look at the activity of angels in response to prayer. As the angel in chapter 10 visited Daniel with the answer to his prayer, he brought Daniel understanding concerning Israel's future destiny, and in so doing he established the prophetic clock for the outworking of that destiny in world events. So we see that as our needs are met through angelic activity, God's Kingdom is established. The Word of God tells us that angels are God's special messengers sent to do His bidding:

> Bless the LORD, you His angels, who excel in strength, who do His word, heeding the voice of the Lord.   Psalm 103:20

…Angelic Authority
There are also a number of other activities associated with angels. For

instance, there are angels that have authority and assignments over men, cities and nations. Daniel 12:1 identifies Michael as "the great prince who stands watch over the sons of your people [the Israelites]." Ezekiel 9 relates the account of the prophet Ezekiel's vision regarding six angels sent by God to bring judgment upon the city of Jerusalem for the abominations that were there. In this vision Ezekiel was visited by a Being who appeared to be a pre-incarnate presence of Christ. Ezekiel writes in verses 1-2:

> *Then He called out in my hearing with a loud voice, saying, "Let those who have charge over the city draw near, each with a deadly weapon in his hand.""And suddenly, six men came from the direction of the upper gate…each with his battle-ax in his hand."*

These "men," or angels, clearly had authority over Jerusalem in the spirit realm. We can be sure if there are God's angels in charge over cities, then there are evil angels assigned to cities also. These are the "principalities" and "powers" and "spiritual hosts of wickedness in the heavenly places" spoken of in Ephesians 6:12.

This hierarchy of "spiritual hosts" extends over *nations*. In Exodus 23 we find an account of the Lord God giving Israel instructions concerning conquest regulations as she goes forth to lay hold of her Covenant land. We see that God gave the nation of Israel an angel to lead her into the Promised Land. The Lord spoke to Moses:

> *"Behold,* I send an Angel before you *to keep you in the way and to bring you into the place which I have prepared."*   verse 20

As we said earlier, in Daniel 10:13, an angel speaking to Daniel identified an evil *"prince of the kingdom of Persia"* who "withstood me twenty-one days; and behold, *Michael, one of the chief princes* [of God], came to help me for I had been left alone there with the *kings of Persia.*" This is a picture of the spiritual warfare that is raging over our cities and nations continually. There are evil princes (with their "principalities," or areas of jurisdiction) and God's princes assigned over every nation and city. The progress of the war for good or evil is largely determined by our prayers — the prayers of God's people arrayed for battle!

…The Ministry of Angels

Hebrews 1:14 describes angels as *"ministering spirits* sent forth to minister for those who will inherit salvation." ~~God dispatches angels, often in response to our prayers, to bring such things as comfort, deliverance and direction.~~ For instance, in Acts 27:22-25 there is an account of Paul sailing at sea in a ship that was tempest tossed. He had a visitation of an angel who **comforted** him, saying, "Do not be afraid, Paul: you must be brought before Caesar; and indeed God has granted you all those who sail with you" (verse 24).

In an instance of divine **deliverance**, when Herod had imprisoned Peter, in Acts 12:1-19, it is recorded that *"constant prayer was offered to God for him by the church"* (verse 5). And as Peter was "sleeping, bound with chains between two soldiers…,an angel of the Lord stood by him, and a light shone in the prison; and he struck Peter on the side and raised him up, saying, 'Arise quickly!' And his chains fell off his hands" (verses 6-7).

An example of a ministering angel giving **direction** occurred, in Acts 8:26-27, when Phillip was sent to minister to the Ethiopian eunuch: "Now an angel of the Lord spoke to Philip, saying, 'Arise and go toward the south along the road which goes down from Jerusalem to Gaza.'… So he arose and went. And behold, a man of Ethiopia, a eunuch of great authority… had come to Jerusalem to worship."

Guardian angels are sent by God to protect His people from the kingdom of darkness. David wrote about such angelic activity in Psalms 91 and 34:

• *"He shall give His angels charge over you, to keep you in all your ways."* (Psalm 91:11)
• *"The angel of the LORD encamps all around those who fear Him, and delivers them."* (Psalm 34:7)

The Bible is also filled with examples of the **destructive** activity of angels against those who oppose God and His Kingdom purposes. These angels, at God's command, bring destruction (Revelation 7:2, 14:19-20, 16:1), curses (Judges 5:23), plagues (2 Samuel 24:15-17), persecution (Psalm 35:5), and death (Acts 12:21-23).

For the intercessor, the important thing to remember about angels is that *prayer activates their activity* on behalf of those who belong to God and for the purpose of establishing His Kingdom in the earth.

CREATING AN ALTAR OF PRAYER

In Scripture, an altar, among other things, was a place to meet with

God. Your "altar," or place of meeting God in prayer, can be a room, a "closet" or simply a chair. The mother of Jonathan Edwards, the great preacher/revivalist, reportedly found her altar under her apron as she retreated to the solace of God's presence amid the busyness of her household. Each person has his own way of entering spiritually and mentally into this place. I have found the following scriptures to be helpful in focusing my thoughts toward prayer. As I gather myself, with Bible and notes, together before my altar to pray, I begin by thanking and praising the Lord through reading a psalm, such as Psalm 29 or 33, which talks about the Lord's mighty voice and the creative power of His Word. Then I spend some time in confession, and reflection on God's goodness and mercy in His forgiveness. Good scriptures to pray are:

- *"Create in me a clean heart, O God, and renew a right spirit within me"* (Psalm 51:10).
- Followed by *"Let the words of my mouth and the meditation of my heart be acceptable in Your sight, O LORD, my strength and my Redeemer."* (Psalm 19:14)

I thank Him, as I confess my sins, that He is faithful and just to forgive me and to cleanse me of all unrighteousness (see 1 John 1:9).

Next, I pray the protecting Blood of Jesus over me and my family, and ask the Lord to strengthen my spiritual armor (previously discussed, in Ephesians 6). I thank Him that no weapon formed against me or mine shall prosper (see Isaiah 54:17) and that He, in me, is greater than he that is in the world (1 John 4:4). And, because the Lord gave me this verse as a personal call to prayer several years ago, I always remind the Lord of His promise in Jeremiah 33:3:

"Call to Me, and I will answer you, and show you great and mighty things, which you do not know."

I then set my mind to *expect* great and mighty things as I pray because *He is a great and a mighty God!*

Then, finally, I ask the Lord to give me His grace to strengthen me in my weakness (see 2 Corinthians 12:9) so that I might pray prayers that will shake nations, move mountains (see Matthew 17:20), and cause principalities and powers to fall (see Ephesians 6:12). I ask Him to anoint my words like He did Jeremiah's, to root out, pull down, destroy and throw down enemy strongholds, and to build and to plant the Kingdom of God (see Jeremiah 1:9-10). I then advance into prayer with the high praises of God in my mouth and a two-edged sword in my hand (see Psalm 149:6) — the sword of the Spirit: the Word of God!

I close my time of prayer with several more scriptural confessions, re-membering that without faith it is impossible to please God (see Hebrews 11:6) and that faith honors and exalts God for who He is. I confess to the Lord that I believe as I now "draw near with a true heart in full assurance of faith" (Hebrews 10:22) that I have the petitions I have asked of Him... and that I "hold fast the confession of [my] hope without wavering, for He who promised is faithful" (Hebrews 10:23). I tell Him that the basis of my con-viction is that I have prayed *in faith, believing* (see Mark 11:24) and *abiding* (see John 15:7) in Him, and I have prayed *in His name* (see John 14:14) and "according to *His will*" (1 John 5:14). My assurance that I have prayed according to His will is that I have prayed *according to His Word*. And His Word does not return void unto Him (see Isaiah 55:11). It is living and powerful and sharper than a double-edged sword (see Hebrews 4:12), able to smash the strategies of darkness (see Jeremiah 23:29) and to "cut asun-der the cords of the wicked" (Psalm 129:4, KJV). I then thank Him for releasing His Word into the earth to bring forth His will and purposes...for His name's sake, that is, that He would receive all the glory, and that the knowledge of the glory of the Lord would cover the earth as the waters cover the sea (see Habakkuk 2:14). And finally, I thank Him that HIS KINGDOM SHALL COME AND HIS WILL BE DONE ON EARTH AS IT IS IN HEAVEN (see Matthew 6:10).

[1] Charles Finney, *Power From God* (New Kensington, PA: Whitaker House, 1996), p. 61.

[2] Herbert Lockyer, *All the Prayers of the Bible* (Grand Rapids, Michigan: Zondervan Publishing House, 1959), p. 154.

[3] Robin McMillan, "From Tragedy to Triumph," *The Morning Star Journal*, (Wilkesboro, NC: Morning Star Publications, Inc., 2003), p. 57.

[4] Herbert Lockyer, *All the Prayers of the Bible* (Grand Rapids, Michigan: Zondervan Publishing House, 1959), p. 156.

[5] Ibid.

[6] Ibid.

PART TWO

❖❖❖

PRAYER STRATEGIES

Specific prayer strategies and principles to enhance prayer life and to assist in being a more effective prayer warrior.

Chapter Five

PROPHETIC INTERCESSION

"In this manner, therefore, pray: Our Father in heaven,...
Your kingdom come. Your will be done on earth as it is in heaven."
Matthew 6:9-10

WHAT IS PROPHETIC INTERCESSION?

DECLARING THE WORD OF GOD

In Chapter Three we said that God has a plan for establishing His Kingdom in the earth. And he has called us as His "Kingdom agents," equipped
us, and delegated to us the authority to partner with Him to bring His plan
to fruition. The means by which we accomplish this is through *prophetic
intercession*, or agreeing in prayer with the *Word* of God to bring forth the
will of God in the earth: "Thy Kingdom come. Thy will be done...." In
other words, it is proclaiming what God has said in the past to bring forth
the purposes of His heart for the future. Derek Prince made the statement
that "the essence of all effective proclamation is to quote God's own word
back to Him."[1] This "word" can be the written Word or God's inspired,
spoken prophetic word. The Scriptures are full of God's prophetic procla-
mations to the Church; such as, "The gates of hell shall not prevail against
the church" (see Matthew 16:18). But we know from experience that all
hell is at war against the Church. The reality is, the promises of God are
not automatic. For the Lord has also said to us that we should "pray without ceasing" (1 Thessalonians 5:17), and that we "do not have because [we]
do not ask" (James 4:2). In the Lord's Prayer we are instructed to pray daily
for our needs ("Give us this day...") — those needs that He already knows
about, and which He already desires to give us, and which He has expressed
in His Word that He *will* give us. But He has set it up that *we must ask Him*

for these things… *continually* and *in faith* (see James 4:2b). God has, indeed, called us to partner with Him in Kingdom building. But He has limited His activity in the lives of men based on our response to Him through prayer. The great man of God, John Wesley, once said, "God does nothing but in answer to prayer."

AUTHORITY IN PRAYER

As we said, God has the master plan — and the way to implement that plan. He shares His plan (will or intention) with His people through a prophetic word or revelation from Scripture. This is given as a call to prayer to bring to pass in the natural what God has spoken in/by the Spirit. For as soon as God gives His word of *intention*, the devil gives his word of *prevention*, and we are at war. The main work of the devil and his kingdom is to hinder the Kingdom of God from being established — in our individual lives and in the earth. Therefore, as God's "Kingdom advancers," we must declare His word in *authority* and *faith* until we see the manifestation of it. Our *authority* is summarized in Luke 10:19, where Jesus said to His disciples, "Behold, I give you authority… over all the power of the enemy, and nothing shall by any means hurt you." We have faith to pray according to God's will based on 1 John 5:14-15: "And this is the confidence that we have in Him, that if we ask anything according to His will, He hears us. And…we know that we have the petitions that we have asked of Him." And as we have said, His Word IS His will.

PERSEVERANCE IN PRAYER

In Acts 1:4, just before His Ascension, Jesus bid a final farewell to His disciples and "commanded them not to depart from Jerusalem, but to **wait** for the Promise of the Father." Then He told them what the promise would bring. He said, in verse 8: *"you shall receive **power** when the Holy Spirit has come upon you; and you shall be witnesses to Me in Jerusalem, and in all Judea and Samaria, and to the end of the earth."* This was the *prophetic word* of what God intended to do to birth His Church in the earth. The disciples' response to this word from the Lord is significant. Notably, they did not return to their homes, their jobs and life as usual to *wait passively* for God to move. The word *wait* in verse 4 in the Greek carries the meaning "to remain or tarry *with expectancy.*" In verses 12-14, it says that after they returned to Jerusalem, "when they had entered, they went up into the upper room where they were staying…[and] *continued with one accord in prayer* *and supplication.*" First, notice that they prayed "with one accord." (We will discuss the power of the corporate prayer of agreement later, in Chapter Eleven.) Secondly, the Scripture says they interceded "in prayer and supplication." *Supplication* is a prayer of great fervency. In other words, they continued (waited), with one accord, in fervent prevailing prayer, until the promise came — the mighty baptism of the Holy Spirit — which would equip them to fulfill their holy commission to be witnesses to take the Gospel to the ends of the earth (see Acts 2:1-4). So out of that season of obedient and expectant waiting and supplication came the mighty outpouring at Pentecost that birthed the Church and changed the world forever.

THE PROPHETIC WORD

Sometimes God gives a prophetic word of blessing, such as His present word to the Church that He is preparing to release revival into the earth, or His scriptural declarations through the Old Testament prophets of His intention to restore Israel to her Covenant land. For example, in Deuteronomy 30, God spoke these words of restoration over Israel:

> *"Now it shall come to pass, when... you return to the LORD your God and obey His voice...that the LORD your God will bring you back from captivity, and have compassion on you, and gather you again from all the nations. ... Then the LORD ...will bring you to the land which your fathers possessed, and you shall possess it. He will prosper you and multiply you more than your fathers."*   verses 1-5, selected

At other times the Lord may bring a word of rebuke or warning to us so intercessors can avert the coming judgment through prayer. The great prophets of the Old Testament, such as Moses, Amos and Ezekiel, were raised up by God to intercede for the errant nation of Israel. Great periods of revival following times of backsliding and judgment were heralded by passionate intercession.

OLD TESTAMENT INTERCESSORS
...Moses

During the time of the Israelite wanderings in the wilderness, the Scriptures recount that "the Lord spoke to Moses face to face, as a man speaks to his friend" (Exodus 33:11). In this favored position, Moses frequently interceded on behalf of his rebellious people. As we said in back in Chapter One, when he ascended Mt. Sinai to commune with God and receive the Ten Commandments, the children of Israel got impatient waiting and made their own "god" in the form of a golden calf. God's wrath then burned against them and He sought to destroy them. You may recall that Moses' intercession caused God to relent from the harm He said He would do (see Exodus 32:11-13). In Deuteronomy 9:25-29 we find Moses reminding the wayward people of Israel of what had happened following their rebellion with the golden calf:

> *Thus I prostrated myself before the* LORD; *forty days and forty nights I kept prostrating myself,* because the LORD had said He would destroy you. *Therefore I prayed to the Lord, and said:* "O LORD GOD, do not destroy Your people and Your inheritance whom You have redeemed through Your greatness, *whom You have brought out of Egypt with a mighty hand.* Remember *Your servants, Abraham, Isaac, and Jacob; do not look on the stubbornness of this people, or on their wickedness or their sin, lest the land from which You brought us should say, 'Because the* LORD *was not able to bring them to the* land which He promised them, *and because He hated them, He has brought them out to kill them in the wilderness.'* "

We can see in the above prayer of intercession that Moses pleaded with God to have *mercy on the people* and to *honor His Name* before the heathen. Additionally, he *brought the Lord in remembrance* of the "everlasting" Covenant He had made with Abraham, Isaac, and Jacob (see Genesis 22:17-18). He then reminded the people of God's merciful response: The Lord relented of the destruction He threatened, and restated His promise that the people would enter in and possess their covenant land (Deuteronomy 10:10-11).

...Amos

Amos is another example of a prophetic intercessor who changed the course of history. Amos, like Daniel before him, appealed to God's great mercy. God gave Amos two visions of coming judgment on rebellious Israel, after which Amos pleaded: "O Lord GOD, forgive, I pray! Oh, that Jacob may stand, for he is small!" The Lord's response was the same in both cases: "So the LORD relented concerning this. 'It shall not be,' said the LORD" (see Amos 7:1-6).

These prayers of Moses and Amos are models of prophetic intercession which averted the judgments of God by putting Him in remembrance of His Word, His Covenant, and the honor of His holy name.

...Ezekiel

About one thousand years after Moses, the Lord spoke through the prophet Ezekiel these words concerning:

- **the wayward nation of Israel:** *"As men gather silver, bronze, iron, lead, and tin into the midst of a furnace, to blow fire on it, to melt it; so I will gather you in My anger and in My fury, and I will leave you there and melt you."* (Ezekiel 22:20)
- **the results of the *lack* of an intercessor:** *" 'So I sought for a man among them who would make a wall, and* stand in the gap before Me on behalf of the land, *that I should not destroy it;* but I found no one. *Therefore I have poured out My indignation on them; I have consumed them with the fire of My wrath; and I have recompensed their deeds on their own heads,' says the Lord GOD"* (Ezekiel 22:30-31)

God is ever looking for someone to "stand in the gap" before Him on behalf of the land and the people.

...Jonah

Jonah is an example of an Old Testament prophet who petitioned God for deliverance on behalf of *himself.* God had given Jonah instructions to take a message of impending judgment to the wicked city of Nineveh. The book of Jonah relates how Jonah ended up in the belly of a great fish as the consequence of running from God and the call to Nineveh. Jonah's impassioned and desperate supplication from the fish's belly is a beautiful example of personal prophetic intercession. For Jonah appealed to God's mercy through poetic images recalled from numerous scriptural references:

Then Jonah prayed to the LORD his God from the fish's belly. And he said:
I cried out to the LORD because of my affliction (Psalm 120:1), *and He answered me* (Psalm 65:2). *Out of the belly of Sheol I cried.... For You cast me into the deep* (Psalm 88:6)...; *all Your billows and Your waves passed over me* (Psalm 42:7). *Then I said, 'I have been cast out of Your sight* (Psalm 31:22); *yet I will look again toward Your holy temple* (1 Kings 8:38). *The waters surrounded me, even to my soul* (Lamentations 3:54)...

You have brought up my *life from the pit, O LORD, my God* (Psalm 16:10).... *But I will sacrifice to You with the voice of thanksgiving. ... Salvation is of the LORD"* (Psalm 3:8).

WHAT DOES GOD SAY ABOUT HIS WORD?

God's Word, the Bible, is neither static nor merely historic. Hebrews 4:12 says that God's Word is "living and active." In Isaiah 55:11 the Lord God says, "So shall My word be that goes forth from My mouth; *it shall not return to Me void*, but it shall accomplish what I please, and it shall prosper in the thing for which I sent it." In Isaiah 46:10-11, the Lord says, "My counsel shall stand, and I will do all My pleasure....Indeed *I have spoken it; I will also bring it to pass.* I have purposed it; I will also do it." And Numbers 23:19 states that "God is not a man, that He should lie, nor a son of man, that He should repent. Has he said, and will He not do? Or *has He spoken, and will He not make it good?"*

GOD WATCHES OVER HIS WORD

In Jeremiah 1:12 (TAB), the Lord says He is watching over His Word to perform it. The prophet Daniel was a man who understood this truth. And he interpreted the times in which he was living through the Word of God. Jerusalem had fallen, and the Israelites had been in captivity in Babylon for seventy years. As a student of the prophetic history and destiny of the nation of Israel, Daniel was aware of what God had said concerning the restoration of His people. In Daniel 9:2 we read:

> *In the first year of his [Darius'] reign, I, Daniel, understood by the books the number of the years specified by the word of the LORD through Jeremiah the prophet, that He would accomplish seventy years in the desolations of Jerusalem.*

Daniel understood, through the writings of Jeremiah, that although his brethren were captives of a hostile empire, their time of deliverance was nigh, and so he prayed to God.

> *"O Lord, great and awesome God,* who keeps His covenant and mercy *with those who love Him, and with those who keep His command-ments, we have sinned..., done wickedly and rebelled.... Neither have*

we heeded… the prophets…. Righteousness belongs to You, but to us shame of face…. To the Lord our God belong mercy and forgiveness, though we have rebelled against Him…. All Israel has transgressed Your law…; therefore the curse and the oath written in the Law of Moses…have been poured out on us…. And now, O Lord our God, who brought Your people out of the land of Egypt with a mighty hand, and made Yourself a name…. Now therefore, our God, hear the prayer of Your servant,… and for the Lord's sake cause Your face to shine on Your sanctuary…; for we do not present our supplications before You because of our righteous deeds, but because of Your great mercies…. O Lord, forgive!… Do not delay for Your own sake, my God, for Your city and Your people are called by Your name."

Like Abraham and Moses, we see in this beautiful prayer Daniel's appeal on the basis of God's mercy, His great name, His Word (promise of restoration) and His Covenant with Israel. Like Daniel, we need to be aware of what the Word of God says concerning future events and also the covenant promises He has made with us, so we can intercede accordingly.

WHAT DOES GOD'S WORD DO?

Hebrews 4:12 goes on to say that not only is God's Word "living and active," but it is "sharper than any double-edged sword" (NIV). This is the sword of the Spirit in Ephesians 6. This sword—the Word of God in your mouth—is able to "cut asunder the cords of the wicked" (Psalm 129:4) and pull down strongholds (2 Corinthians 10:4). Marsha Burns gives us a glimpse of the *sword of the spirit* in action:

I heard in the Spirit the sound of the spoken Word echoing through the habitation of demons. I saw the Word of God as it manifested as the wind of the Spirit storming through the caverns and striking fear in the hearts of Satan's minions. I was aware that the devils were taking cover and hiding from this great power. And, I knew that we must speak forth the Word, which is the sword of the Spirit, our offensive weapon of warfare against the enemy. [2]

In addition, the Word establishes righteousness (see Ephesians 4:24) and faith (see Romans 10:17). It brings healing (see Psalm 107:20) and sets the captives free (see John 8:32). The Word has creative and regenerative power (Hebrews 11:3 and James 1:18). And it brings reconciliation (see 2 Corinthians 5:19). The Word illumines our minds (see Psalm 119:130) and brings forth spiritual life and fruit (see 2 Peter 1:3,4 and 8), thus equipping us to be better soldiers. ~~The Word of God is not only "living," but it generates life.~~ Pastor Rick Warren, of Saddleback Church in Lake Forest, California, declares that the Word "generates life, creates faith, produces change, frightens the devil, causes miracles, heals hurts, builds character, transforms circumstances, imparts joy, overcomes adversity, defeats temptation, infuses hope, releases power, cleanses our minds, brings things into being, and guarantees our future forever!"[3]

The psalmist tells us that God's Word is eternal, forever settled in heaven (see Psalm119:89). As intercessors we need to declare into the heavenlies what the Lord has said in His Word. We need to come into agreement with His Word and put Him in remembrance of it, so that it can be released to bring forth the fruit for which He sent it. As God's holy people arise and take the authority that they have been given by God to take dominion and declare His will and Word in the earth, the Kingdom of God will arise and His enemies will be scattered (Psalm 68:1). Truly it is time to activate the weapons we have been given and take back the land! The following prophetic word was released by Bill Burns of Trumpet Ministries (Kremmling, Colorado) on March 22, 2004:

I sound the trumpet, says the Lord, for these are the days of glorious victory in My house. *I shall give heavenly weapons, the prophetic word.* Corporate power has never been exercised in the history of mankind as it is now being activated. *It will come forth as a mighty sword against the enemy and destroy his devices, tear down his strongholds, and establish My rule in the land. It is My land,* and I will take back the title deed to planet earth. *I am establishing it now through the voice of My servants.* I will bring forth a victory in the land that will astound even the greatest of intercessors, for they have desired to see My Kingdom established. You have the sword of the Spirit, the torch, the glory, and the anointing by which you will break the power of the enemy. It is written that the anointing breaks the yoke. *Go forth in the power of My might and become that which I have spoken. You are My priests and kings, My warriors ordained for victory, says the Lord. Walk it out and perform My will in the land, but begin where you are by taking dominion back from the enemy.* [4]

[1] Derek Prince, "War in Heaven: God's Epic Battle with Evil", *Intercessors for America Newsletter*, Vol. 30, No. 11, November 2003.

[2] Marsha Burns, *Spirit of Prophecy Bulletin,* Kremmling, CO., Internet Article, March 13, 2006.

[3] Rick Warren, *The Purpose-Driven Life* (Grand Rapids, Michigan: Zondervan, 2002), p. 186.

[4] Bill Burns, *Trumpet Ministries*, Kremmling, CO., Internet article, March 22, 2004.

Chapter Six

MAKING DECREES: GOVERNMENTAL AUTHORITY

"Thou shalt also decree a thing, and it shall be established...."
Job 22:28, KJV

WHAT IS GOVERNMENTAL AUTHORITY?

We have been talking about authority through Christ and the Kingdom of God. Since kingdoms are ruled by governments, it follows that our authority in God's Kingdom is a *governmental authority*. A key scripture on the government of God is Isaiah 9:6-7:

> *For unto us a Child is born, unto us a Son is given;*
> And the government will be upon His shoulder.
> *And His name will be called*
> *Wonderful, Counselor, Mighty God, Everlasting Father, Prince of Peace.*
> Of the increase of His government and peace there will be no end.
> Upon the throne of David and over His kingdom,
> To order it and establish it with judgment and justice
> *From that time forward, even forever.*
> The zeal of the Lord of hosts will perform this.

This scripture tells us that Jesus, the Mighty God, entered the earth realm 2,000 years ago with the ultimate goal of establishing His Kingdom (government) in the earth through a people called and set apart to be His own. He was crucified, buried and rose again to take His rightful place at the right hand of the Father as the King of kings and Lord of lords. His throne is the throne established through covenant with David three thousand years ago, and, one day, His government of justice and peace shall have no end (verse 7).

Government may be defined as "rule and administration exercised over a people giving direction and control to society." The Kingdom of God exists in the earth through a *progression* of government. First of all, Jesus must rule in the individual heart of *every Believer*. We each must consider: "Is Jesus on the throne of my heart exercising sovereign control and direction in my life?" If not, then we are a lawless citizen of His Kingdom. The next level of Kingdom sovereignty is *the Church*: Is Jesus the true head of the Church in the world today? At this point in time, because of the secularization of the Church through sin and ignorance, God's Kingdom authority in the earth has been abdicated to a governmental organization of man. But the Kingdom Age is upon us, and the time is fast approaching when the Church will arise triumphant in all her glory (see Isaiah 60:1-3). When this happens, *the whole world* will bow to God's government, for the "kingdoms of this world [shall] become the kingdoms of our Lord and of His Christ, and He shall reign forever and ever" (Revelation 11:15).

THE "KEY OF DAVID" (ISAIAH 22:22)

A key scripture on governmental authority is Isaiah 22:22:

> *"The* key of the house of David *I will lay on his shoulder; so he shall open, and no one shall shut; and he shall shut, and no one shall open."*

These words were spoken by the prophet Isaiah over a man named Eliakim, who was identified as a steward over King Hezekiah's house. Eliakim is described as "a father to the inhabitants of Jerusalem and to the house of Judah" (verse 21). He can be regarded as a type of the Messiah. The phrase "key…of David" in verse 22 is repeated in Revelation 3:7 (to the church in Philadelphia, and speaking of the Messiah):

> *"These things says He who is holy, He who is true, 'He who has the* key of David, *He who opens and no one shuts, and shuts and no one opens.'"*

This "key" (of David) principle works like, and in tandem with, the "binding and loosing" principle in Matthew 18:18. Quoting Jesus:

"Assuredly, I say to you, whatever you bind on earth will be bound in heaven, and whatever you loose on earth will be loosed in heaven."

In other words, whatever is bound or loosed on earth is bound or loosed in Heaven; and whatever is closed or opened on earth is closed or opened in Heaven.

A MANTLE OF AUTHORITY

Back to Isaiah 22:22, the "house of David" is the royal line of descent from which Jesus was born (see Matthew 1:1). We, as born-again Believers, are grafted into that line. It is also the royal line on which God's government shall rest, according to Isaiah 9:6-7 (quoted earlier):

And the government will be upon His shoulder.... Of the increase of His government...there will be no end, upon the throne of David *and over His kingdom.*

Isaiah 22:22 speaks of the "key" being laid on his shoulder. The word shoulder here refers to a *"mantle of authority."* A mantle is a cloak worn over the shoulders. It is also a term designating a "weight" of authority which rests upon a person. For instance, when Elijah was taken up into Heaven on the chariot of fire, his mantle fell off and was picked up by Elisha. When Elisha then struck the water with the mantle, the water divided and he walked across. The sons of the prophets who were watching said, "The spirit of Elijah rests on Elisha," as evidenced by the authority of the mantle (see 2 Kings 2:11-15). In Isaiah 22:22, this mantle of authority is a *governmental* authority, because it relates to the house of David. This governmental authority gives us authority with God over all that opposes Him. We have already quoted Luke 10:19, which says Jesus has given Believers authority over all the power of the enemy. Isaiah 22:22 tells us that *as we are grafted into the house of David, upon which His government shall rest, His mantle of governmental authority is released on us to open and shut things in the spirit realm.*

Jesus instructed His followers to occupy till He comes (see Luke 19:13, KJV).

The "key of the house of David" gives us governmental authority to occupy by opening and closing doors in the spirit realm. And as we exercise His divine authority on earth, He seals it in Heaven! (see Revelation 3:7).

MAKING DECREES

JESUS

In Luke chapter 4, Jesus was led by the Spirit into the wilderness to be tested by satan. His response to the devil is a model for intercessors. For at each point of temptation, Jesus answered with the words: "It is written...." He countered every ploy and word of the enemy with the Word of God — and so should we. There is no more powerful prayer than one which begins with the words: *"It is written...."* This is how we take up our "sword" (Ephesians 6:17) and "wage the good warfare" (1 Timothy 1:18).

MARY

Mary, the mother of Jesus, also had a test. The angel Gabriel appeared to her and told her that something miraculous was going to happen to her: She was going to have a baby without knowing a man. The angel assured her that "with God nothing will be impossible" (Luke 1:37). Mary chose to believe the word of the Lord. *She agreed with God for what was impossible with man*, and said, "Let it be to me *according to your word* " (Luke 1:38). This is a model for intercessors. We, too, can say, "Let it be unto _____ according to Your Word!" In this account of Mary's annunciation, verse 45 is key:

> *"Blessed is she* who believed, *for* there will be a fulfillment *of those things which were told her from the Lord."*

I wonder what would have happened if Mary *hadn't* believed? All roads, in prayer, come back to FAITH. We receive *by* faith, and we pray *in* faith. Indeed, there is fulfillment for those who believe the Word, but "without faith it is impossible to please God" (Hebrews 11:6).

DECLARING THE WORD

Both Jesus and Mary believed God, and secured the promise and the victory through the words of their mouth. By declaration they aligned themselves with the Word of the Lord. Jesus said: *"It is written...."* Mary said: *"...according to your word."* We, too, need to declare with our mouth the truth of God in prayer to bring our need into alignment with God's provision. The Spirit of Truth is at work in us to accomplish this on a personal and a national level. For *"before God moves in the earth, He first moves in the hearts of a few to make intercession for what He wills to do."* [1]

BEING IN RIGHT RELATIONSHIP WITH GOD

Job 22:23-28 gives us further instruction for making declarations and decrees:

> "If you return to the Almighty, *you will be built up; you will remove iniquity far from your tents. Then you will lay your gold in the dust,...and the Almighty will be your gold.... For then you will have your delight in the Almighty, and lift up your face to God. You will* make your prayer to Him, He will hear you.... You will also declare [King James: "decree"] a thing, and it will be established for you."

We see from this passage another key to prevailing prayer: *being in right relationship with God* ("IF you return to the Almighty"). For as we return and submit to the Lord, our sin is dealt with, our faith gets built up, and our priorities come into order. Then, instead of worldly pursuits and wealth, the Almighty will be our precious "gold." Obedience and love unto God raise our level of authority when making decrees. For then, as we *delight* in Him, His will becomes ours and our prayers get results: We will "decree a thing, and it will be established."

THE "ESTHER DECREE" (ESTHER 8:8)

There is a verse in the book of Esther that works hand in hand with Isaiah 22:22 in making decrees. Esther was a young Jewish woman who was among the many wives of King Xerxes of the Persian Empire, about 480 B.C. The Scripture records that a wicked man named Haman devised a plan to annihilate all the Jews in Persia. With the king's permission, he made a decree concerning his plan. And because it was sealed with the king's signet ring, the decree could not be revoked. But God had raised up

Esther "for such a time as this," to intercede on behalf of her people before the king. King Xerxes then gave Esther permission to make a *counter decree* and seal it with his signet ring. We read in Esther 8:8 the words of King Xerxes:

"You yourselves write a decree *concerning the Jews, as you please, in the* king's name, *and seal it with the* king's signet ring; for whatever is written in the king's name and sealed with the king's signet ring no one can revoke."

SEALED WITH THE BLOOD

Now, if we put Isaiah 22:22 together with Esther 8:8, we then see that we have been given authority to "make a decree," in the name of our King, which cannot be revoked, and that is binding in Heaven and on earth. King Xerxes' signet ring was sealed with wax. Our King has given us a signet ring sealed with *the Blood of the Lamb*. At the time of the first Passover, in Exodus 12, the Hebrew people were instructed by God through Moses to anoint the lintels and doorposts of their houses with the blood of the sacrificial lamb. This acted as a "seal" to keep out the death angel as he "passed over" all the homes in Egypt. As an extension of the Isaiah 22:22 strategy, after taking authority to open or close doors in the spirit realm, we then put the "seal" of the Blood of the Lamb over the doorposts and lintels of these spiritual doors of access that the enemy has used to gain influence in a situation or life. In this way we insure that the "death angel" (demonic power) can no longer enter. So, we "decree a thing" from the Word of God, opening and closing doors in the spirit realm, and seal it with the Blood of the Lamb. This word then cannot be revoked, and is binding in Heaven and on earth until the appointed time at which God performs it.

CAUTION IN CONFRONTING THE ENEMY

There needs to be caution whenever challenging the enemy, especially at the level of principalities and powers over cities and nations. We must come well girded in our armor: the breastplate of righteousness and shield of faith must be polished and secure. The *Blood* of Jesus is our covering and the *sword of the Spirit* our offensive weapon. As we stand on the authority of God's Word, we must remember that the battle is the Lord's (see 1 Samuel 17:47). Our work is to **stand, declare** and **petition**. His work is to pull down strongholds, to set the captives free, and to establish His Kingdom in the earth.

A "New Season" of Advancing God's Kingdom

Barbara Wentroble, a recognized prophetic voice in the Church, had this to say about governmental authority and prophetic intercession in her article entitled "Governmental Intercession — Our Nuclear Weapon Against Satanic Hosts!"[2] (emphasis added):

> God's *governmental intercession* will be released through powerful proclamations and decrees to overcome powers of darkness. As our faith comes to new levels, we operate in strong creative faith that brings to manifestation the invisible things that have not yet been seen in the earth. An inner energy by the Spirit of God causes us to believe the things we say will be birthed in the earth. *There is a commanding aspect of governmental prayer that speaks not so much to God as it does to the things that need to be manifested in the earth.* For too long the Church has been bound by natural thinking.... However, she is rising up and receiving revelation that releases her from natural thinking and propels her into the supernatural.... *This is a new season: the day for the advancing of God's Kingdom throughout the earth. A new mantle of governmental authority must be received for the task at hand... Powerful prophetic proclamations and apostolic decrees will cause us to possess what God has promised us. We have the ability to now see the answer to the prayer Jesus taught His disciples:* "Your kingdom come. Your will be done on earth as it is in heaven."
>
> Matthew 6:10

---

[1] Ed Corley, *Hagar, Outraged Mother of the Arab World* (Elk Park, NC: Berean Publications, 2004)

[2] Barbara Wentroble, "Governmental Intercession—Our Nuclear Weapon Against Satanic Hosts!", Internet article, February 2002.

Chapter Seven

THE POWER OF THE BLOOD AND THE NAME OF JESUS

"And being found in appearance as a man, He humbled Himself and became obedient to the point of death, even the death of the cross. Therefore God also has highly exalted Him and given Him the name which is above every name." Philippians 2:8-9

THE BLOOD

THE AUTHORITY OF THE BLOOD

Not only is the *Blood of the Lamb* the means to our salvation, it is the **foundation** of our authority and power in prayer. And that Blood alone is what brings our prayers "through the veil" (Hebrews 10:19-20) directly to the throne of God. John Calvin once said, "If we wish to pray in a profitable manner, we must learn ever to set before us the death of Christ, which alone sanctifies our prayers." Revelation 12:11 says that "they [the brethren] *overcame him* [the devil] *by the blood of the Lamb* and by the word of their testimony." As covenant children of Almighty God we have benefits (i.e., redemption, healing, cleansing, deliverance, victory, etc. — see Isaiah 53:4-6) that Jesus' Blood has bought for us, and which we appropriate through our declaration of faith (the "word of our testimony"). Our authority over the devil comes not from our own righteousness, but from the righteousness of Christ imparted to us (see 2 Corinthians 5:21) and through the power of His *cleansing Blood:*

- *"If we walk in the light as He is in the light, we have fellowship with one another, and the blood of Jesus Christ His Son cleanses us from all sin."* (1 John 1:7)

- "[Jesus] *loved us and* washed *us from our sins in His own blood.*" (Revelation 1:5)

BLOOD HEIRS WITH CHRIST

This Blood of the Covenant represents for us both a covering of protection and a mantle of authority. For through the Blood we are brought into God's family and share in the inheritance of Christ:

> *For as many as are led by the Spirit of God, these are sons of God...,and if children, then heirs — heirs of God and joint heirs with Christ.*
>   Romans 8:14 and 17

What this means for us, practically, is that all that Jesus has and does belongs to, and is available to, us — not by virtue of our own goodness or our own righteousness, but through His blood Covenant with us. And so to His followers He has delegated His authority:

- "*Behold,* I give you the authority... *over all the power of the enemy, and nothing shall by any means hurt you.*" (Luke 10:19)
- "*Most assuredly, I say to you, he who believes in Me, the* works that I do he will do also; *and greater works than these will he do.*" (John 14:12)

VICTORY IN THE BLOOD

The Scriptures extol the victory we have through the Blood of Jesus over all the power of death and sin:

- Christ is "*the Mediator of the new covenant.... He has appeared to put away sin by the sacrifice of Himself.... With His own blood He entered the Most Holy Place once for all, having obtained eternal redemption.*" (Hebrews 9:15, 26 and 12)
- "*The sting of death is sin, and the strength of sin is the law. But thanks be to God, who gives us the* victory *through our Lord Jesus Christ.*" (1 Corinthians 15:56-57)

Just as Jesus commanded the evil spirits, so can we. Satan, and all his evil horde are already defeated foes, anyway, so we are just reminding them of their sealed destiny. According to Colossians 2:13-15, Jesus triumphed over all the powers of darkness by the **Blood of His cross**:

> *He has made [you] alive together with Him....* Having disarmed principalities and powers, He made a public spectacle of them, triumphing over them in it [the cross].

These defeated demonic spirits act by deception and counterfeits, and they have no authority except what is given them through the doors that we open by our sin or ignorance. And then they are allowed to further prosper in the lives of men and nations because of the abdication of the Christians' God-given dominion-taking authority.

THE BLOOD AS A WEAPON

We can, and should, declare often that the Blood of the Lamb prevails against all the power of the enemy, and whatever plans he may be bringing against us or the situation we are praying for. Praying a "Blood" covering/line over/around people, cities, nations and situations is a strategic weapon in spiritual warfare (see Chapter Twenty-One). It is the Blood of the Lamb that paralyzes the devil, and the Blood line of Jesus he cannot cross.

TESTIMONY OF THE POWER OF THE BLOOD

International evangelist Mahesh Chavda has had much personal experience in deliverance and intercession. He shares the following testimony in his book *The Hidden Power of Prayer and Fasting*[1]:

> *I had been fasting, and I went into the room where this man was waiting. The man had been a homosexual for eighteen years, and when I entered the room, he was standing there as if waiting for a chance to intimidate again. I could see that the demon had come to the surface. He was literally staring out of the man. You could see it because the man's whole countenance had been transformed into a mask of evil. He saw me and said in an incredibly evil tone, "Oh, another man. Come in, I'd like to have fellowship with you." Now it was my turn to do the talking by the power of the Holy Spirit. "You want to have fellowship with me? Do you know what the Scriptures say? ...*

'If we walk in the light as He is in the light, we have fellowship with one another, and the blood of Jesus Christ cleanses us from all sin' (1 John 1:7). *Now, demon, can you say, 'The blood of Jesus'? (The thing could only growl at this point.) Demon, say 'The blood of Jesus' now, come on!"*

The man's hand started twisting, and I could literally hear bones cracking. Then the man's ankles began to twist in a contorted manner, and he fell on the floor and started writhing. I said, "Stop doing that. Say, 'The blood of Jesus' — say it now!" Finally he went, "The bl—, the bl—." Then the man seemed to regurgitate and the demon came out screaming.

I returned to that area five years later, and a man knocked on my hotel door.... He said, "Brother Chavda, I want to introduce you to someone." He stepped aside so I could see the young lady who was with him and he said, "We have been married for five years, and I want you to know that when you prayed for me that day, I was totally delivered. Now I am married and have normal desires."

What an awesome testimony of the power of the Blood of Jesus! The fact that Brother Chavda had been fasting was significant also, as we shall see further in Chapter Thirteen.

THE NAME

The Authority of the Name

The Blood goes in tandem with the *name of Jesus*, which carries authority above every other name, as we see in Philippians 2:9-11:

> *Therefore God also has highly exalted Him and given Him the name which is above every name, that at the name of Jesus every knee should bow, of those in heaven, and of those on earth, and of those under the earth, and that every tongue should confess that Jesus Christ is Lord, to the glory of God the Father.*

The Bible tells us that Jesus has been given all authority in Heaven and on earth (see Matthew 28:18). Because the name of Jesus carries with it His authority, we are instructed to pray in *His name:*

- *"He who believes in Me, the works that I do he will do also; and greater works than these will he do.... And* whatever you ask in My name, *that I will do, that the Father may be glorified in the Son. If you ask anything* in My name, *I will do it."* (John 14:12-3 and 14)
- *"If you abide in Me, and My words abide in you, you will ask what you desire, and it shall be done for you.... You did not choose Me, but I chose you and appointed you that you should go and bear fruit, and that your fruit should remain, that whatever you ask the Father* in My name *He may give you."* (John 15:7 and 16)
- *"Whatever you ask the Father* in My name *He will give you."* (John 16:23)

We could substitute the word *authority* for *name* in these scriptures and see the power of the name of Jesus.

The Power of the Name

In Acts 3, you may remember, is the account of Peter and John healing a lame man. In response to the people's amazement at the miracle, Peter said, "Why look so intently at us, as though by our own power or godliness we had made this man walk?... *His* [Jesus'] *name*, through *faith in His name*, has made this man strong" (Acts 3:12 and 16).

Continuing to chapter 4, we see that the Sanhedrin (Jewish religious leaders) felt threatened by this display of power:

> *"What shall we do to these men? For, indeed, that a notable miracle has been done through them is evident to all who dwell in Jerusalem, and we cannot deny it. But so that it spreads no further among the people, let us severely threaten them, that from now on they speak to no man in this name."*
> Acts 4:16-17

In response to this threat, the apostles went to God in prayer:

> *"Now, Lord, look on their threats, and grant to Your servants that with all boldness they may speak Your word, by stretching out Your hand to heal, and that signs and wonders may be done* through the **name** of Your holy Servant Jesus."
> Acts 4:29-30

USING THE NAME IN PRAYER

In Acts 16:16-18, Paul gives us an example of how to use the name of Jesus in prayer. In this account a slave girl who was possessed by a spirit of divination brought her masters much profit through fortune-telling. After she had harassed Paul and Silas for many days, Paul turned to her and said to the spirit who was controlling her, "I command you *in the name of Jesus Christ* to come out of her." And it came out of her that very hour.

We see from Scripture that, in prayer, the authority that the name of Jesus carries comes through delegation. It is mighty in the hands of those who are called by His name — of those who abide in, and believe in, Him. However, the authority is not *automatically* intrinsic to the name. In Acts 19, some Jewish exorcists attempted to use the name of Jesus without the authority behind it. The results were disastrous:

> *The evil spirit answered and said, "Jesus I know, and Paul I know; but who are you?" Then the man in whom the evil spirit was leaped on them, overpowered them, and prevailed against them, so that they fled out of that house naked and wounded.*   Acts 19:15-16

So what is it that causes evil spirits to recognize legal authority? — the victorious Blood of Jesus, and the power of His name invoked through a Spirit-filled Believer. Demons, and all powers of darkness, cannot stand against that Blood or that name.

---

[1] Mahesh Chavda, *The Hidden Power of Prayer and Fasting* (Shippensburg, PA: Destiny Image Publishers, Inc., 2000), pp. 34-35.

Chapter Eight

PRAYING THE NEWS/HEADLINES

*"Be anxious for nothing, but in everything by prayer and supplication,
with thanksgiving, let your requests be made known to God." Philippians 4:6*

PRAYER PROMPTS FROM THE HEADLINES

Whether we are reading bad news or good, we can turn a headline into a
prayer: "God, have mercy…" or "Thank You, Lord…." Imagine the impact if every time someone read a disturbing article, he would intercede for
the situation instead of getting angry. Anger, even righteous anger, cannot
produce good fruit unless it is submitted to God in prayer. By reading the
headlines we can get clues to target quick "arrow" prayers or to receive direction for broader intercession.

GOD SPEAKS THROUGH THE NEWS

God, Himself, can even *speak to us* through the news…. One morning
as I was walking through the kitchen on the way to my prayer room, a
picture on the front page of *The Washington Post* caught my eye. It was a
photograph of a large (many-thousand-seated) entertainment center being
demolished to make way for the construction of a shopping center. The
photographer caught the moment in time immediately after the explosion/
implosion as the huge structure began collapsing to the ground in a cloud
of rubble and dust. As I stood transfixed, gazing at the picture, the Lord
spoke to my spirit: "This is what I am doing." I sensed that He was speaking about destroying enemy strongholds. However, I always like God's spoken word to be confirmed in His written Word. Minutes later while I was
praying, Isaiah 25 just happened to be the highlighted chapter in my devo-

tional reading for that morning. These are the concluding verses of that chapter (which, by the way, I had never noticed before):

> *And He will spread out His hands in their midst [that is, in the midst of His enemies]...and He will bring down their pride together with the trickery of their hands. The fortress of the high fort of your walls* He will bring down, lay low, and bring to the ground, down to the dust.   Isaiah 25:11-12

What a mighty visual description of what happens to enemy strongholds when God's people pray! Indeed, we are the prayer warriors, but *the battle is the Lord's!* (see 1 Samuel 17:47).

PROLONGED PRAYER ASSAULT

Sometimes an article gives information that requires a more prolonged prayer assault. For instance, the following article appeared in *The Washington Times* on January 12, 2002:

KANDAHAR COMES OUT OF THE CLOSET

Our correspondent sees the gay capitol of south Asia throw off structures of the Taliban. Now that Taliban rule is over in Mullah Omar's former southern stronghold, it is not only television, kites, and razors which have begun to emerge. Visible again, too, are men with their *ashna*, or "beloveds": young boys they have groomed for sex. Kandahar's *Pashtuns have been notorious for their homosexuality for centuries*, particularly their fondness for naïve young boys. It is called *"the homosexual capitol of south Asia."* Such is the Pashtun obsession with sodomy. Locals tell you that the rape of young boys by warlords was one of the key factors in Mullah Omar mobilizing the Taliban. Men accused of sodomy faced the punishment of having a wall toppled on them, usually resulting in death. "In the days of the mujahideen, there were men with their *ashna* everywhere;...it was completely open, a part of life," said Torjan, 38, one of the soldiers loyal to Kandahar's new governor." They are emerging again," Torjan said. "The fighters too now have the boys in their barracks. The boys live with the fighters very openly. *In a short time, and certainly within a year,* it will be like pre-Taliban: *They will be everywhere.*"

As we examine this article, we see points at which to target our intercession. First of all, we are told that the Pashtuns "have been notorious for their homosexuality for centuries." So this is not just a modern problem, but has deep generational roots. There is a spiritual stronghold of sodomy here similar to the situation in Sodom and Gomorrah during the time of Abraham and Lot (see Genesis 18-19). You may recall that God poured out His wrath of fire and brimstone upon that evil place because their sin (of homosexuality) was very great (see Genesis 18:20).

Also, notice that the article closes with a declaration: "In a short time, and certainly within a year, it will be like pre-Taliban: They will be everywhere." As intercessors we can counter that declaration with one of our own. The following decree is an example of how we can pray into such a situation with authority and power. This decree confronts the stronghold of evil with Scripture, declares the city redeemed, and makes a faith declaration of what God can do to set the captives free:

In the name of Jesus Christ of Nazareth, I demolish the stronghold of sodomy in Kandahar, and declare that the Blood of Jesus has triumphed over you (see Colossians 2:15). *I take the key of the house of David* (according to Isaiah 22:22) *and I close the door to perversion and bondage and I open the door to freedom. I say to you, Kandahar, you are no longer the "gay capitol of south Asia"; you are the "Deliverance and Salvation Capitol" of south Asia! I declare that the Lord God has delivered your young boys from "the power of darkness and conveyed [them] into the kingdom of the Son of His love"* (Colossians 1:13). *I "demolish arguments and every pretension that sets itself up against the knowledge of God, and...take captive every thought to make it obedient to Christ* (2 Corinthians 10:5, NIV). *"For thus says the Lord: Even the captives of the mighty will be taken away, and the prey of the terrible will be delivered; for I will contend with him who contends with you, and I will give safety to your children and ease them"* (Isaiah 49:25, TAB). *Father, have mercy on these young boys and deliver them (and all children everywhere who are victims of violence) out of the grip of evil!*

DERAILING DISASTER: A Real-life Testimony

Another example of praying the news concerns the relationship between Israel and the United States and its impact on our nation. As is explained further in Chapter Seventeen (under the heading "A Word About Israel"),

God blesses those who bless Israel and judges those who don't. John McTernan, who wrote the book *Israel: The Blessing or the Curse*,[1] has followed the interactions between the U.S. and Israel for over twenty years and has documented an amazing pattern: Whenever the U.S. does anything to disfavor Israel, we experience a crisis such as severe weather (tornadoes, hurricanes, etc.), earthquakes, or economic shock (stock market plunges, etc.). The week of September 15 through 19, 2003, the U.S. was threatened by a category 5 hurricane following an extended time of trying to negotiate peace in Israel by encouraging land concessions to the Palestinians. The U.S. representatives had recently condemned Israel for wanting to deport the terrorist PLO leader, Yasser Arafat. On the day that this happened, the hurricane amazed meteorologists by leaping from a category 3 to a category 5 (with 160-mile-an-hour winds) in only a few hours. Intercessors were activated by the frightening news reports of impending disaster, for the hurricane was on a track that would take it directly up the Chesapeake Bay and over Washington, D.C.! As I was in prayer on the morning of September 16, the following scriptures were brought to mind, and became the basis of a prayer of supplication for mercy in response to the impending crisis:

- *"He has made the earth by His power; He has established the world by His wisdom, and stretched out the heaven by His understanding. When He utters His voice — there is a multitude of waters in the heavens; He causes the vapors to ascend from the ends of the earth; He makes the lightnings for the rain; He brings the wind out of His treasuries."* (Jeremiah 51:15-16)
- *"The LORD is slow to anger and great in power [and mercy]…. The LORD has His way in the whirlwind and the storm…. Who can stand before His indignation? And who can endure the fierceness of His anger?…The LORD is good, a stronghold in the day of trouble; and He knows those who trust in Him."* (Nahum 1:3, 6a and 7)

First of all, I knew that God is the One who creates the storms, and so He would be able to deflate and derail them. Also, I knew I could remind the Lord about His great mercies. With all of these scriptures in mind, I wrote a petition for mercy to the "Father of mercies":

Father, I pray, forgive this nation for touching the apple of Your eye, Israel. Forgive our leaders for pressuring Israel to divide up Your covenant land and for aligning with Israel's enemies. Surely, no one can endure the fierceness of Your anger. O Sovereign Lord, "in wrath remember mercy" (Habakkuk 3:2), *for "mercy triumphs over judgment"* (James 2:13). *And as You have brought this "whirlwind" out of Your treasuries, I beseech You to utter Your mighty voice to thunder over the waters* (see Psalm 29:3) *and remove its power and derail its course. I beseech You, "Father of mercies"* (2 Corinthians 1:3), *have mercy on us according to Your Word:*

- *"Through the LORD's mercies we are not consumed, because His compassions fail not. They are new every morning; great is Your faithfulness.... For the Lord will not cast off forever. Though He causes grief, yet He will show compassion according to the multitude of His mercies. For He does not afflict willingly, nor grieve the children of men."* (Lamentations 3:22-23 and 31-33)
- *"The LORD is gracious and full of compassion, slow to anger and great in mercy. The LORD is good to all, and His tender mercies are over all His works."* — *"For His mercy endures forever!"* (Psalm 145:8-9 and Psalm 136)
- *"Now therefore, our God, hear the prayer of Your servant, and cause Your face to shine on [us]. Incline Your ear and hear; open Your eyes and see our desolations...for we do not present our supplications before You because of our righteous deeds, but* because of Your great mercies. *O Lord, hear! O Lord, forgive! O Lord, listen and act! Do not delay for Your own sake, my God."* (Daniel 9:18-19)

TRUSTING GOD FOR THE OUTCOME

Sometimes in the news there are stories that are very tragic, and you wonder where God is in it. At such times we need to remember that God sees a much larger picture than we do. And if He has allowed something horrific to happen to good people, then we must trust Him for the outcome, and for His larger plan to emerge: always that His Kingdom come and His will be done. Joseph, the son of the patriarch Jacob, led a life of great tribulation. He was sold into slavery at a young age by his jealous brothers, living most of his life separated from his family. He was wrongly accused and imprisoned. After many years, Joseph was reunited with his brothers and his family. In Genesis 50, Joseph reassured his brothers who had wanted to kill him so long before. Joseph had every "right" to harbor feelings of bitterness and revenge toward his brothers. And his brothers feared the worst, saying, "Perhaps Joseph will hate us, and may actually repay us for the evil which we did to him" (verse 15). Instead, Joseph had a godly perspective. He said, "Do not be afraid, for am I in the place of God? But as for you, *you meant evil against me; but God meant it for good*, in order to bring it about as it is this day, to save many people alive" (verses 20-21). God had given Joseph great favor and wisdom. Pharaoh had promoted him over his house, and stated that "all my people shall be ruled according to your word; only in regard to the throne will I be greater than you" (Genesis 41:40). God gave Joseph much wisdom to prepare for a great famine that was to come to the land. Thus, he was able to "save many people alive." Joseph understood that his life was ordered by God and that everything he had suffered was not only for his ultimate good, but for the saving of the whole nation of Egypt, and even surrounding nations, including his estranged family.

The point we need to grasp is that we don't see the whole picture, and we must trust that God does, especially when we see things happening that we don't understand. A good prayer strategy in cases like this is to confess that what the devil means for evil, God means for good. And He, our Redeemer, will redeem (bring good out of) the situation. For example, when the space shuttle *Columbia* exploded on reentry in January of 2003, no one could imagine any good in it. Neither could I. But when I heard the news broadcast and saw the headlines, I prayed that what the devil meant for death and destruction, God would turn to good, to the salvation of many. God's divine manifest purpose is to build His Kingdom in the earth. We are not to judge or question how He works to accomplish that, but just to pray it in: His Kingdom come and His will be done...*however* He sees fit to accomplish it.

---

[1] John McTernan and Bill Koenig, *Israel: The Blessing or the Curse* (Oklahoma City, OK: Hearthstone Publishing, 2001).

Chapter Nine

BINDING AND LOOSING

"And I will give you the keys of the kingdom of heaven, and whatever you bind on earth will be bound in heaven, and whatever you loose on earth will be loosed in heaven." Matthew 16:19

THE "KEYS OF THE KINGDOM"

In Matthew chapter 16 there is recorded a profound conversation that Jesus had with His disciples. When He questioned them about who He was, Peter said, "You are the Christ, the Son of the living God." Jesus answered him by saying that on this revelation of who Jesus was, He would build His Church (see verses 15-18). Then Jesus made this amazing statement in verse 19:

"And I will give you the keys of the kingdom of heaven, and whatever you bind on earth will be bound in heaven, and whatever you loose on earth will be loosed in heaven."

This same statement is recorded in Matthew 18:18:

"Assuredly, I say to you, whatever you bind on earth will be bound in heaven, and whatever you loose on earth will be loosed in heaven."

A NEW PERSPECTIVE

The conventional way of applying the principle of "binding and loosing" in intercession is to "bind" the work/power of satan and "loose" the work/power of God. But there is another perspective on this which I would like to validate through a personal story of how I came into this information. One day during my early morning prayer time I found myself desiring greater insight on "binding and loosing" as described in these verses in Matthew. I had some limited understanding of this principle, but always sensed that there was much more to it than I had so far realized and practiced. In fact, I wasn't sure that what I was practicing was even the correct interpretation. Well, that morning I had no further revelation from the Lord. However, I had been out of town, and upon returning home on that very same day, I discovered in my mail a package from a friend. It was a book called *Shattering Your Strongholds*, by Liberty Savard. It was an exposition and teaching on "the keys of the kingdom" described in Matthew 16:19 and 18:18. I realized then that God had placed the burden for understanding on my heart earlier, so that I would appreciate the importance of this information when I found it. Therefore I have taken the words from this book as from the Lord Himself. The following information in this chapter is garnered from Ms. Savard's teachings in that book.

PRACTICAL APPLICATION

Going back to Matthew 16:19, Jesus said:

> *"And I will give you the keys of the kingdom of heaven, and whatever you bind on earth will be bound in heaven, and whatever you loose on earth will be loosed in heaven."*

Christ's giving of these keys, Ms. Savard points out, "represents the giving of permission, authority, and ability to enter into the kingdom of heaven to transact business. The remainder of the verse tells the believer how to transact that spiritual business."[1]

…The problem of strongholds

This is the "business" of "binding and loosing." This strategy involves releasing people from strongholds that have kept them bound, and connecting them in the spirit to what they need to be delivered. Ms. Savard goes on to explain that "sustained faith in a wrong belief can cause the erecting of a stronghold which will effectively block the receiving of God's truth."[2] A *stronghold* can be defined as a "fortification (in the mind) around and defense of what you believe," even when that belief may be "dead wrong." "Strongholds not only allow access for demonic torment and torture, they also affect the believer's right standing with the Lord by protecting wrong attitudes, thoughts, and feelings."[3] Along with worldly thinking, wrong teaching, especially in church, can create powerful strongholds in the minds of God's people. Until strongholds are broken, even scripturally correct teaching will not automatically correct wrong ideas. Truth may be twisted as it is filtered through minds influenced by strongholds. So it is the mindsets of our old nature which are the problem. "Binding and loosing makes it possible to crucify that old nature and receive God's full healing and restoration."[4] The "keys" Jesus spoke of are the keys to unlock strongholds and then set the captives free. Here is how we use them.

...Using the "keys"

First of all, we need to understand that "binding" has two sides — positive and negative. The positive side of binding is a "binding to," much like a mother might bind her infant to her body to carry it around with her into the fields to work.[5] In this sense we "bind" ourselves to the Truth. The negative binding is a "restraining," and is used to "bind the strong man" and take back the plunder he has stolen (see Matthew 12:29 and Luke 11:22). This type of negative binding *temporarily* deactivates the spiritual power at work. But Satan will not be truly "bound" until he is bound and cast into the bottomless pit by the angel of God for one thousand years (see Revelation 2:1-3). Strongholds must be pulled down and destroyed for deliverance to be complete.[6] Here is the typical pattern of how a stronghold is erected in the life of one who has not been completely surrendered to the will and purposes of God:

*"Something traumatic happens (which is a **fact**) — which leads me to develop a **wrong pattern of thinking** — which helps me justify a **wrong behavior** — which causes me to erect a **stronghold** to protect my right to do so — which **perpetuates my pain by keeping the trauma locked in and God locked out**."*[7]

Strongholds are pulled down through the "loosing" prayer. Loosing destroys the access ("spiritual bridges") of the demonic influence in a person's mind. We must remember that spiritual battles are waged in the mind. That is why the Bible is so insistent on the command to renew our minds.

For example, Romans 12:2 says, "Do not be conformed to this world, but be transformed by the *renewing of your mind*." As we have said, many times strongholds are just bad habits or mindsets from our "old nature" (or, that we have learned from the world) that have not yet been corrected, brought under conviction, or repented of. Ephesians 4:17-32 instructs us to put off this old nature ("old man") and put on the new:

> *You should no longer walk as the rest of the Gentiles walk, in the futility of their mind, having their understanding darkened, being alienated from the life of God, because of the ignorance that is in them, because of the blindness of their heart.... But you have not so learned Christ,...as the truth is in Jesus: that you* put off, *concerning your former conduct,* the old man *which grows corrupt according to the deceitful lusts, and be* renewed *in the spirit of your mind, and that you put on the new man which was created according to God, in true righteousness and holiness.*

We need to loose wrong things from the old nature and then destroy the strongholds that have been built to protect those things.[8] Loosing someone (or yourself) from these characteristics of the "old man" — the false teachings of this world — and binding him to the character of the "new man" — the truth of God's Word — is a powerful and strategic way to pray. For this is the truth that sets the captives free! (see John 8:32).

---

[1] Liberty Savard, *Shattering Your Strongholds* (North Brunswick, NJ: Bridge-Logos Publishers, 1998), p. 11.

[2] Ibid., p. 28.

[3] Ibid., p. 28.

[4] Ibid., p. 30.

[5] Ibid., p. 54.

[6] Ibid., p. 70.

[7] Ibid., p. 168.

[8] Ibid., p. 90.

Chapter Ten

PROPHETIC IDENTIFICATION

"A good name is to be chosen rather than great riches." Proverbs 22:1

SCRIPTURAL MODELS

The Word of God is rich with characters and scenarios that model for us how we can pray in certain situations. Jesus' parables used prophetic identification to teach spiritual principles. For example, in Luke 18, He told of the woman who appealed to the unjust judge for justice from her adversary. Jesus said that though the judge was resistant for a while, because she persisted, she won favor with the judge and received justice. In this prophetic lesson, Jesus said that we are to *identify* with the woman's experience and pray without ceasing, until we get what we need, for:

> *"Shall God not avenge His own elect who cry out day and night to Him, though He bears long with them? I tell you that He will avenge them speedily. Nevertheless, when the Son of Man comes,* will He really find faith on the earth?" Luke 18:7-8

The key to the woman's success was that she had faith to press through until the answer came. We need to pray with that same faith.

There are many people from Scripture whom we could emulate, and whose character we can pray into the lives of others. For instance, there is the humility of Paul, the passion of David, the faith of Abraham, the patience of Job, the wisdom of Solomon, the devotion of John, and the zeal of Peter.

PRESENT-DAY APPLICATION

Placing this in a present-day scenario, I have been praying, from an insight garnered from Bob Jones, for the current United States President, George Bush, to have the grace of Abimelech concerning the issue of dividing up Israel's covenant land in an effort to bring peace to the Middle East. In Genesis 26, there is an account of Isaac and his wife, Rebekah, in the land of Gerar, where the Philistine king, Abimelech, ruled. Isaac, fearing for his life, passed off Rebekah as his sister. Later, when Abimelech found out that Rebekah was really his wife, he wisely rebuked Isaac, saying, "What is this you have done to us? One of the people might soon have lain with your wife, and you would have brought guilt on us" (verse 10). By defiling Rebekah, Isaac's wife by covenant, guilt and its consequences would have fallen on the Philistines. The grace of God is evident in Abimelech's wisdom in protecting the sanctity of the marriage vow. We can then pray, in prophetic identification with Abimelech, the same grace for our President regarding the treatment of Israel, God's covenant people, and their "covenant connection" to their biblical land. For "it is written" in Scripture (for example: Genesis 13:14-18; Joshua 1:3-6 and Deuteronomy 34:1-4) that God gave Israel the land of Canaan for their inheritance *forever,* and further, that whoever divides up this covenant land will be judged by God (see Joel 3:2). By praying for the "grace of Abimelech" for our President, we are asking that God would not allow him to bring guilt and judgment upon our nation by dividing up Israel's covenant land, but that he would honor Israel's land covenant much like Abimelech honored Isaac's marriage covenant.

PERSONAL APPLICATION

Another example of prophetic identification is using the model of King David. David was a very courageous man who learned the secret of living in the presence of God. He was, as Scripture describes, a man after God's own heart (see 1 Samuel 13:14). Above all else, David was a worshiper, as evidenced by his confession in Psalm 34:1: "I will bless the Lord at *all* times; His praise will *continually* be in my mouth."

David danced before the Lord (see 2 Samuel 6:14) and extolled Him in more than seventy-five psalms and songs recorded in the Old Testament. But David was not only a poet and worshiper. He was also a mighty warrior. He boldly and victoriously fought in over one hundred battles, losing none, as God was with him. I pray for my son to have the "heart of David"

— that is, a heart of boldness and courage, victorious through God, and one that has a passion for Jesus.

PROPHETIC ALIGNMENTS IN CURRENT EVENTS: IRAQ

As we pray through current events of our day, we can find innumerable prophetic alignments. For instance, during the 2003 war for Iraqi freedom, I prayed passages from the book of Jeremiah toward the downfall of the terrorist regime in that country. Present-day Iraq is on the land occupied by biblical Babylon (the area surrounding the confluence of the Tigris and Euphrates rivers). Babylon represented all that was anti-God in the ancient world. The spiritual roots of that kingdom are still active in the land today, and were empowering the government of evil under Saddam Hussein. Jeremiah 50 and 51 record the word of destruction that the Lord spoke against Babylon. We can use these scriptures to make decrees against those spiritual powers: "It is written...." "The Lord has said...."

"Declare among the nations... 'Babylon is taken, Bel the title of Marduk, the chief god of the Babylonians is shamed....' I will punish Bel...and I will bring out of his mouth what he has swallowed....Yes, the wall of Babylon shall fall.... For behold, I will raise and cause to come up against Babylon an assembly of great nations..., *and they shall array themselves against her; from there she shall be captured.... Shoot at her, spare no arrows, for she has sinned against the LORD. Shout against her all around...her foundations have fallen, her walls are thrown down;* for it is the vengeance of the LORD.... *A sound of battle is in the land, and of great destruction....* The LORD has opened His armory, *and has brought out the weapons of His indignation....* Behold, I am against you, *O most haughty one!" says the Lord GOD of hosts; "for your day has come, the time that* I will punish you."

Jeremiah 50:1-31 and 51:44, selected

And continuing on, the Scripture decrees defeat to Babylon's armies and its king:

"The most proud shall stumble and fall, and no one will raise him up;...her young men shall fall in the streets, and all her men of war

shall be cut off in that day," says the LORD.... The mighty men of Babylon have ceased fighting, they have remained in their strongholds; their might has failed,...the bars of her gate are broken.... "The king of Babylon has heard the report about them, and his hands grow feeble; anguish has taken hold of him, pangs as of a woman in childbirth."

Jeremiah 50:30, 32, 43 and 51:30, selected

Repeatedly throughout the Old Testament the Lord used nations to judge nations. Notice in the above passages that it is GOD who is the avenger, and GOD who brings the armies to judge the sins of Babylon. As I prayed like this, using prophetic identification, again, I was not praying against people, but against the spiritual powers of darkness who manipulate and deceive people. I was declaring the victory of God in this present-day situation just as He was victorious in ancient Babylon. As the allied forces thundered through Baghdad, one of the first demonstrations of victory was the toppling of the statue of Saddam Hussein. As Hussein had brazenly identified himself with Nebuchadnezzar, the ancient Babylonian king, one could look at this as an outward sign of the beginning demise of this spiritual kingdom empowering the Hussein regime.

Chapter Eleven

THE PRAYER OF AGREEMENT

"If two of you agree on earth concerning anything that they ask, it will be done for them by My Father in heaven." Matthew 18:19

OLD TESTAMENT EXAMPLE: DANIEL

The Prophet Daniel knew of the power of united prayer. When King Nebuchadnezzar of Babylon made a decree to destroy all the wise men of the land because they could not interpret his dream, the lives of Daniel and his companions were in danger. The Scripture says that Daniel spoke with "counsel and wisdom" to the captain of the guard (Daniel 2:14). He then "asked the king to give him time, that he might tell the king the interpretation" (verse 16). And then it says, "Daniel went to his house, and made the decision known to...his companions, *that **they** might seek mercies from the God of heaven* concerning this secret, so that Daniel and his companions might not perish with the rest of the wise men of Babylon. *Then the secret was revealed* to Daniel in a night vision" (verses 17-19).

NEW TESTAMENT EXAMPLE: "WITH ONE ACCORD"

The power of agreement in prayer was experienced by New Testament Believers as well. As mentioned in Chapter Five, following the resurrection of Jesus, the disciples *"continued with one accord in prayer and supplication"* waiting for "the Promise of the Father," the baptism of the Holy Spirit (Acts 1:4-5 and 14). Later, on the Day of Pentecost, as the disciples were again gathered *"with one accord* in one place," the glory of God fell on them, baptizing them with the Holy Spirit and fire. They were thus empowered to become the apostles, prophets, pastors, teachers and evangelists who would then transform the world of their day with the gospel of salvation through Jesus Christ (see Acts 2:1-4). Mighty things happen when God's people agree in prayer!

OLD TESTAMENT INSIGHT

There is actually a mathematical model in the Scriptures for this principle of the power of agreement. Two key verses to consider are from the Old Testament:

- (Speaking of God's judgment of Israel for disobedience) *"How should one chase a thousand, and two put ten thousand to flight, except their Rock had sold them, and the Lord had shut them up?"* (**Deuteronomy 32:30**)
- (Speaking of God's blessings to Israel for obedience) *"And ye shall chase your enemies, and they shall fall before you by the sword. And five of you shall chase a hundred, and a hundred of you shall put ten thousand to flight"* (**Leviticus 26:7-8**)

The Key Is Grace

If you examine these scriptures carefully, you will see that they are not mathematically correct. In the Leviticus verse, if 1 could chase 1,000, then 2 would put 2,000 to flight, not 10,000. And in the Deuteronomy verse, if 5 chase 100, then 100 would chase 2,000, not 10,000. But a closer look reveals a pattern: In the Leviticus verse, 5 chased 100 and 100 chased 10,000. In the Deuteronomy verse, 1 chased 1,000 and 2 chased 10,000. In each case (each scripture) there is an increase of five times: 100 chased **five times** as may as five; and 2 chased **five times** as many as one. There is significance in the number five. In Scripture, this is the number for GRACE. Concerning grace, the Scripture tells us in James 4:6-8:

> *"But He gives more grace. Therefore He says: 'God resists the proud, but gives grace to the humble.' Therefore submit to God. Resist the devil and he will flee from you. Draw near to God and He will draw near to you...."*

In Leviticus 26:7-8, the soldiers put the enemy to flight as they resisted in battle. ("Resist the devil and he will flee from you.") When more soldiers were fighting together (agreement), the **grace** of God enabled them to increase their victory *five times* beyond what the natural result should be. However, when you read the Deuteronomy verse in context, you see that this was referring to God giving Israel's *enemies* the same victory over Israel, as punishment for their disobedience: "God resists the proud." In this case, God's grace is *still* at work. *For His judgments are His grace — they are always designed to bring us back to Him.* God was judging Israel so that her heart would turn back to Him and He could release His covenant blessings on her once again.

These scriptures are lessons from the natural field of battle. But they are also lessons for the prayer warrior during spiritual battles. As we *humble* ourselves before God to intercede, and as we *join in the prayer of agreement* with other intercessors, God draws near and *His grace is released, causing an* **exponential explosion** *of power against the camp of the enemy!*

THE PRAYER OF AGREEMENT

Looking to the New Testament, we find that Jesus taught specifically on the "prayer of agreement." Matthew 18:19-20 is a key passage:

> *"Again I say you that if two of you **agree** on earth concerning anything that they ask, it will be done for them by My Father in heaven. For where two or three are gathered together in My name, I am there in the midst of them."*

So how does the prayer of agreement work? And what does it mean to "agree" in prayer? First of all, this doesn't mean simply that we agree to pray *about* the same thing, such as "pray for our church." "Agreement" in this sense is not merely general consent about something. It is more specific than that. It is agreement grounded in Scripture. We need to find God's will and wisdom in His Word as it relates to our needs or the burden we carry for others. Then we "gather around" this word and agree on it by corporately praying, in the authority of His name (John 14:13-14), God's word back to Him, believing that we will get what we ask because we know it is His will (see 1 John 5:14-15). This is praying in agreement. This is praying prayers that God is waiting to answer (see Jeremiah 1:12).

Chapter Twelve

THE POWER OF PRAISE, WORSHIP AND COMMUNION

"Let the high praises of God be in their mouth, and a two-edged sword in their hand." Psalm 149:6

PRAISE AND WORSHIP

Worship is a mighty weapon of spiritual warfare. As we shall see, "worship builds our spirit man, takes us into the presence of the King, changes the atmosphere, and defeats our enemies."[1] Intercessors fight spiritual battles, but Jehoshaphat, one of the righteous kings of Judah, experienced the power of praise and worship on the battlefield of war.

THE BATTLE IS THE LORD'S

When the people of Moab and Ammon came against Judah, Scripture tells us that Jehoshaphat "feared, and set himself to seek the LORD." He said, "O our God, will You not judge them? For we have no power against this great multitude that is coming against us; nor do we know what to do, but our eyes are upon You" (2 Chronicles 20:3 and 12). God's answer was:

> *"Do not be afraid nor dismayed because of this great multitude, for the battle is not yours, but God's."*   verse 15

This is a significant reality for the intercessor. In all spiritual warfare, the battle IS the Lord's. We war with our words, and our prayers activate the angelic hosts to come against the powers of darkness on our behalf, and on behalf of those for whom we pray. But it is God who changes hearts, heals bodies, and moves mountains (see Matthew 17:20) *in response to our petitions.*

THE HIGH PRAISES OF GOD ON THEIR LIPS

Getting back to Judah's situation, when the Lord told them not to fear, that the battle was His, their response was that "all Judah and the inhabitants of Jerusalem *bowed before the* LORD, *worshiping the* LORD" (verse 18). This is the posture of one who has a need before the Lord: the posture of humility and worship. When the army went out the next morning to face the enemy, the worshipers led the way with the praises of God on their lips:

> *[Jehoshaphat] appointed those who should sing to the* LORD, *and who should praise the beauty of holiness, as they went out before the army and were saying: "Praise the* LORD, *for His mercy endures forever."* Now when they began to sing and to praise, the LORD set ambushes against the people…*who had come against Judah; and they were defeated.*
>
> verses 21-22

Hallelujah! But the victory didn't end there. The narrative continues in verse 25:

> *When Jehoshaphat and his people came to take away their spoil, they found among them an abundance of valuables on the dead bodies,…which they stripped off for themselves, more than they could carry away; and* they were three days gathering the spoil because there was so much.

RESTORATION

The devil, "the strongman," comes to steal, kill and destroy (see Matthew 12:29 and John 10:10). Whatever he steals from us we can demand back, and God will restore, in its fullness, as He did for Israel following His judgment of locusts and famine during the time of the prophet Joel:

> *"I will restore to you the years that the swarming locust has eaten, the crawling locust, the consuming locust, and the chewing locust."*
>
> Joel 2:25

Through spiritual warfare we can expect to take back spoil from the enemy — health of body, peace and joy, family relationships, finances, homes, jobs, whatever we have lost. Praise the Lord!

Praise Sets the Captives Free

In the New Testament, Paul and Silas endured beatings with rods and being thrown into prison for teaching and ministering the Gospel of Jesus Christ. The Scripture relates how God released them in response to their worship and prayers:

> *But at midnight Paul and Silas were praying and singing hymns to God, and the prisoners were listening to them. Suddenly there was a great earthquake, so that the foundations of the prison were shaken; and immediately all the doors were opened and everyone's chains were loosed.* Acts 16:25-26

Now consider this picture: Paul and Silas were seriously wounded and undoubtedly in great pain as they sat chained to the floor in the jail cell. From a natural perspective, there was not much hope. *But they chose to praise God in their bad circumstance.* Now, several things happened when they began to praise God. First an earthquake shook the foundations of the building: Praise not only brings the release (the answer), but also it destroys the foundations of evil that imprison God's people (the cause of the problem). Next, *all* the doors flew open and *everyone's* chains fell off, not just Paul's and Silas': *Praise sets the captives free.* Your attitude of praise and thankfulness to God affects those around you.

Praise Is a Commandment

Not only is praising God a blessing and a privilege, it is a commandment. We are told to give thanks always in all things, "for this is the will of God in Christ Jesus concerning you" (1 Thessalonians 5:18, KJV). Taking this a step further, we are instructed in Ephesians 5:18-20 to "be filled with the Spirit,…giving thanks *always for all things* to God the Father in the name of our Lord Jesus Christ."

Scripture commands us to praise the Lord because, most importantly, *He is worthy* to receive our praise, and praise honors Him. Praise has a personal benefit as well. For it strengthens and edifies us to do battle with

the enemy. Nehemiah 8:10 says: "The joy of the LORD is your strength."
Like Paul and Silas, praising God even in hard times is a demonstration of
faith and trust that God is in control and will work out all things together
for our good (see Romans 8:28). Faith, through praise, releases power to
bring prayer answers from Heaven.

PRAISE BANISHES DARKNESS

As a weapon of warfare, praise not only releases the power of God into a
situation, but it *banishes darkness* and everything associated with it. According to Wade Taylor, "The heart of spiritual warfare is worhip. It is not
our pronouncements, casting out, or our trying to command principalities,
that will *cleanse* the heavens. Rather, it is our worship that flows up and
unites with the harmony of heaven that will defeat them. When we come
together in union, and enter into this high level of worship, we literally
'bring down' principalities from their place of control."[2]

As it cleanses the atmosphere of heaven, worship declares and establishes
the sovereignty of God over all the objects of prayer. Since God inhabits
the praises of His people (see Psalm 22:3, KJV), the devil and his demons
won't hang around very long where God is being praised! According to
Psalm 149, the saints are honored to execute vengeance and *bind the powers
of darkness through the high praises of God:*

> *Let Israel rejoice in their Maker....*let them praise His name with the
> dance; let them sing praises to Him with the timbrel and harp. *For
> the LORD takes pleasure in His people; He will beautify the humble
> with salvation. Let the saints be joyful in glory....Let the* high praises
> of God be in their mouth, *and a two-edged sword in their hand, to
> execute vengeance on the nations, and punishments on the peoples; to
> bind their kings with chains, and their nobles with fetters of iron....*
> This honor have all His saints. verses 2-9

Psalm 149 introduces another powerful form of praise and worship: *the
dance* (verse 3). Psalm 150:4 also admonishes us to "praise Him with the
timbrel and dance." Dancing in worship delights the Lord, but it also dam-
ages the enemy. Romans 16:20 (NIV) says, "The God of peace will soon
crush Satan under your feet." While this speaks of the defeat of Satan in

general (Psalm 110:1 tells us that God will make His enemies His footstool), it also is a picture of the victory dance: As we dance in worship, God defeats the enemy. Isaiah 30:29-32 describes another victory dance — of Israel over her enemies:

> You shall have a song as in the night when a holy festival is kept, and gladness of heart as when one goes with a flute, *to come into the mountain of the LORD, to the Mighty One of Israel. The LORD will cause His glorious voice to be heard, and show the descent of His arm.... For through the voice of the LORD Assyria will be beaten down, as He strikes with the rod. And in every place where the staff of punishment passes, which the LORD lays on him,* it will be with tambourines and harps; *and in battles of brandishing He will fight with it.*

"INTERCESSORY WORSHIP"

Along with the Blood of the Lamb, praise and worship are the most powerful weapons available to the intercessor. This is not only because of the warfare element previously described, but also because worship is the vehicle that carries intercession before the throne of God. World evangelist Dick Eastman, in his book *Heights of Delight,* uses the term "Intercessory Worship" to describe "concentrated worship that becomes intercessory in nature, because it carries the prayers of God's people, like the fragrance of incense, before God's throne. As a result, God releases His power."[3] Revelation 5:8 describes this scenario, as the worshipers come before the Lord with harps in one hand (symbols of worship) and bowls in the other (symbols of prayer and intercession):

> *Now when He [The Lamb] had taken the scroll, the four living creatures and the twenty-four elders fell down before the Lamb, each having a* harp [worship], *and golden bowls full of incense, which are* the prayers of the saints [intercession].

Psalm 37:4 (which we have mentioned previously) states: "Delight yourself also in the LORD, and He will give you the desires of your heart." As we delight in Him through our worship and adoration, He causes our thoughts, desires and petitions to come into agreement with His. Then as we lift our prayers to the throne of grace, He, in turn, delights to grant our requests.

COMMUNION

We have already talked about the power of the Blood of Jesus in Chapter Seven. His Blood was given to ransom the souls of men, and Communion was given to the Church as a celebration of this glorious truth. As we celebrate the sacrifice of His precious Blood, we are also celebrating Christ's victory over the powers of darkness (see Colossians 2:15). As such, Communion is a powerful preamble to spiritual warfare. The celebration of the Body and Blood of our Lord, is an intimate act of worship which identifies us with the power source of our authority. Jesus said, "He who eats My flesh and drinks My blood abides in Me, and I in him" (John 6:56). The Enemy recognizes the presence of the Lord and the power of His Blood — and trembles. The atoning sacrifice of the Lord Jesus won new life for us. Similarly, His Body and Blood, received through Communion, continues to have life-giving power. My personal experience has been that, if I have been fasting, receiving the Body and Blood during Communion is strengthening to both spirit AND body. I believe that the Spirit of God can take one quarter of a saltine cracker and multiply it just like the loaves and fishes to feed every cell in our body! The Blood of Jesus is the most powerful antidote we have against sin and the most powerful weapon we can wield against our adversary. Indeed, like the old hymn says, there is wonder-working power in the Blood of the Lamb!

[1] Ken Malone, U.S. Strategic Prayer Network (State Apostolic Coordinator for Florida), Internet article, ("Glory of Zion International" September 10, 2004).

[2] Wade Taylor, "Worship for Spiritual Warfare," Internet article, July, 2006.

[3] Dick Eastman, *Heights of Delight* (Ventura, CA: Regal Books, 2002), pp. 27-28.

Chapter Thirteen

THE POWER OF FASTING

"However, this kind does not go out except by prayer and fasting."
Matthew 17:21

WHY DO WE FAST?

We see the discipline of fasting exercised throughout Scripture, from Abraham to Jesus. Jesus said, "*When* [not "if"] you fast, anoint your head and wash your face, so that you do not appear to men to be fasting, but to your Father who is in the secret place; and your Father who sees in secret will reward you openly" (Matthew 6:17-18). For Jesus, fasting was part of a normal, regular discipline of prayer. It should be for us, too.

FASTING "CHASTENS THE SOUL"

Psalm 69:10 says that *fasting chastens the soul*. In other words, fasting is one way to deny the flesh in our being, and put it in its place. Paul charged Timothy: "Exercise yourself toward godliness. For bodily exercise profits a little, but godliness is profitable for all things" (1 Timothy 4:7b-8a). Fasting is one way in which to "exercise yourself toward godliness." Paul said further, "I discipline my body and bring it into subjection" (1 Corinthians 9:27). We cannot be Spirit-led and flesh-driven people at the same time. The "flesh" component is that part of our human person that is still tied to, and the servant of, the passions and demands of the worldly life. It is "self" centered instead of God-centered. It is that disposition toward sin that continues to reside within our being and that opposes the work of God within us to bring forth faith and righteous living. Its character is *natural and carnal* as opposed to *spiritual and redemptive*. And its fruit brings forth death instead of life. Paul described the continual inner conflict between the Spirit and the flesh in his epistle to the Galatians:

For the flesh lusts against the Spirit, and the Spirit against the flesh; and these are contrary to one another, so that you do not do the things that you wish.   Galatians 5:17

This is why Jesus admonished His disciples: "If anyone desires to come after me, let him *deny himself,* and *take up his cross,* and follow Me" (Matthew 16:24). Just as Jesus conquered sin through His holy life of *self-denial* which culminated in the cross, we conquer sin and its destructive influence by surrendering daily to the crucifixion of *self* within us. Paul said again to the Galatians, "Those who are Christ's have crucified the flesh with its passions and desires" (Galatians 5:24). The personal faith declaration of every serious intercessor should be Galatians 2:20 (KJV):

I am crucified with Christ: nevertheless I live; yet not I, but Christ liveth in me: and the life which I now live in the flesh I live by the faith of the Son of God, who loved me, and gave himself for me.

In the Greek, the phrase above rendered "I am crucified with Christ" expresses an *ongoing process of continually being crucified.* We must *continually* submit to the Spirit's dealings with us to bring us to total submission to His sovereignty. This includes, among other things, the regular discipline of fasting.

FASTING STRENGTHENS THE SPIRIT

After Jesus' baptism by John in the Jordan River, the Scripture says that He was *"filled with the Holy Spirit...* and was led by the Spirit into the wilderness, being tempted for forty days by the devil. And in those days *He ate nothing"* (Luke 4:1-2). After these forty days of testing, verse 14 tells us that "Jesus returned *in the power of the Spirit* to Galilee, and news of Him went out through all the surrounding region." Notice that Jesus went into the wilderness being *filled* with the Spirit and came out in the *power* of the Spirit. The first test He received after not eating for forty days was the devil challenging Him to turn the stones into bread (verse 3). Jesus' response was: "Man shall not live by bread alone, but by every word of God" (verse 4). Fasting had helped to strengthen Him against every temptation the devil brought. Fasting will do the same for us. After Jesus left the place of testing,

THE POWER OF FASTING

He emerged in the power of the Spirit to begin His three years of ministry that would change the world forever.

OTHER REASONS TO FAST

In addition to following the example and command of Scripture to fast, and the previous benefits, there are a number of other reasons to fast:

FOR POWER IN INTERCESSION

Through fasting we can tap into God's power. Paul said, "Most gladly I… boast in my infirmities, that the power of Christ may rest on me…. For *when I am weak, then I am strong*" (2 Corinthians 12:9 and 10). As we crucify the flesh our spirit man grows. Our discernment and other spiritual "receptors" and gifts are sharpened, as are our focus and dependency on God. For the less we depend on ourselves, the more we depend on, and press into, God. Our inadequacy is God's opportunity to glorify Himself. As John the Baptist said, "He must increase, but I must decrease" (John 3:30). John was speaking of Jesus' ministry versus his, but this is applicable to our personal lives as well. The more of God we have (and the less of self), the more impact our intercession will have.

FOR DIRECTION AND DECISION MAKING

During the period of the Judges in the Old Testament, there was a war between the tribes of Israel and Benjamin. Judges 20:26-28 records that "all the people went up and came to the house of God and wept. *They sat there before the LORD and fasted that day until evening*…. So the children of Israel inquired of the LORD,…and Phinehas…stood before [the ark],…saying, 'Shall I yet again go out to battle against the children of my brother Benjamin, or shall I cease?' And the LORD said, 'Go up, for tomorrow I will deliver them into your hand.' " This was God's hand of judgment upon the tribe of Benjamin for their immorality and rebellion.

FOR REPENTANCE AND TO HUMBLE ONESELF BEFORE GOD

David was a man who was very familiar with the discipline of fasting. For instance, in Psalm 35:13 he expressed his humility in fasting for his enemies: "But as for me, when they were sick, my clothing was sackcloth; *I humbled myself with fasting.*"

During the period of the Judges, when Israel was being threatened by the Philistines, the prophet Samuel brought a word from the Lord, "saying, 'If you return to the Lord with all your hearts, then put away the foreign gods and the Ashtoreths [idols] from among you, and prepare your hearts for the LORD, and serve Him only; and He will deliver you from the hand of the Philistines.' So the children of Israel put away the Baals and the Ashtoreths, and served the LORD only. And Samuel said, 'Gather all Israel to Mizpah, and I will pray to the LORD for you.' *So they gathered…. And they fasted that day, and said there, 'We have sinned against the LORD' "* (I Samuel 7:3-6). And so it was that repentance with fasting brought Israel deliverance from the Philistines.

DURING A CRISIS

The prophet Elijah brought a word from the Lord to Ahab, the wicked king of Samaria, saying: "…you have sold yourself to do evil in the sight of the LORD: Behold, I will bring calamity on you. I will take away your prosperity, and will cut off from Ahab every male in Israel…. I will make your house like the house of Jeroboam…and like the house of Baasha…because of the provocation with which you have provoked Me to anger, and made Israel sin…. So it was, when Ahab heard those words, that *he tore his clothes and put sackcloth on his body, and fasted and lay in sackcloth, and went about mourning.* And the word of the LORD came to Elijah…, saying, 'See how Ahab has humbled himself before Me? *Because he has humbled himself before Me, I will not bring the calamity* in his days" (1 Kings 21:20,21,22, and 27-29). And so it was that by humility and fasting disaster was averted in the life of Ahab.

FOR HEALING

King David had a son with Bathsheba through an adulterous affair. However, because this deed gave occasion to the enemies of the Lord to blaspheme, God had said the child would die (see 2 Samuel 12:14-17 and 20). However, knowing that the Lord was a God of great mercy and forgiveness, David *"pleaded with God for the child, and [he] fasted and went in and lay all night on the ground."* Even though the child later died, David, also knowing of God's justice, "went into the house of the Lord and worshiped."

TO RECEIVE REVELATION FROM GOD

In Chapter Four we talked about a troubling vision Daniel received from

God concerning the future of Israel which led him into an extended period of prayer and fasting for further revelation: "I ate no pleasant food, no meat or wine came into my mouth, nor did I anoint myself at all" (Daniel 10:3). The Scripture goes on to say that after twenty-one days of fasting Daniel had an angelic visitation: "Then he said to me, 'Do not fear, Daniel, for from the first day that you *set your heart to understand, and to humble yourself before your God*, your words were heard; and I have come because of your words.... I have come to make you understand what will happen to your people in the latter days' " (verses 12 and 14). And so it was that fasting brought Daniel the revelation from God that he sought.

TO RECEIVE FAVOR WITH GOD AND MAN
Following the Jews' dispersion to Babylon, the walls of Jerusalem were destroyed. When Nehemiah, a dispersed Jew and cupbearer to the Persian king, Artaxerxes, heard about the city, he was forlorn: "When I heard these words, I sat down and wept, and mourned for many days; *I was fasting and praying before the God of heaven....* 'O Lord, I pray, please let Your ear be attentive to the prayer of Your servant...; and let Your servant prosper this day, I pray, and grant him mercy [favor] in the sight of this man' [the king]. For I was the king's cupbearer" (Nehemiah 1:4 and 11). Nehemiah then requested, and was granted from the king, permission, provision and protection for the massive project of rebuilding the walls of Jerusalem.

SPIRITUAL BENEFITS OF FASTING IN PRAYER

FASTING INCREASES SPIRITUAL AUTHORITY
Just look at the life of Jesus. He lived a life of fasting and intimacy with God. And the demons trembled in the authority of His presence. One day when He entered the country of the Gergesenes, "there met Him two demon-possessed men...,exceedingly fierce, so that no one could pass that way. And suddenly they cried out, saying, 'What have we to do with you, Jesus, You Son of God? Have You come here to torment us before the time?' " (Matthew 8:28-29). All Jesus apparently did was to pass by them, and the demons were stirred up by His holy presence. They knew His name ("Jesus, You Son of God") and they recognized His authority ("Have you come here to torment us before the time?") What "time"? Apparently they were aware of their ultimate judgment. Similarly, demons recognize the presence

and authority of the Holy Spirit of Jesus in us, especially when accompanied by fasting. For a present-day testimony of the power of fasting in enhancing spiritual authority, recall the experience of Mahesh Chavda from Chapter Seven, and the power of the Blood.

FASTING INCREASES THE EFFICACY OF PRAYER

There is an account in Mark 9:14-29 of a demon-possessed boy who was healed by Jesus. Initially, Jesus' disciples prayed, but could not deliver him of the demon. But when Jesus commanded the deaf and dumb spirit to "come out of him and enter him no more," the boy was delivered. When the disciples questioned Jesus why they were unsuccessful, He told them: "This kind can come out by nothing but prayer *and fasting.*" Apparently, there are situations where fasting is necessary to bring the breakthrough in intercession.

PERSEVERANCE IN FASTING

Fasting is not easy for most people. It is best to "start simple" and build up slowly. One of the keys to avoid weariness is to keep your eyes on the "mark." That is, stay focused on Jesus by staying in His Word. When struggling with fatigue and hunger, the *Bread of Life* (see John 6:48) and the *meat of the Word* (see Hebrews 5:12-14, KJV) can be satisfying to spirit, soul and body. There are some wonderful scriptures that have strengthened me over the years. When Jesus, after forty days of fasting in the wilderness, was being tempted by Satan to turn stones into bread, He said, "It is written, 'Man shall not live by bread alone, but by every word of God' " (Luke 4:4). When I am fighting physical weariness and I am tempted to break my fast, I remind the devil, and myself, of Luke 4:4. Additionally, IT IS WRITTEN:

- *"My food is to do the will of Him who sent Me, and to finish His work"* (John 4:34).
- *"I have esteemed the words of His mouth more than my necessary food"* (Job 23:12, KJV).
- *"You satisfy me more than the richest of foods. I will praise You with songs of joy"* (Psalm 63:5, paraphrased).
- *"I am the Bread of Life"* (John 6:35, MES, TAB).
- *"My grace is sufficient for you, for My strength is made perfect in weakness"* (2 Corinthians 12:9).

- *"My strength you have exalted like a wild ox; I have been anointed with fresh oil"* (Psalm 92:10).
- *"They that wait upon the LORD shall renew their strength..."* (Isaiah 40:31, KJV).
- *"The joy of the LORD is [my] strength"* (Nehemiah 8:10).
- *"In the day when I cried thou answeredst me, and strengthenedst me with strength in my soul."* (Psalm 138:3, KJV).
- *"But You, O LORD, are a shield for me, my glory, and the One who lifts up my head"* (Psalm 3:3).
- *"The LORD is my strength and my shield"* (Psalm 28:7).

Chapter Fourteen

THE POWER OF REPENTANCE AND TRAVAIL

"Repent therefore and be converted, that your sins may be blotted out, so that times of refreshing may come from the presence of the Lord."
Acts 3:19

REPENTANCE

"IF MY PEOPLE..."

Historically, throughout Scripture, there were many cycles of rebellion-repentance-revival-restoration of the children of Israel. The Lord God instructed Solomon that the remedy for judgment for sin was *repentance*:

> *"IF My people who are called by My name will humble themselves, and pray and seek My face, and turn from their wicked ways, THEN I will hear from heaven, and will forgive their sin and heal their land."*
> 2 Chronicles 7:14

This is a powerful promise that was tested and proven many times over during Israel's pre-Christ history. And it is still applicable today. If God's people in any nation will turn to Him in humility and repentance, He *will* heal their land. What a powerful word for prophetic intercession — calling God's people to repentance that will lead to revival and restoration!

MERCY FOR THE HEATHEN

The Bible shows us that God's mercy extended even to pagan nations. The pagan city of Nineveh, the capital of the Assyrian Empire in the Old

Testament, was a wicked and ruthless place in a nation that had repeatedly invaded and pillaged the homeland of the Israelites. But God, in His great mercy and compassion, sent the prophet Jonah to bring a word of impending doom to spur the people to repentance. The word had the desired effect:

> *So the people of Nineveh believed God, proclaimed a fast, and put on sackcloth, from the greatest to the least of them.*　　　　Jonah 3:5

Even the king participated in this act of repentance, and decreed:

> *Who can tell if God will turn and relent, and turn away from His fierce anger, so that we may not perish?*　　　　verse 9

God did indeed relent when He saw their great contrition:

> *Then God saw their works, that they turned from their evil way; and God relented from the disaster that He had said He would bring upon them, and He did not do it.*　　　　verse 10

MERCY FOREVER TO ALL

The Bible tells us throughout that God's mercy endures forever, and to all generations. Not that God is slack toward sin. But even in His judgments there is mercy, for His judgments are, many times, redemptive. That is, they are intended to turn a wayward people back to Him. This turning of heart and direction is what repentance is all about. So, our part is repentance, and in His graciousness, His mercy brings forgiveness and restoration. From the beginning of His earthly ministry, Jesus preached the message: "Repent [turn away from sin], for the kingdom of heaven is at hand" (Matthew 4:17). For only in the ground of a repentant heart can seeds of revival be sown. And transformation through revival is what will usher in the Kingdom of God to the earth.

TRAVAIL

Travailing in the natural is most often associated with the labor of childbirth. Travailing in the spirit has many of the same symptoms: deep agony, with sobbing and wailing. There may also be a birthing sensation in the belly with pain or sense of pushing. There is a "birthing" in the spirit, which brings forth the purposes of God. The Church is going through a state of spiritual birthing now, which will likely involve travailing, as we enter into revival and, ultimately, the Kingdom Age. Just like in the natural, the process will be painful as the Church comes forth as the Bride of Christ in all her resplendent glory. There is always pain as the old, comfortable flesh must be crucified to make way for the new and vibrant life in the Spirit. And just like the mother-to-be cannot direct her labor, spiritual travailing is a work of the Spirit of God. Travail can come upon an intercessor at any time that the Spirit so moves. The best thing to do is just go with it and not resist, and know that God is doing something mighty in the spirit realm.

"THE WEEPING PROPHET"

Jeremiah is sometimes called "the Weeping Prophet" because of his broken heart and travailing intercession over his homeland of Judah:

> *Oh, that my head were waters, and my eyes a fountain of tears, that I might weep day and night for the slain of the daughter of my people!*
> Jeremiah 9:1

Jeremiah 9:17-21 is a very descriptive passage on the power of travail. The Lord had pronounced judgment on the wayward nation of Israel:

> *"Because they have forsaken My law..., but they have walked according to the dictates of their own hearts and after the Baals [false gods].... I will scatter them.... And I will send a sword after them until I have consumed them."*
> verses 13,14 and16

To avert this catastrophe the Lord then gave the command in verses 17-21:

> *"Consider and call for the mourning women, that they may come; and send for skillful wailing women, that they may come. Let them make haste and take up a wailing for us, **that our eyes may run with tears, and our eyelids gush with water.** For a voice of wailing is heard from Zion: 'How we are plundered! We are greatly ashamed, because we have forsaken the land, because we have been cast out of our dwellings.' Yet hear the word of the LORD, O women, and let your ear receive the word of His mouth;* teach your daughters wailing, *and everyone her neighbor*

a lamentation. For death has come through our windows, has entered our palaces, to kill off the children — no longer to be outside! and the young men — no longer on the streets!"

The purpose of the wailing in verse 18 was to bring forth repentance ("that our eyes may run down with tears") and bring the nation back to God. The women were called to travail for the sake of the violence which has come upon the land because of the people's rebellion and idolatry. Even the children were suffering: "For death is come up into our windows,…to cut off the children…, and the young men from the streets" (verse 21, KJV). Sounds like a modern-day scenario. God is calling again for the wailing women…and men!

REVIVAL FIRE

There are sparks of revival fires burning around the world today. In this country, such places as Pensacola, Florida, and Albany, Oregon, have experienced revival-type visitations in spiritual renewal and deliverance. But what is it going to take for these isolated "camp" fires to ignite into a blazing inferno that will sweep across continents? Pastor Denny Kline, of the Vineyard Church in Albany, said this of the ongoing outpouring of the Holy Spirit there: "We have contended as a congregation for the ministry of Jesus for five and one half years, and have been to the brink of a revival-type outpouring at least four other times since our beginnings." In Pensacola, Pastor John Kilpatrick had developed an exceptionally strong local church prayer ministry that had been in place for two and a half years before revival broke out there in 1995. We are hearing from prophetic voices everywhere that God is about to break forth with the most awesome, earth-shaking revival that the world has ever seen. So, what will it take to bring such a revival to the earth?

I believe the Lord would say to the Church today: "The HEAD is crowning!" The King of kings and Lord of lords, the Head of the Body, is getting ready to be crowned in the Church today — on earth as He is in Heaven. And God is calling His Church to *push through in the spirit realm* in sustained intercession until we see this come forth. The time has never been more urgent for God's people to get into their prayer closets and pray for a spirit of travail.

Chapter Fifteen

THE POWER OF PRAYING IN THE HOLY SPIRIT

"I indeed baptize you with water unto repentance, but He who is coming after me is mightier than I... He will baptize you with the Holy Spirit and fire." Matthew 3:11

HOLY SPIRIT BAPTISM

There is another dimension of prayer that needs to be mentioned if the intercessor desires to be fully equipped with every tool available for spiritual warfare and personal edification. John the Baptist mentioned an experience called *the Baptism in the Holy Spirit*. The fact that this experience is recorded in all the gospels indicates its significance to the Christian:

I indeed baptize you with water unto repentance, but He who is coming after me is mightier than I, whose sandals I am not worthy to carry, He will baptize you with the Holy Spirit and fire.

Matthew 3:11
(see also Mark 1:7-8, Luke 3:16, and John 1:33)

THE HOLY SPIRIT WITHIN—"THE HELPER"

We are not, at this time, given details of this particular experience. But later in Jesus' ministry, our Lord spoke of another Holy Spirit experience. He told the disciples that He would *send* (not *baptize* with) the Holy Spirit to them after He left the earth:

It is to your advantage that I go away, for if I do not go away the

Helper [or Counselor] *will not come to you; but if I depart, I will send Him to you.*   John 16:7

This work of the Holy Spirit, Jesus said, was the following:

- *"He will convict the world of sin, of righteousness and of judgment."* John 16:8
- *"He, the Spirit of Truth, will guide you in all truth…He will tell you things to come."* John 16:13
- *"He will testify of Me…and glorify Me."* John 15:26 and 16:14

Then on the evening of His resurrection, the fulfillment of this promise of *the Helper* came. Jesus appeared to the disciples who were gathered behind closed doors for fear of the Jews. At this time He commissioned them and *filled* them with His Holy Spirit. They were now "Christians" ("anointed ones") being filled with the Spirit of Christ:

Peace to you! As the Father has sent me, I also send you.
                    (see Matt. 28:19-20—the Great Commission)

And when He had said this, He breathed on them, *and said to them,* 'Receive *the Holy Spirit.*'"   John 20:19-22

THE "PROMISE OF THE FATHER"

Luke records an interesting statement of Jesus following the issuance of the *Great Commission,* and before His ascension, in Luke 24. From these words below, we can deduce that whatever He had given them so far, there was something more they needed to fully equip them with power for the job He had called them to. And so He instructed them to go to Jerusalem and wait for it :

Behold, I send the Promise of My Father *upon you; but tarry in Jerusalem until you are endued with* power from on high.
                                                                        Luke 24:49

Acts 1 picks up this scene, and further explains what the *Promise* and the

Baptism are. It is clear here that this experience with the Holy Spirit is different from the *infilling* they already had. This time the Spirit will come *upon* them in *power*. The following analogy may be helpful in understanding the difference between these two experiences. If we think of the Holy Spirit as water, receiving the infilling of the Spirit at salvation would be like drinking a glass of water, while receiving the Baptism of power in the Holy Spirit would be like jumping into a swimming pool of water—and being immersed, completely covered over, or *baptized*. According to the passage below, this new Baptism of Power was primarily for more effective service and witnessing to fulfill the *Great Commission*. :

And being assembled together with them, He commanded them not to depart from Jerusalem, but to wait *for the* **Promise of the Father,** *'which,' He said, 'you have heard from Me; for John truly baptized with water, but you shall be* baptized *with the Holy Spirit not many days from now'* .... [and] *'you shall receive power when the Holy Spirit has come upon you; and you shall be witnesses to Me in Jerusalem, and in all Judea and Samaria, and to the end of the earth.'*

Acts 1:4, 5 and 8

The above phrase "witnesses to Me" suggests not merely needing power to preach the Gospel and *tell about* Jesus, but the importance of *demonstrating the life and works* of Christ: Witnessing to the power of a holy life baptized with the Spirit of God. As some wise person once said, "preach the Gospel and sometimes use words." The Apostle Paul depended upon this Holy Spirit empowerment in his ministry:

And my speech and my preaching was not with enticing words of man's wisdom but in demonstration of the Spirit and of power.

1 Corinthians 2:4

Jesus said of the ministry of the Believer:

He who believes in Me, the works that I do he will do also; and greater works than these will he do....

John 14:12

PENTECOST BAPTISM

And so the disciples obediently returned to Jerusalem and gathered in prayer waiting for this *Promise* to come:

Then they returned to Jerusalem…and they went up into the upper room…and continued with one accord in prayer and supplication…

Acts 1:12-14

Acts 2 records the day of the Holy Spirit Baptism that they had been waiting for. This was the celebration of the feast of Pentecost. It was no coincidence that the Lord chose this particular day to send His empowerment to the fledgling Church. The day of Pentecost did not originate with the New Testament Church. For centuries the *Feast of Pentecost* on the Jewish calendar had been a celebration of the *barley harvest*. So on this day, while the Jews were gathered in Jerusalem to celebrate the agricultural harvest, God was equipping them to bring in the *Harvest of souls* from the nations. Jerusalem, Judea, Samaria, and the end of the earth!

"When the day of Pentecost had fully come, they were all with one accord in one place. And suddenly there came a sound from heaven, of a rushing mighty **wind,** *and it filled the whole house where they were sitting. Then there appeared to them divided tongues, as of* **fire,** *and one sat upon each of them. And they were all filled with the Holy Spirit and* began to speak with other tongues, as the Spirit gave them utterance."*

(verse 4)

BAPTISM FOR PRAYER POWER

WHY TONGUES?

Here was the "baptism of Holy Spirit and fire" that the gospel accounts mentioned earlier. We see from the passage above that the evidence of the Baptism was "speaking with other tongues." In this particular case, it goes on to explain that the *tongues* were given to these Galilean men so that all who were gathered in Jerusalem (from other nations) could hear "in our own tongues the wonderful works of God." (verse 11)

In Romans 8:26 we see another function of *tongues*: empowering prayer:

Likewise the Spirit also helps in our weaknesses. For we do not know what we should pray for as we ought, but the Spirit Himself makes intercession for us with groanings which cannot be uttered."

The word "weaknesses" (or in the King James version, "infirmities") in this passage literally means *dullness of perception and inability to achieve results.* We do not know how to pray as we ought because we lack spiritual perception and discernment. And so we cannot, in our own strength, achieve the results we, and God, desire. Therefore, He has given us His Spirit to pray through us and for us, as we yield our tongues to Him. Praying in *tongues* is, indeed, a powerful weapon of spiritual warfare.

Not only does the Spirit pray *through* us and *for* us in intercession, but He also prays *in* us to edify and build up our faith. Even when we are baptized in the Spirit, we need "recharging" from time to time. We know that all that God has provided for us we access by FAITH, and so we need to have our faith continually rejuvenated. We see in Jude that one of the ways to accomplish this is to *pray in the Holy Spirit*:

"But you, beloved, building yourself up on your most holy faith, praying in the Holy Spirit…"   Jude 20

So we see from these passages that praying in *tongues* (or praying in the Holy Spirit) is given for power in service, for power in prayer, and for personal edification.

BAPTISM FOR MINISTRY GIFTS

Besides *tongues*, there are other power and revelatory ministry gifts that are manifested through the Baptism in the Holy Spirit. Paul listed a total of nine such spiritual gifts in 1 Corinthians 12:7-10:

"…the manifestation of the Spirit is given to each one for the profit of all: for to one is given the word of wisdom through the Spirit, to another the word of knowledge…to another faith…to another gifts of healings…to another the working of miracles, to another prophecy, to another discerning of spirits, to another different kinds of tongues, to another the interpretation of tongues."

BUILDING UP THE BODY

Paul taught much about the use of these spiritual gifts in 1 Corinthians chapters 12-14. He instructed that in the worship service the gifts should be focused on *building up the Body of Christ*. For instance, in giving instruction on exercising *tongues* in corporate worship, he emphasized, "God is not the author of confusion, but of peace" (1 Corinthians 14:33). Therefore, he taught that, though *tongues* was very significant, prophecy was more edifying than *tongues* in the *corporate* worship setting:

- *"I thank my God I speak with tongues more than you all; yet in the church I would rather speak five words with my understanding, that I may teach others also, than ten thousand words in a tongue."* 1 Corinthians 14:18-19
- *"He who speaks in a tongue edifies himself, but he who prophecies edifies the church. I wish you all spoke with tongues, but even more that you prophesied...*that the church may receive edification." 1 Corinthians 14:4-5
- *"Since you are zealous for spiritual gifts, let it be for* the edification of the church *that you seek to excel. Therefore let him who speaks with a tongue pray that he may interpret. For if I pray in a tongue, my spirit prays but my understanding is unfruitful...(therefore) I will pray with the spirit, and I will also pray with the understanding."* 1 Corinthians 14:12-15

He concluded, "Therefore, brethren, desire earnestly to prophesy (and interpret), and *do not forbid to speak with tongues.*" (1 Corinthians 14:39)

EMPOWERING THE CHURCH

...*THE BAPTISM IS FOR ALL*

The book of Acts is designated in Scripture as the "Acts of the Apostles," but could also be titled: the "Acts of the Holy Spirit." For throughout the pages of this book are the glorious accounts of the ministry of the Holy Spirit empowering the Church. Through these scriptures we see that God is no respecter of persons: "But in every nation *whoever* fears Him and works righteousness is accepted by Him." (Acts 10:30) We see in these ac-

THE POWER OF PRAYING IN THE HOLY SPIRIT

counts how the Baptism came upon the Samaritans, Gentiles, and Jews alike. We also see clearly the difference between Holy Spirit Baptism and water baptism, or the "baptism of John" for salvation. In Acts 8:14-17, for example, we read the account of the Samaritans, who had already received salvation, receiving the Holy Spirit Baptism:

When the apostles... heard that Samaria had received the word of God, they sent Peter and John to them, who... prayed for them that they might receive the Holy Spirit. *For as yet He had fallen upon none of them. They had only been baptized in the name of the Lord Jesus.*

Then in Acts 10:44-48 we read the account of the Gentiles receiving the Holy Spirit Baptism, even *before* they received water baptism. Apparently there was belief among the Jews that the salvation experience was not for uncircumcised Gentiles. But God taught them a lesson. While Peter was preaching to the Gentiles, the Holy Spirit moved:

While Peter was still speaking these words, the Holy Spirit fell upon all those who heard the word. *And (the Jews) who believed were astonished... because the gift of the Holy Spirit had been poured out on the Gentiles also. For they heard them speak with other tongues and magnify God. Then Peter answered, 'Can anyone forbid water that these should not be baptized who have received the Holy Spirit just as we have?' And he commanded them to be baptized in the name of the Lord.*

How did the Jews know that the Gentiles had received the Baptism? They spoke with other tongues and magnified God.

In Acts 19:2-6, we read an account of Jewish disciples receiving the Holy Spirit Baptism, like the Samaritans, after being baptized with a baptism of John, or the baptism of repentance:

(Paul) said to them, 'Did you receive the Holy Spirit when you believed?' So they said to him, 'We have not so much as heard whether there is a Holy Spirit.' And he said to them, 'Into what then were you baptized?' So they said, 'Into John's baptism.' Paul said, 'John baptized

with a baptism of repentance, saying to the people that they should believe ...on Jesus Christ.' When they heard this, they were baptized in the name of the Lord Jesus. And when Paul laid hands on them, the Holy Spirit came upon them, and they spoke with other tongues and prophesied.''

...THE BAPTISM IS FOR TODAY

Just like the growing church in the book of Acts, there are those today who don't understand that there is a Pentecostal experience - the Holy Spirit Baptism - to empower the Church in these last days. According to the words of the Lord through the Apostle Peter in Acts 2:16-18:

"This (Holy Spirit Baptism with evidence of speaking in tongues) is what was spoken by the prophet Joel*: And it shall come to pass in the last days, says God, That I will pour out My Spirit on all flesh; your sons and your daughters shall prophesy, your young men shall see visions, your old men shall dream dreams, and on My menservants and on My Maidservants I will pour out My Spirit in those days..."

*Joel 2:28-32

We are now living in the days that Joel was writing about nearly 3000 years ago. This prophetic manifestation is not something sensational to build personal ministries or to bring attention to any man. This is not about those who "have" and those who "have not." The Baptism in the Holy Spirit was given by God to His Church, His Body, so we can be fully equipped for spiritual warfare and personal ministry to advance His Kingdom in the earth.

The weapons, tools and strategies we have been talking about in Part Two are indeed "mighty in God for pulling down strongholds," casting down everything that exalts itself against the knowledge of God, and bringing every thought obedient to Christ. (2 Corinthians 10:4-50) Use them often in "offensive" warfare and watch the enemy flee! (James 4:7)

PART THREE

❖ ❖ ❖

PROPHETIC DECREES AND SCRIPTURAL DECLARATIONS

Over the Church and Over the Nations

Principles and strategies from Parts One and Two are used to craft model scriptural declarations and prophetic decrees to be used as tools for the intercessor, and to inspire the writing of such decrees to be used in personal and corporate prayer and intercession.

Among the gods there is none like You, O Lord;
Nor are there any works like Your works.
All nations whom You have made
shall come and worship before You, O Lord,
And shall glorify Your name.
For You are great, and do wondrous things;
You alone are God.
Psalm 86:8-10

Chapter Sixteen

THE CHURCH

"And He is the head of the body, the church,...
that in all things He may have the preeminence."
Colossians 1:18

THE CALL TO REVIVAL AND TRANSFORMATION

THE CONDITION FOR REVIVAL

As we saw in the last chapter, 2 Chronicles 7:14 makes this promise:

If MY people who are called by My name will humble themselves, and
pray and seek My face, and turn from their wicked ways, then I will
hear from heaven, and will forgive their sin and heal their land.

From this scripture it is clear that America won't see revival or restoration until the Church wakes up and turns back to God in genuine *repentance*. That God holds His Church responsible is also evident in the scripture, "For the time has come for *judgment to begin at the house of God*: and if it begins with us first, what will be the end of those who do not obey the gospel of God?" (1 Peter 4:17). From the recent sexual abuse scandals in the Roman Catholic Church, to the outrageous "Gospel of Inclusion" (concerning the blessing of homosexual leadership and marriages) rampant in the Episcopal Church, and the worldliness and immorality in *all* churches, the Body of Christ in this nation is a shameful, hypocritical representation of our Lord. We have embraced the ways of the world and abdicated the love and holy living of the biblical Christian. Journalist Katherine Kersten had this observation of the present-day Church: "Mainline American churches are losing their theological moorings, and increasingly falling prey to the prevailing winds of secular doctrine."[1] The apostle Paul admonished the Church at Ephesus to:

> *Come into the unity of the faith and of the knowledge of the Son of God, to a perfect man, to the measure of the stature of the fullness of Christ;* that we should no longer be children, tossed to and fro and carried about with every wind of doctrine, *by...the cunning craftiness of deceitful plotting."* Ephesians 4:13-14

HARBINGERS OF COMING APOSTASY?

The lawlessness, carnality and religious spirit which have permeated the Church are harbingers of the coming apostasy that Paul spoke of in his second epistle to Timothy:

> *But know this, that in the last days perilous times will come: For men will be lovers of themselves, lovers of money, boasters, proud, blasphemers, disobedient to parents, unthankful, unholy, unloving, unforgiving, slanderers, without self-control, brutal, despisers of good, traitors, headstrong, haughty, lovers of pleasure rather than lovers of God,* having a form of godliness but denying its power. 2 Timothy 3:1-5

Now poised at the end of the age, we are on the brink of some wonderful, and terrible, happenings in the earth. The wars raging in the earth today are the physical manifestations of a spiritual war that is raging in the heavenlies for the souls of men. Jesus said, "The harvest truly is plentiful, but the laborers are few. Therefore pray the Lord of the harvest to send out laborers into His harvest" (Matthew 9:37-38). This fallen creation "groans and labors with birth pangs" (Romans 8:22) for redemption, while, at the same time, the Church is rising.... Though the future looks dark, for the praying Christian who seeks after God, the best is yet to come! For it is written that the gates of hell shall not prevail against the Church (see Matthew 16:18), and she shall arise with the glory of God upon her for all the world to see! (see Isaiah 60:1-2). The Kingdom of God will be established and the Harvest will be brought in — as God's people pray!

A CALL TO REPENTANCE

THE LAODICEAN CHURCH

As I have prayed for repentance for the Church, the Lord has given me a present-day picture of the Laodicean church described in **Revelation 3:16-19:**

> *"Because you are lukewarm, and neither cold nor hot, I will vomit you out of My mouth. Because you say, 'I am rich, have become wealthy, and have need of nothing' – and do not know that you are wretched, miserable, poor, blind, and naked. – I counsel you to buy from Me gold refined in the fire, that that you may be rich; and white garments, that you may be clothed, that the shame of your nakedness may not be revealed; and anoint your eyes with eye salve, that you may see.* As many as I love, I rebuke and chasten. Therefore be zealous and repent."

...Fool's gold

The picture I have is that many in the Church are buying fool's gold from the world and substituting it for **pure gold**, refined in the fire (see Malachi 3:2-3). The Lord is looking for those with clean hands and pure hearts (see Psalm 24:4), those who are weeping with broken and contrite hearts (see Psalm 51:17) — broken for the sins of compromise, impurity and rebellion.

As I meditated on this, He began to reveal things to me about this fool's gold. I discovered that in the natural there is a compound made up of iron and sulfur which has the appearance of real gold, but it is worthless. Its scientific name is *pyrite,* but it is referred to as fool's gold because of the many people who have been duped by its deceptive shiny gold color. Pyrite is readily available in nature, unlike gold, which is a very precious and rare metal. Because pyrite is really a compound of two other elements, it breaks down when it is heated, giving off a very offensive smell.

In this day and time there are many how-to books, conferences and programs on becoming men and women of faith and on moving in greater spiritual power. Partaking of these, we are duped into thinking our spiritual lives are rich and our fast-track faith, sufficient. But while many are working to "get in shape" under their own strength, they are not taking the time to develop *intimacy with God.* Neither are they seeking His refining fire in their lives. For this is what will bring forth what He desires: *His* beauty and purity, and *His* strength tempered by humility and love. God is saying that our efforts, instead of making us more holy, are making us more "wretched, miserable, poor, blind, and naked." Instead of doing it our way, and buying fool's gold, He is saying to us, "Do it My way: Submit to My purification processes and buy from Me gold refined in the fire." Like fools, many have gone their own way, and not received His counsel. ("The way of a fool is right in his own eyes, but he who heeds counsel is wise," according to Proverbs 12:15.) We have compounded something that looks like gold but is counterfeit. And when His holy refining fire comes, it will be consumed, bringing a stench to the nostrils of God.

...True gold

Gold, on the other hand, is a basic chemical element containing only one kind of atom, which means it cannot be broken down any further. That is why *heating gold only serves to purify it,* making it more beautiful, burning off all the dross, or impurities that may attach themselves to it. In its purest state gold is a relatively soft metal, making it very pliable and easy to work with and fashion into different shapes. However, gold is very resistant to chemical changes, so it doesn't tarnish or discolor. This is the gold that God requires — precious, genuine, pure, beautiful, pliable, enduring.

But God is ever gracious: "As many as I love, I rebuke and chasten. Therefore be zealous and repent" (verse 19). The Church needs to be willing to repent and pay the price that God requires for purity — to be subjected to His purging and refining processes to remove all the dross so that only pure gold — pure, soft and pliable — is left, so that He can make us whatsoever He wills.

...Eye salve

The previous passage in Revelation also speaks of the Church needing to "anoint your eyes with **eye salve** that you may see" (verse 18). We need vision. Proverbs 29:18 says, *"Where there is no revelation [prophetic vision], the people cast off restraint;* but happy is he who keeps the law." Vision keeps us on the right path and helps us to discern truth from falsehood and error. Lawlessness, on the other hand, abounds where there is no direction or restraint. In the world today many adhere to situation ethics: everyone doing what is right in his own eyes. This scenario was prevalent even in the days of the judges of Israel, when Israel was without the leadership of a king: "In those days there was no king in Israel; *everyone did what was right in his own eyes*" (Judges 17:6 and 21:25).

We need God's *eye salve* for vision to see and do what *God* requires of us.

...White garments

Verse 18 additionally speaks of the Church buying from God "*white garments*, that you may be clothed, that the shame of your nakedness may not be revealed." In Revelation 19:8, the Bride of Christ is arrayed in "fine linen, clean and bright, for the fine linen is the righteous acts of the saints." In the days of Moses and in the Tabernacle wilderness, the priests had to put on consecrated garments of white linen before going into the presence of the Lord (see Exodus 29:39-43). God is saying to the Church that we must likewise "put on" righteousness and holy living.

..."White-hot, enthusiastic lovers of our God!"

Verse 16 of the Revelation 3 passage reads: "Because you are lukewarm, and neither cold nor hot, I will vomit you out of My mouth." For many so-called Christians, spiritual life exists for one hour on Sunday. Content with hay and stubble, they don't long to adorn their lives with the riches of Christ (see 1 Corinthians 3:12-15). They may even substitute sports and recreation for worship on Sunday morning. Their passion is reduced to lukewarm as their life focus is self-centered instead of God-centered. David said, "My heart was hot within me; while I was musing, the fire burned" (Psalm 39:3). David had an undivided and passionate heart for the Lord. Songwriter and worship leader Eric Herron described this call to passionate surrender in his song *"Revive Your Fame Forever"*[2]:

We are white-hot, enthusiastic lovers of our God.
We agree our passion for Him goes unmatched.
We are called to eternal purposes in Jesus Christ.
We believe His name is branded on our hearts.
.....And we will shine unfading lights until
Our passionate surrender revives His fame forever.

This picture of the Laodicean church gives us much direction for our intercession for repentance and purity within the Church.

PRAYER FOR REPENTANCE AND PURITY
Purifying the Bride

Lord Jesus, heal us of our carnal, aberrant Christianity. Cause us to rise up in authentic Christianity that glorifies You in the world. May Your pure, spotless Bride come forth in all her splendor (see Ephesians 5:27). May the Church arise out of fear and doubt into overcoming faith to sit with You on Your throne (see Revelation 3:21). Father, purge the Church of our complacency, compromise and apathy (see Malachi 3:3). May we turn back to You in true repentance, with a holy fear of God, a holy hatred of sin, and a holy passion for Jesus in our hearts. Forgive us, Lord, for filling the soccer fields, football stadiums and amusement parks on Sunday mornings instead of filling Your churches. Raise us up out of lukewarmness to be "white-hot, enthusiastic lovers of our God." May we be clothed with humility instead of being driven by pride. May the Church humble herself in Your sight and give up her prideful ways (see James 4:10). May we put away childish things and be perfected in Your holiness and love (see 1 Corinthians 13:10-11). Forgive us, Father, for our friendship with the world that has made us Your enemies (see James 4:4.) Help us, instead, to hunger and thirst after righteousness (see Matthew 5:6). Lord, increase our appetite for the things that attract Your presence: love and compassion for our neighbors (see Matthew 22:39), love and devotion to You (see Matthew 22:37), repentant and contrite hearts (see Psalm 51:17), obedience (see John 14:15), holiness (see 1 Peter 1:15-16), unity (see Ephesians 4:3), faith (see Hebrews 11:6), effective, fervent praying (see James 5:16), and true spiritual worship that will tear down idols and strongholds (see John 4:23). And send Your holy refining fire to purge from us all of those things that repel Your presence: complacency, compromise, apathy (see Ephesians 5:11), bitterness (see Hebrews 12:15), anger (see Ephesians 4:31), unforgiveness (see Mark 11:25), offense (see Romans 14:13), envy (see Romans 1:29), impurity (see Hebrews 12:14), pride (see 1 John 2:16), lukewarmness (see Revelation 3:16), and every other work of the flesh that stifles spiritual life and withholds Your blessing and manifest presence from us. Lord, may we be the salt and light in the world that You have called us to be (see Matthew 5:13-14).

Putting on the "New Man"

Most Holy Father, I pray that the Church would "purify ourselves from everything that contaminates body and spirit, perfecting holiness out of reverence for God" (2 Corinthians 7:1, NIV). May a deep conviction and repentance come upon us so that we would have eyes to see our nakedness and be willing to pay the price that You require for purity. That we would submit to Your refining fire to bring forth pure gold: "the beauty of holiness" (Psalm 96:9) *within us* (see Revelation 3:16-18). *Father, may we put on the character of Your chosen people, clothing ourselves with compassion, kindness, humility, gentleness, patience, forgiveness, love, unity, peace, and thankfulness"* (see Colossians 3:12-17). *I pray that we would "put off, concerning [our] former conduct, the old man which grows corrupt according to the deceitful lusts, and be renewed in the spirit of [our] mind" — that we might "put on the new man which was created according to God, in true righteousness and holiness"* (Ephesians 4:22-24). *For the hour has come…to wake up from slumber…. So let us put aside the deeds of darkness and put on the armor of light. Let us behave decently, as in the daytime, not in orgies and drunkenness, not in sexual immorality and debauchery, not in dissension and jealousy. Rather, [let us] clothe [ourselves] with the Lord Jesus Christ, and do not think about how to gratify the desires of the sinful nature"* (Romans 13:11-14, NIV).

A prophetic call to the Laodicean (Revelation 3:14-21) Church…

Church! I say to you, wake up and arise to your destiny! — "Awake, you who sleep, arise from the dead, and Christ will give you light"! (Ephesians 5:14) — *"You are the light of the world…. Let your light so shine before men, that they may see your good works and glorify your Father in heaven."* (Matthew 5:14 and 16) — *"Arise, shine; for your light has come! And the glory of the* Lord *is risen upon you."* (Isaiah 60:1)

AN UNHOLY TRINITY

Jonas Clark speaks of an anti-Christ confederation, an "unholy trinity" as it were, working against and through the Church that needs to be challenged. The three spiritual forces are identified as *Jezebel, Balaam and Religion.*[3]

JEZEBEL SPIRIT

Jezebel was the evil pagan wife of King Ahab. She hated the people of God and manipulated to have the prophets of the Lord, and other godly men, massacred (see 1 Kings 18:4 and 21:7). She was a conniving, controlling woman who would stop at nothing to get her way. She was also a Baal worshiper, and influenced her husband, Ahab, to follow after her in her abominations: "But there was no one like Ahab who sold himself to do wickedness in the sight of the LORD, because Jezebel his wife stirred him up" (1 Kings 21:25). Because of her sin and rebellion before the Lord, her destiny was that she would be eaten by dogs at the wall of Jezreel (see 1 Kings 21:23). The fact that the Jezebel spirit is still influencing the church today can be seen in Revelation 2:20. Jesus said to the church at Thyatira, "Nevertheless I have a few things against you, because you allow that woman *Jezebel,* who calls herself a prophetess, to teach and seduce My servants to commit sexual immorality and eat things sacrificed to idols." *Jezebel is the voice of a false prophet who personifies the spirits of control, witchcraft and perversion in the Church.*

BALAAM SPIRIT

Balaam literally means, "destroyer of the people." Balaam was a soothsayer from Mesopotamia who was hired by Balak, the king of Moab, to bring a curse against the children of Israel (see Numbers 22-24). Balaam professed to be a prophet of God, but he was covetous, and willing to sell his prophetic gift for money. And though he brought blessing instead of curses to God's people, he did lure the men of Israel into sin with the Moabite women. Peter spoke of this spirit in 2 Peter 2:12-17 in referring to *false teachers* who "speak evil of the things they do not understand, and will utterly perish in their own corruption, and will receive the wages of unrighteousness …having eyes full of adultery and that cannot cease from sin, enticing unstable souls…. They have forsaken the right way and gone astray, following the way of Balaam." Jude also spoke of *false teachers* who "have run greedily in the error of Balaam for profit" (verse 11). "*The fundamental error of the Balaam spirit is the desire to become personally wealthy by making a business out of the service of God.*"[4]

RELIGIOUS SPIRIT

The spirit of *Religion* has nothing to do with genuine spirituality. It is that "religion" of works that desires to impress men and has nothing to do with what pleases or honors God. This "pharisee" spirit of legalism is what crucified Jesus and is still killing genuine spiritual life in the Church today. It is covetous and prideful, and persecutes genuine Spirit–filled religion and genuine prophets of God. This "religion" involves an outward demonstration of piety, with a spiritual void on the inside. Jesus called such people "whitewashed tombs which indeed appear beautiful outwardly, but inside are full of dead men's bones and all uncleanness" (Matthew 23:27). Paul said to the Corinthians that the new covenant is superior to the old because "the letter kills, but the Spirit gives life" (2 Corinthians 3:6). In other words, the letter of the Law of Moses kills because it only shows failure and demands punishment, but the law of Christ is one of victory and life through the Spirit. This is the only true religion.

DECREE AGAINST THIS ANTICHRIST CONFEDERATION

In the authority and name of Jesus Christ of Nazareth who came in the flesh (see 1 John 4:2), *I decree failure to the unholy trinity of Jezebel, Religion, and Balaam that seeks to destroy the Church and the Kingdom of God in the earth. Father, I ask you to bring confusion and disunity into their unholy alignment. For it is written: "Every kingdom divided against itself is brought to desolation, and every...house divided against itself will not stand"* (Matthew 12:25). *I take the "key of the house of David"* (Isaiah 22:22) *and close the door in the spirit realm to the continued operation of this unholy confederation within the Church. And I declare that the Blood of Jesus has triumphed over, and prevails against, these wicked powers to bind their influence and to render their authority null and void* (see Colossians 2:15 and Matthew 16:19). *I decree victory and prosperity to the Church as mighty overcomers by "the blood of the Lamb and the word of* [our] *testimony"* (Revelation 12:11). *For as it is written, the gates of hell shall not prevail against the Church* (see Matthew 16:18).

HOLY ALIGNMENT

THE BODY IS OUT OF ORDER

Another significant adjustment that needs to come into the Church is in the area of spiritual and functional *alignment.* To put it simply: the Body is out of order, and thus it is "sick." People are serving in places that God hasn't called them to, thus displacing others; and on it goes, so the whole body is "out of joint." The apostle Paul had this advice to the Ephesian church concerning this matter of church alignment and maturity:

> *May* [we] grow up in all things *into Him who is the head — Christ — from whom the whole body,* joined and knit together by what

every joint supplies, *according to the effective working by which* every part does its share, *causes growth of the body for the edifying of itself in love.* Ephesians 4:15-16

The Bible teaches that "God has set the members, each one of them, in the body just as *He* pleased" (not just as *we* pleased),... "that there should be no schism in the body, but that the members should have the same care for one another" (1 Corinthians 12:18 and 25). Within this Body there is also to be an order of *functional* gifts:

> *But to each one of us, grace was given according to the measure of Christ's gift.... And He Himself gave some to be apostles, some prophets, some evangelists, and some pastors and teachers, for the* equipping of the saints *for the work of ministry, for the edifying of the body of Christ, till we all come to the* unity of the faith *and of the knowledge of the Son of God, to a* perfect man, *to the measure of the stature of the fullness of Christ.* Ephesians 4:7 and 11-13

FUNCTIONAL GIFTS FOR EQUIPPING AND UNITY

These functional gifts are given, as it says in the above passage, for three reasons. First, in verse 12, it says these gifts are for the *equipping and edifying of the saints*. And further, in verse13, it is to bring *unity of the faith*. And thirdly, the functional gifts are to bring perfection, or maturity, to the Body into the fullness of Christ's character.

In addition to the *functional* gifts, there are *spiritual* gifts given individually to the Body, to profit all. These are outlined in 1 Corinthians 12:4, 7-10 and 28:

> *There are diversities of gifts, but the same Spirit.... The manifestation of the Spirit is given to each one* for the profit of all:*...the word of wisdom, the word of knowledge, ...faith, ...gifts of healings, ...working of miracles, ...prophecy, ...discerning of spirits, ...tongues, ...interpretation of tongues, ...helps, ...administrations.*

LOVE IS ESSENTIAL

Paul continues his teaching on spiritual gifts in 1 Corinthians 13. Having these gifts, he says, means nothing, and profits nothing, unless they are exercised through **love** (see verses1-3). In order for the Body of Christ to come into proper alignment under the headship of Christ, with each member in his own place and with his own function in ministry, the Church will have to grow up in love. According to the previous passage in Ephesians 4, the Church is edified and built up through the *love* we have for one another (see verse16). Jesus prayed to the Father:

> *"I have declared to them Your name, and will declare it,* that the love with which You loved Me may be in them, *and I in them."*
>
> John 17:26

The measure of the indwelling Christ (the personification of love) in the Church is in the love we show for one another. The apostle Peter said, "Above all things *have fervent love for one another,* for 'love will cover a multitude of sin' " (1 Peter 4:8). It is only when love overcomes our self-centeredness that the unity which Jesus prayed for the Church will begin to manifest:

> *"...that they all may be one, as You, Father, are in Me, and I in You; that they also may be one in Us, that the world may believe that You sent Me. And the glory which You gave Me I have given them, that they may be one just as We are one."*
>
> John 17:21-22

It is this unity, and the love of Jesus, which will draw the lost: "that they [the Church] may be made perfect in one, and that the world may know that You have sent Me, and have loved them as You have loved Me" (verse 23). The Church's unity, expressed by our love and nurtured through alignment, will be God's end-time witness to the world.

PROPHETIC CALL FOR UNITY AND HOLY ALIGNMENT WITHIN THE CHURCH

Forgive us, Lord, for dissension, division and competition within the Body of Christ. Pour out Your glory upon us to bring us into a spirit of unity, so that we might become one as You and the Father are one, as a witness to the world of Your great love (see John 17:20-23).

I call the Church into Your divine order under the apostolic headship (see Ephesians 4:11). *I call forth apostles, prophets, evangelists, pastors and teachers for our equipping and edification, for the unity of the faith, and for the perfecting of Your character within us* (see Ephesians 4:11-13). *Help each member of the Body to take his own place in the assembly, being "fitly joined together"* (Ephesians 4:16, KJV) *so as to please You, and not us* (see 1 Corinthians 12:18). *I beseech You, Lord, to stir up and activate the gifts that You have deposited within the Church: words of wisdom and knowledge, faith, gifts of healings, working of miracles, discerning of spirits, prophecy, tongues and interpretation, helps and administrations* (see 1 Corinthians 12:7-10 and 28). *Father, I confess that, as a whole, Your Church has been an impotent spiritual force in the world, "bringing forth wind," and not accomplishing any deliverance in the earth* (see Isaiah 26:18). *Help us, Lord, to arise as a mighty army, well-equipped for battle and for labor in Your harvest fields, in Jesus' name and for His glory!* (see Ephesians 6:10-11 and Luke 10:2).

CHURCH LEADERSHIP

In order for the Church to be strong, and to fulfill her destiny, she needs strong leadership. We need to pray for our Pastors to be established in faith and fully equipped for their calling. Following are some scriptures to pray to this end.

SCRIPTURAL DECLARATIONS FOR PASTORS
That by the enabling grace of God...

- *They would be built up in their most holy faith,* (see Jude 20), *so that they would persevere as Nehemiah did rebuilding the wall of Jerusalem* (see Nehemiah)
- *They would endure chastening, knowing that God deals with them as sons* (see Hebrews 12:7-11)
- *They would stand on the truth that nothing can separate them from God's love, and that they are more than conquerors through Jesus* (see Romans 8:35-37)
- *They would hold fast the confidence and rejoicing of hope firm to the end* (see Hebrews 3:6)
- *As they have received Christ, so shall they walk in Him, rooted and built up in Him and established in the faith, as they have been taught, abounding in it with thanksgiving* (see Colossians 2:6)

- *They would be strong, immovable, always abounding in the work of the Lord, knowing their labor is not in vain* (see 1 Corinthians 15:58)
- *They would fully submit to God and victoriously resist the devil; remaining steadfast, knowing that Jesus and their brothers have experienced the same sufferings* (see James 4:7 and Peter 5:9)
- *They would stand fast in liberty, not being entangled again with a yoke of bondage* (see Galatians 5:1)
- *They would press on toward the goal of the prize of the upward call of God in Christ, laying aside every weight and besetting sin, and running the race with endurance to receive the crown* (Philippians 3:14 and Hebrews 12:1-2)
- *Freedom of utterance would be given them that they would open their mouths boldly, to make known the mystery of the gospel, and that signs and wonders would follow the preaching of the Word* (see Ephesians 6:19 and Acts 4:29-30)
- *They would have great boldness in the faith which is in Christ Jesus* (see 1Timothy 3:13)
- *They would be clothed with humility, which brings grace; and the fear of the Lord, which brings wisdom* (see 1 Peter 5:5; Proverbs 22:4 and Proverbs 1:7)
- *They might be strengthened, perfected and established in the power of God's might and by the glory of God's grace* (see 1 Peter 5:10 and Ephesians 6:10)

Also, other church leaders, such as deacons, elders and the like, need to be covered in prayer. We can use the "binding and loosing" strategy from Chapter Nine to pray effectively for all church leaders. Many of the following words and phrases are from Scripture.

BINDING AND LOOSING FOR CHURCH LEADERS
I LOOSE them from all demonic and fleshly influences over every part of their body, mind and spirit, including: a carnal mindset (anything that exalts itself against the knowledge of God), worldliness in all forms, vain imaginations, busyness, distraction, confusion, depression, weariness, anxiety, fear, intimidation, workings and manipulations of the flesh: all confidence in the flesh, profane and idle babblings, ungodliness, false humility, all unhealthy soul ties,

unholy vows and covenants, contention and strife, deceit, hypocrisy, envy, evil speaking, DECEPTION in all forms

I BIND their mind, will and emotions to the will and purposes of God, including binding them to: the mind of Christ (bringing every thought captive to Christ), freedom of utterance to preach the gospel, a hunger and thirst after righteousness, knowledge of God's will, discernment, fruitfulness, not busyness, spiritual strength and might: a spirit of revelation, knowledge, wisdom, under-standing, counsel, power, and the fear of the Lord (see Isaiah 11:2), being rooted and grounded in love, true humility, meekness, godliness, holiness, wisdom to rightly divide the word of truth, faith that moves mountains, sound doctrine, sobriety, vigilance, steadfastness in faith, divine nature: fruit of the Spirit, grace and mercy, holy boldness, spirit of unity, TRUTH

ISRAEL AND THE CHURCH

One last thing that the Church needs specific prayer for is regarding her spiritual connection and destiny with Israel. As we said in Chapter One, it is God's holy plan for Israel and the Church *together* to be a dwelling place for Him in the earth. The problem is that many in the Church do not understand this truth. We need, first of all, to repent for this ungodly atti-tude, and then to pray for God to bring this revelation into the Church.

PRAYER FOR THE CHURCH REGARDING ISRAEL
One New Man
Father, I pray that our spiritual leaders within the Church would have a true burden and love for Israel, Your chosen people and the "apple of Your eye" (see Zechariah 2:8). I repent for the anti-Semitic spirit which has pervaded the Church, and for the false belief that the Church has replaced Israel in God's prophetic and redemptive plan. Forgive us, Father, and give us hearts that love Israel as You do. Give Your Church revelation from Your Word that You are shaping history for two groups of covenanted people, Israel and the Church, whom You are bringing together as ONE NEW MAN (see Ephesians 2:11-16). Help the Church to understand that both her heritage and her destiny lie with the Jewish people. May the Jews and the Gentile Christians be built to-gether into a glorious holy temple fit for Your dwelling place in the earth! (see Ephesians 2:21-22).

[1] Katherine Kersten, article in *The Wall Street Journal*, August 8, 2003.

[2] Eric Herron (Eric Herron Publishing, 2000), CCL1#3716551.

[3] Jonas Clark, Internet article (Hallandale, FL: Spirit of Life Ministries, January 1, 2003).

[4] William McDonald, *Believers' Bible Commentary* (Nashville, TN: Thomas Nelson Publishers, Inc., 1995), p. 2343.

Chapter Seventeen

THE UNITED STATES

"Blessed is the nation whose God is the LORD, the people He has chosen as His own inheritance." Psalm 33:12

REPENTANCE AND MERCY FOR NATIONAL SINS

OUR GODLY HERITAGE

In the year 1620, our forefathers journeyed to this land with the covenanted purpose of establishing a nation to the glory of God and the advancement of the Christian faith. This is set forth in the words of the Mayflower Compact, signed by forty-one brave Pilgrims upon their landing at Plymouth, Massachusetts:

> *Having undertaken,* for ye glory of God, and advancements of ye Christian faith…*a voyage to plant ye first colonie in the northerne parts of Virginia, doe by these presents solemnly and mutually in* the presence of God, *and one of another, covenant and combine our selves together into a civill body politick; for our better ordering, and* preservation and furtherance of ye ends aforesaid.

America has a godly heritage. And our God is a covenant-making God who doesn't forsake or forget the covenants that He makes with His people. For instance, even though Israel is struggling today to maintain her national land, God has covenanted with her regarding the land originally promised to her forefathers, Abraham, Isaac and Jacob (see Genesis 12:1-3 and 15:6-21). That covenant is an *everlasting covenant* (see Genesis 17:7) which, though man may forget, or try to override, God will not. Israel and the United States of America are the only two nations in history that have ever made covenants with Almighty God. That we have covenanted with Him regarding our land is foundational to our intercession. Because we know that GOD has predetermined that the United States will be "one nation under God," we can pray with confidence that we are, in fact, praying His will. But it will take much prayer, for with a certainty the enemy has his own agenda to try to derail the covenanted destiny of this nation — and he has done a pretty good job of it so far. We have lost our moral compass and have been reaping the consequences of following after our own ways. We have slipped off of our righteous foundation, but it is still there. The job of the intercessor is to pray us back onto our foundation, and re-dig those deep wells of revival from the First and Second Great (spiritual) Awakenings (in the seventeen and eighteen hundreds, respectively) that will bring us back on track as a nation that honors God once again.

God Is Looking for Those Who Will Stand in the Gap

Ezekiel 22 records a message of judgment sent by God to Jerusalem through the prophet Ezekiel. God's mercy is evident in verse 30 as He looks for an intercessor who would stand in the gap and pray on behalf of the wayward nation:

> *"So I sought for a man among them who would make a wall, and* stand in the gap before Me on behalf of the land, *that I should not destroy it; but I found no one."*

Sadly, there was no one to intercede for the nation, so the God of justice was forced to pour out His indignation on them (see verse 31). Our nation is in a similar place: embroiled in sin and rebellion against God, and in desperate need of intercessors to stand in the gap so God does not have to pour out His wrath upon us. Isaiah 59 describes our situation:

> *Your iniquities have separated you from your God; and your sins have hidden His face from you. ...For your hands are defiled with blood, and your fingers with iniquity; your lips have spoken lies, your tongue has muttered perversity. No one calls for justice, nor does any plead for truth. They trust in empty words and speak lies; they conceive evil and bring forth iniquity....* For our transgressions are multiplied before You, and our sins testify against us.... Justice is turned back, and

righteousness stands afar off; for truth is fallen in the street, and equity cannot enter.   verses 2-4, 12 and 14

GOD IS CALLING FOR REPENTANCE

The Lord God said to Israel, and He says to us:

"Repent, turn away from your idols, and turn your faces away from all your abominations..., that the house of [America] *may no longer stray from Me, nor be profaned anymore with all their transgressions, but that they may be My people and I may be their God."*
Ezekiel 14:6 and 11

"Return to the LORD your God, for He is gracious and merciful, slow to anger, and of great kindness; and He relents from doing harm."
Joel 2:13

Psalm 81 speaks of God's plea for Israel's obedience. He ends His exhortation by telling Israel that because they would not heed His voice He "gave them over to their own stubborn heart" (verse12). America is presently in a similar state of reaping what we have sown. But the Lord, our Redeemer, further declared to His wayward nation, "Oh, that My people would listen to Me…[and] walk in My ways! I would soon subdue their enemies" (verses 13-14). Repentance and turning to God alone will bring the revival and restoration that we need.

MODEL PRAYER FOR THE NATION

Following the model of the prayer of Moses in Exodus 32, that we discussed in Chapter One, we can pray accordingly. Moses pleaded with God to *honor His name* before the heathen and he *brought the Lord into remembrance* of the covenant He had made with Abraham, Isaac and Jacob. We can use these same strategies today as we go before the Father on behalf of our nation. And as Daniel laid Israel's sins before the Lord and asked for mercy (see Daniel 9), so should we. For indeed, it is time to "seek the LORD while He may be found" and "call upon Him while He is near." We need to pray that the "wicked forsake his way, and the unrighteous man his thoughts," and that we would all "return to the LORD and He will have mercy on [us]; and to our God, for He will abundantly pardon" (Isaiah 55:6-7).

Though there is much lawlessness and unrighteousness in this nation, there are certain *defining* sins. The following prayer of supplication contains prayer points for America.

PRAYER FOR THE UNITED STATES
Mercy, Restoration, Revival!

Father, I stand in the gap on behalf of this nation (see Ezekiel 22:30), *beseeching You to remove the yoke of wickedness from us and establish in us a passion for holiness.*

Holy Spirit, move upon the Church in America with a spirit of conviction so that God's people will humble themselves, and pray, and seek Your face, and turn from their wicked ways so that You will hear from Heaven, forgive our sin, and heal our land (see 2 Chronicles 7:14).

O most merciful God, we are a stiff-necked and rebellious people who have run after other gods. We have lusted after pleasures, money, fame and power, and have been men-pleasers instead of God-pleasers.

O Lord, break our hearts with godly sorrow that brings forth repentance and righteousness (see 2 Corinthians 7:10). *Have mercy on us and forgive us for our national sins.*

Father, forgive this nation for touching "the apple of Your eye," Israel. Forgive our leaders for pressuring Israel to divide up her covenant land and for aligning with Israel's enemies. May America bless Israel and not curse her, so You can withhold Your hand of judgment from us concerning Israel (see Numbers 24:9).

And, Lord, forgive us and cleanse us of the abominations that have defiled this land (see 1 John 1:9). — *Some defining sins...*

- **The shedding of innocent blood** *through PERSECUTION (of races, gender, nationality) and ABORTION: Father, You are "a God of justice"* (Isaiah 30:18), *so "Arise, O Lord, in Your anger.... Awake, my God; decree justice"* (Psalm 7:6, NIV). *for the unborn who cannot speak for themselves! Move upon the hearts of those doctors who perform these wicked procedures, and upon the hearts of the women who seek them. May those women who demand the freedom to "choose," choose to be chaste! And grant victory to those who are seeking to overturn Roe v. Wade through the court system.*
- *Our violent and perverse TV and movie industries*

- *Exportation of evil, violence and filth around the world*
- *Glorification of external beauty while our souls and spirits are destitute of the inner beauty of integrity and holiness* (see 1 Peter 3:3 and 4)
- ***Sexual perversion:*** *incest, adultery, fornication, pornography, homosexuality. Decree failure to the political agendas of homosexuality and pornography. Repent for the validation of sodomy by the highest court of our land, and for the validation of homosexual leaders and "gay" unions within the Church.*
- ***Idolatry and greed:*** *Freemasonry (uproot this wicked seed with its root and fruit, and deliver all those caught up in its deception), being lovers of money and power and pleasure instead of lovers of God* (see 2 Timothy 3:4), *bribery, manipulation, corruption, abandonment of God and children to careers*
- ***Pride, rebellion, lawlessness:*** *self-reliance, self-indulgence (while others suffer need), broken covenants (especially concerning marriage and Native Americans), lack of personal integrity*
- ***Taking the Word of God and prayer out of schools and public places: turning to humanistic ways and false religions:*** *O Lord, bring us back to the one true and living God of the Bible. Father, forgive us for embracing the lie that Islam is a peaceful, God-honoring religion. (For more on this, see Chapter Eighteen.) In the name of "diversity" and "religious tolerance" we have enabled the enemy to establish a stronghold in our nation. Heal us of our spiritual blindness. I pray for revelation, beginning with our President, concerning the dangers and deceptions of Islam. And Father, I cry out in supplication, and for the sake of Your holy name, that You would stop the advancement of this insidious spiritual plague from usurping our religious freedoms and destroying our Christian heritage.*

Though we deserve judgment, O Lord, for these and all of our sins, I ask that "in wrath [You would] remember mercy" (Habakkuk 3:2). For "mercy triumphs over judgment" (James 2:13). May the power of Your mercy overcome the wickedness of our sin! I beseech You, "Father of mercies" (2 Corinthians 1:3), to extend Your mercy and compassion to us according to Your Word in:

- Lamentations 3:22-23 and 31-33: *"Through the LORD's mercies we are not consumed, because His compassions fail not. They are new every morning; great is Your faithfulness.... For the Lord will not cast off for-*

ever. Though He causes grief, yet He will show compassion according to the multitude of His mercies. For He does not afflict willingly, nor grieve the children of men."
- Psalm 145:8-9: *"The LORD is gracious and full of compassion, slow to anger and great in mercy. The LORD is good to all, and His tender mercies are over all His works."* — *"For His mercy endures forever"* (Psalm 136).
- Daniel 9:17-19: *"Now therefore, our God, hear the prayer of Your servant, and...cause Your face to shine on [us]...incline Your ear and hear; open Your eyes and see our desolations, ...for we do not present our supplications before You because of our righteous deeds, but because of Your great mercies. O Lord, hear! O Lord, forgive! O Lord, listen and act! Do not delay for Your own sake, my God..."*

Lord, I put You in remembrance of the blood of the martyrs upon this land — and of our godly heritage. Lord, remember the faith of our founding fathers, and their holy covenant with You for the dedication of this land to the glory of God and the Gospel of the Lord Jesus Christ. O Lord, do not forget or forsake this covenant, I pray. For the sake of Your mighty name, do not allow our enemies to triumph over us! Your Word says that "when the enemy comes in like a flood, the Spirit of the LORD will lift up a standard against him" (Isaiah 59:19). Lord, I pray that You would raise up a standard of repentance and righteousness across this land, so that "the Redeemer will come to...those who turn from transgression" (Isaiah 59:19-20). Father God, may America "turn to [You] with all of our heart with fasting, weeping and mourning" (Joel 2:12). So that You can uncap the wells of Revival...Uncap the wells of Revival and let them gush forth with rivers of living water across this land. May the spirit of intercession and evangelism of Jonathan Edwards, Dwight L. Moody, Charles Finney, Mary Lyon, David Brainerd, George Whitfield, and John Elliot be released upon us once again. Father, reestablish justice as the measuring line and righteousness as the plumb line (see Isaiah 28:17, NIV). Lord, You said that when we return to You, You will heal our backslidings (see Jeremiah 3:22). Come and shake the earth so that the ungodly structures of men may be removed and Your Kingdom, which cannot be shaken, will remain (see Hebrews12:26-28). I declare over America that the LORD is our Judge, the LORD is our Lawgiver, the LORD is our King"! (Isaiah 33:22).

Restore us, O God of our salvation, and cause Your anger toward us to

*cease. Will You be angry with us forever? Will you prolong Your anger
to all generations? Will You not REVIVE us again, that Your people
may rejoice in You? Show us Your mercy, LORD, and grant us Your salvation.* Psalm 85:4-7

*Father, I pray for a mighty outpouring of Your Holy Spirit to bring forth
REVIVAL and a great harvest of souls into this land. May it sweep across this
nation like a holy fire and a mighty river — in Jesus' Name and to His glory!*

A Prophetic Call to America, taken from Ezekiel 14:6 and Psalm 62:5-8:

*America! Repent and turn from your idols and turn away your faces
from all your abominations. Your expectation is from God alone. He
only is your rock and your salvation; He is your defense; you shall not be
moved. In God is your salvation and your glory; the rock of your strength,
and your refuge, is in God. Trust in Him at all times, you people; pour
out your heart before Him; God is a refuge for you.*

A WORD ABOUT ISRAEL

GOD'S COVENANT AND REDEMPTIVE PLAN

Because the heritage and the destinies of the Church and Israel are so
bound together, we need to understand the significance of Israel to our
national security and well-being. Romans 11 explains the connection between Israel and the Church:

*For I do not desire, brethren, that you should be ignorant of this
mystery…that blindness in part has happened to Israel until the fullness of the Gentiles [the Church] has come in. And so all Israel will be
saved, as it is written: "The Deliverer will come out of Zion, and He
will turn away ungodliness from Jacob [Israel];* for this is My covenant with them, *when I take away their sins."* verses 25-27

It is God's covenant with Israel that guarantees her national and geo-
graphical restoration (see Genesis 17:7-8). Paul, writing to the Ephesians,
explains the shared destiny of Israel and the Church:

But now in Christ Jesus you who once were far off [Gentile peoples] *have been brought near* [to God] *by the blood of Christ. For He Him-self is our peace, who has made both ONE, and has broken down the middle wall of separation...so as to create in Himself ONE NEW MAN from the two, thus making peace, and that He might reconcile them both* [Jews and Gentiles] *to God in ONE BODY through the cross."*

Ephesians 2:13-16

And further, we see that there is being built a new "household of God":

...having been built on the foundation of the apostles and prophets, Jesus Christ Himself being the chief cornerstone, in whom the whole building, being fitted together, grows into a holy temple in the Lord, in whom you are also are being built *together for a dwelling place of God in the Spirit.*

Ephesians 2:19-22

This is God's holy plan: Israel and the Church, being fitted together as a dwelling place for Him in the spirit!

SIGNIFICANCE TO OUR NATIONAL SECURITY

So how does this impact the United States? First of all, the Scripture tells us that, because Israel is God's specially chosen covenant people and "the apple of His eye" (Zechariah 2:8), the nation that blesses Israel will be blessed, and the nation that curses Israel will be cursed (see Numbers 24:9). And because God has guaranteed the complete restoration of Israel's covenant land (see Amos 9:13-15), the nations that seek to scatter the people of Israel and divide up her covenant land will ultimately receive severe judgment from the Lord (see Joel 3:2).

Because of these facts, it is imperative that our leaders stand with Israel and not participate in the current "land for peace" initiative in the Middle East. For he who touches Israel, to harm or diminish her in any way, touches "the apple of God's eye" and incurs His wrath. The only real and lasting peace will come to Israel when she receives the *"Prince of Peace"* (Isaiah 9:6), Messiah Jesus.

OUR LEADERS

The Bible is very clear about the importance of praying for our leaders. 1 Timothy 2:1-4 states:

Therefore I exhort first of all that supplications, prayers, intercessions, and giving of thanks be made for all men, for kings and all who are in authority, *that we may lead a quiet and peaceable life in all godliness and reverence. For this is good and acceptable in the sight of God our Savior, who desires all men to be saved and to come to the knowledge of the truth.*

There are several things to consider here. First, the command is to pray for "all" men in authority. Whether we deem them "good" or "bad" makes no difference. "God is the Judge: He puts down one, and exalts another" (Psalm 75:7). Our job is to PRAY. Secondly, this passage gives us the reasons why we should pray: that we might "lead a quiet and peaceable life..." (verse 2) and so that "all men [might] be saved" (verse 4).

THE PRESIDENT

With this in mind, the following prayer is a model for how to pray for our highest leader, the President of the United States.

PRAYER FOR THE PRESIDENT

Protection: *Father, I pray the precious blood of Jesus over the President, his family and his staff. May your angels watch over them and keep them in all their ways today* (see Psalm 91:11). *May the angel of the Lord encamp around the President and deliver him from every evil. May You deliver him from all his fears and save him out of all his troubles* (see Psalm 34:7, 4 and 6). *I declare that no weapon formed against the President shall prosper, and every tongue that rises up against him in judgment he shall condemn* (see Isaiah 54:17). *I pray that You would hide him from "the secret plots of the wicked, from the rebellion of the workers of iniquity, who sharpen their tongue like a sword"* (Psalm 64:2-3). *Lord, close the mouths of those who would shoot out bitter words, and cause them to stumble over their own tongue* (see verses 3-9). *Blessed be the Lord, who has not given the President as prey to their teeth, but has enabled him to escape as a bird from the fowler's snare* (see Psalm 124:6-7). *Keep him from the snares the enemy has laid for him, and from the traps of the workers of iniquity. Let the wicked fall into their own nets, while he escapes safely* (see Psalm 141:9-10). *Bless the President, Lord, and surround him with Your shield of favor and with mercy* (see Psalms 5:12 and 32:10).

Wisdom: *Father, may the President be given wisdom liberally from above to* *make the decisions that he needs to make today* (see James 1:5). *Each morning, awaken his ear to hear as the learned* (see Isaiah 50:4), *and quicken his heart to be willing and wise to do the work that You have given him to do* (see Exodus 35:5 and 36:2). *May he "be filled with the knowledge of [Your] will in all wisdom and spiritual understanding"* (Colossians 1:9), *and may the eyes of his understanding be enlightened with Your truth* (see Ephesians 1:18). *Your Word says that "he who rules over men must be just, ruling in the fear of God"* (2 Samuel 23:3). *I pray that the President would rule in the fear of God rather than men. I loose him from the influence of falsehood, deception and ungodly counsel, and I bind his mind, will and emotions to truth and to the will and purposes of God. I loose him from the passions of the flesh and worldly thinking and bind him to the mind of Christ* (see 1 Corinthians 2:16). *Thank You for giving him discernment to know Your voice so he will not follow the voice of a stranger* (see John 10:4-5). *I pray that You would empower him with all wisdom and knowledge so that he will be able to excel in all his endeavors* (see Ephesians 3:20) *to uphold righteousness, truth and justice across this land* (see Isaiah 28:17).

Salvation and godly character: *Father, I pray that the President, if he doesn't already know You, would come to a saving knowledge of You. I pray that he would have the "excellent spirit" of Daniel* (Daniel 5:12) *and that he would "put on the Lord Jesus Christ and make no provision for the flesh"* (Romans 13:14). *I loose him from fear and intimidation, and bind him to power, love, and a sound mind* (see 2 Timothy1:7). *I pray that discretion will protect him and understanding will guard him, and that wisdom will save him from the ways of evil and from wicked men* (see Proverbs 2:10-12). *I pray that he would walk worthy of the Lord, fully pleasing Him, being fruitful in every good work and increasing in the knowledge of God. Lord, may You strengthen him with might by Your glorious power, giving him patience, joyful endurance, and a thankful heart* (see Colossians 1:10-12). *I pray that he would be an instrument for noble purposes, useful to You for accomplishing every good work for the sake of this nation* (see 2 Timothy 2:21).

OTHER NATIONAL LEADERS

This would include people like the President's Cabinet and policy advisors (secretary of defense, national security advisor, secretary of state, attorney general, senior advisor to the President, chief of staff, FBI director, CIA director), military leaders, congressional leaders, Supreme Court justices, and ambassadors to foreign nations (including the United Nations).

PRAYER FOR OUR NATIONAL LEADERS

Father God, I lift up our national leaders and ask You to save the souls of those who don't know You, and to bring them all into alignment with Your holy will and purposes for this nation. May the Spirit of the Lord give them the Spirit of wisdom, understanding, counsel, might, knowledge and the fear of the Lord. And may their delight be in the fear of the Lord so they will not judge by the sight of their eyes, nor the hearing of their ears, but with righteousness and equity (see Isaiah 11:2-4).

THE ECONOMY

Rick Joyner made the point following the September 11 terrorist attacks that we should pray especially for our economy and our military, as these targets were represented by the plane crashes destroying the World Trade Center and part of the Pentagon. Our economy has been undergoing a shaking the past few years, and will likely continue to do so, as God continues to expose evil and corruption in our corporate structure. We need to pray that, in His mercy, He will keep the economy from collapsing under the shaking.

Osama Bin Laden, the international terrorist leader, reportedly has said that allah's order is to "kill the Americans and plunder their money." The fact is, much of America's financial wealth is in the hands of international individuals and corporations, and many of these are Muslim. We need to pray for God's mercy regarding our economy and that He would transfer the wealth back into the hands of American corporations. Through Islamic entrepreneurs and others, the "strong man" has plundered the "house" of America. We need to pray for God to release upon us the anointing to plunder HIM and take back what he has stolen (see Matthew 12:29). With these in mind, following is a prayer model for our economy.

PRAYER DECLARATION FOR THE ECONOMY

In the name of Jesus, I condemn the judging and cursing words decreed against our economy by Islamic terrorists and others. I command them to fall to the ground null and void. Father, I thank You for the ongoing exposure of evil and corruption in America's corporate structure. But in Your mercy, I pray You would not allow it to destroy our economy. Lord, may we remain fiscally strong to be able to continue to send out missionaries, support and resources for the building of Your Kingdom around the world and to bring in the end-time Harvest. And may we be enabled to continue to support and protect Israel. Lord, I pray that You would transfer America's wealth now in the hands of the international/ Islamic entities into the hands of Americans. And I call forth a corporate America owned and managed by righteous men and women. I declare that this wealth WILL come into the hands of the righteous, for it is written: "the wealth of the sinner is stored up for the righteous" (Proverbs 13:22). *Lord, I ask that You release to Your intercessors the anointing to plunder the strong man and take back what he has stolen from America!* (see Matthew 12:29).

THE JUDICIAL SYSTEM

The judicial system in America has passed down some very dangerous decisions in the past thirty or so years. Beginning with taking prayer out of public schools, and *Roe* v. *Wade* (which legalized abortion on demand), our nation has been in a steady moral downward spiral. This, unfortunately, has been facilitated by the Church's complacency, compromise and lack of involvement. Reverend Dutch Sheets has stated that we are now at the "crisis point of our generation," which involves a spiritual war for the very heart of our nation. He says:

> *The war of which I speak is for* the turning of the courts, *with its obvious connection to many critical issues. The Church of America in the 60's and 70's, by allowing the courts to remove God from our culture, prayer from our schools, and by legalizing abortion, sent us on a downward spiral from which we have not recovered. The outcome of the spiritual war we are entering into is probably going to be the single most important deciding factor in whether or not we see revival and the healing of America in our generation. If we do not win this battle, we will lose the war. We have reached the pivotal point; all we have gained is on the line. There will be no grace extension for our generation if we falter on this one. The question for us, prompted by Isaiah 37:3, is about to be answered: we have come to the point of birth; will there be strength to deliver?[1]*

This is the challenge to us as intercessors: Do we have the strength and perseverance to pray this through until we see victory? There are some key issues. First of all, it is likely that two conservative Supreme Court justices will soon retire. If they are not replaced by like-minded Justices, that will sway the power over to the liberal side. This would have horrific repercussions in our judicial decisions, with an increasing downward spiral into moral and spiritual decadence. On the other hand, if the President nominates pro-choice justices, the Senate will likely continue to filibuster, President Bush nominated a number of conservative judges to benches across the land that were not confirmed by the Senate, because of a *filibuster.* But all hope is not lost. As Dutch Sheets has said, "We **can** win this war, shift the judicial system of America, and see God heal our land. But it will require much prayer and effective spiritual warfare!"

PRAYER DECLARATION FOR THE JUDICIAL SYSTEM

O Lord, You are our Judge, our Lawgiver, and our King (see Isaiah 33:22). *You set up governments and rulers* (see Romans 13:1) *and You founded the government of the United States as "one nation under God." But the enemy has been trying to destroy our righteous foundation through our court system and the rule of law. I declare, in the authority and power of Jesus' name, that every plan and scheme of the devil to divert and dismantle God's model for the United States judiciary is null and void. I call every judge in this nation to salvation and submission to the Lordship of Jesus Christ. I call every judge, from the highest court in our land to the lowest precinct, to come into alignment with the purposes and the laws of God. Father, may our judges fulfill their constitutional roles of upholding justice through interpreting the law, and not legislating it. I call each judge to make rulings according to God's justice and Word of Truth. I call upon You, our "righteous Judge"* (2 Timothy 4:8), *to abolish judicial tyranny from our land. I declare justice the measuring line and righteousness the plumb line* (see Isaiah 28:17) *over this nation. May the Spirit of the Lord give every judge a Spirit of wisdom, understanding, counsel, might and knowledge. May the fear of the Lord be their delight, so they will not judge by the sight of their eyes, nor the hearing of their ears, but with righteousness and equity* (see Isaiah 11:2-4).

*O **Master of Breakthroughs*** (see 2 Samuel 5:19), *break through the filibustering spirit and any other hindrances that are preventing any righteous judges from being confirmed into their God-appointed positions. In the authority of Jesus Christ, I crush, smash and destroy the spiritual strongholds that are preventing God's will and purposes from going forth through our judicial system,* *and that are denying or threatening the integrity of the U.S. Constitution. I rebuke, bind and cast out every partisan spirit, and spirits of witchcraft (intimidation and control), obstruction, destruction, lawlessness, perversion and murder. And I declare that their assignment against the judicial system of the United States is cancelled, in Jesus' name, and by the power of His shed Blood. Sovereign Lord, "the heavens are Yours, [and] the earth also.... You have a mighty arm; strong is Your hand, and high is Your right hand. Righteousness and justice are the foundation of Your throne" (Psalm 89:11, 13 and 14). Establish the dominion of Your throne over our courts, our lives and our wayward nation — in Jesus' name and for His glory!*

NATIONAL SECURITY

OUR CITIES

There are a number of cities that seem to be vulnerable for one reason or another: geographic location, cultural/population centers, political significance, etc. Some of these cities are: San Diego, El Paso, Chicago, Minneapolis, Buffalo, Atlanta, Los Angeles, Denver, Key West, Miami, Orlando, Tampa, Mobile, New Orleans, Houston, San Francisco, Seattle, Portland, Boston, Philadelphia, Pittsburgh, Cleveland, Dallas, Norfolk and Hampton Roads.

PRAYER OVER OUR CITIES

I put the Blood of Jesus over our cities and declare that the Blood has triumphed over, and prevails against, all the plans of the enemy and any spiritual forces sent to bring terror and destruction. I declare that all such evil plans are exposed and cancelled in Jesus' name, and by the power of His shed Blood (see Colossians 2:15). *Father, I pray that You would station Your warring angels over the borders of the United States and all of its cities, especially Washington, D.C. and New York City.*

NATIONAL SECURITY AND AGENCIES

Our national security is ultimately in the hands of God. And so we beseech Him to have mercy and to intervene on our behalf. We must also lift up *to* God our various security agencies which are dedicated to preserving the safety of our people and our nation. It is strategically imperative that they all work together in a spirit of cooperation and teamwork to accomplish this job.

PRAYER FOR NATIONAL SECURITY

O most merciful Father, I lift up America and ask You to hold her in Your "secret place" (Psalm 91:1) "under the shadow of Your wings" (Psalm 17:8). As You raised Your mighty voice to call the world into being (see Psalm 33:6), I beseech You to raise Your mighty voice to "roar" (Joel 3:16) against the spirit of death and the tactics of terror and destruction. May You "frustrate the devices of the crafty so that their hands cannot carry out their plans" (Job 5:12). According to Your mercy, O God, please protect this nation from natural disasters as well as terrorist, biochemical and nuclear attacks. I pray the Blood of Jesus over our defense and telecommunication systems, particularly satellite, computer, Internet, telephone and all media networks. Also, I pray the Blood of Jesus over our energy systems and nuclear power plants. Lord, please set your angelic host to encamp around and protect (Psalm 34:7) our high-risk and strategic locations: subway and rail systems, airports and airplanes, oil refineries and storage areas, bridges, reservoirs, seaports, waterways, dams, shipyards, and military bases. I pray for the efficiency of the "bio-watch" systems around our cities and the heightened security systems around our airports. I beseech You, Father, to enable America to fulfill her God-ordained destiny in the earth. May Your Kingdom come and Your will be done — in Jesus' name!

PRAYER FOR OUR SECURITY AGENCIES

Father, I lift up the Homeland Security Department, the FBI (Federal Bureau of Investigation), the CIA (Central Intelligence Agency), the DIA (Defense Intelligence Agency) and the Terrorist Threat Integration Center and pray that they would all work together in a spirit of cooperation and teamwork. May You give them Your strategies for securing this nation from all threats of aggression and ambushments. I pray that these personnel would have "wisdom and strength,...counsel and understanding" (Job 12:13) as they seek to protect this nation from danger and terrorism. I pray that You would enable them to uncover deep things out of darkness, and to bring the shadow of death to light (see Job 12: 22). Father, help them to expose all evil and terrorist activity and bring it to justice. I declare that "there is nothing hidden which will not be revealed, nor has anything been kept secret but that it should come to light" (Mark 4:22) that threatens our national security.

"NOT MY WILL, BUT YOURS, BE DONE"

Having said all of this concerning the importance of praying for God's mercy and protection for our nation, we must also make room for the sovereignty of God. On the night before the crucifixion, Jesus was in such agony, Luke tells us, that "His sweat became like great drops of blood falling down to the ground" (Luke 22:44). He faced an unimaginably horrific ordeal: He had to drink the cup of judgment for the sins of all mankind. His humanity wondered if He could get through it; His deity knew He must. Love and obedience propelled Him forward. He prayed, "Father, if it is Your will, take this cup away from Me; nevertheless *not My will, but Yours, be done*" (22:42). This must be the stance of the intercessor when praying for God to protect this nation from disaster. We must face the possibility that the very thing that will bring about the revival we desire may be the judgment we fear. God sent His redemptive judgments many times in Scripture to draw people to Himself and to fulfill His purposes. We *want* revival, but we *need* change. Surely we have offended God and done everything possible to incur, and deserve, His wrath. Therefore, we must make room for a merciful God to do *whatever is necessary* to effect change. We pray that, if it is possible, He would let the "cup of judgment" be taken from us — however, not our will, but HIS be done. And so we will continue to pray that darkness be pushed back and evil be defeated, because that is our calling. But HOW that is done we must leave up to God.

TERRORISM

Even as we pray *for* America's safety, we need to pray *against* the forces of terrorism. The threat of terrorism exists on local, regional, national and international levels. And so we must target each level in our warfare, including the spiritual level. So first we need to address terrorism at the root: the *spiritual forces that incite terrorism*. Then, since terrorism is an international threat, and since terrorism in America is largely funded and directed from outside of the U.S., we need to pray against w*orldwide terrorism*. Further, since it is God's stated will that He desires for ALL men to come to repentance and salvation, we must pray for God's mercy, deliverance and *salvation for the terrorists*.

We also need to be aware that much demonic control in the world is concealed by occult activity, through curses and witchcraft. Rick Ridings, director of *Succat Hallel* in Jerusalem, brings us a strategy for intercession concerning the exposure of terrorists. He reports that the Lord has given their intercessors a clear call to prayer for the removal of the "occult shield of protection" surrounding terrorist leaders.[2]

PRAYER AGAINST TERRORISM

Against the Spiritual Forces Inciting Terrorism...

"*Arise, O Lord, in your anger; rise up against the rage of [our] enemies*" (*principalities, powers, rulers of darkness, spiritual wickedness in high places* — see Ephesians 6*). "Awake, my God, decree justice....O righteous God,...bring an end to the violence of the wicked and make the righteous secure*" (Psalm 7:6 and 9, NIV). *For, Lord, the wicked "gather themselves together against the soul of the righteous and condemn the innocent blood." Mighty God, "cut them off in their own wickedness*" (Psalm 94:21 and 2, KJV) *O Lord, "give us help from trouble, for the help of man is useless. Through God we will do valiantly, for it is He who shall tread down our enemies*" (Psalm 60:11-12).

Concerning the Network of Terrorist Cells in America...

Lord, You know where every terrorist cell is located across this nation. Father, I ask You to cut asunder the cords of this wicked net (see Psalm 129:4). *And bring disarray, confusion, defection, and a holy fear of God into the enemy camp. Sever their communication network, their financial backing and their tracking systems. Diffuse their power and expose their evil schemes and terrorist activities and bring them to justice, in Jesus' name.*

Against Worldwide Terrorism...

In the authority of Jesus Christ of Nazareth and by the power of His name, I decree destruction over the worldwide terrorist network. I say, "Let God arise over terrorism and His enemies be scattered!" (see Psalm 68:1). *I decree that every terrorist-sponsoring-and-supporting government shall be dismantled and uprooted. Father, I ask You to cause ambushments to come from within the terrorist network so that it will begin to self-destruct from the inside out* (see 2 Chronicles 20:22-24). *May the infrastructure of terrorism collapse in on itself as the ambushments are set by Your mighty hand and the leadership is divided and destroyed. For it is written: "Every... house divided against itself will not stand*" (Matthew 12:25).

Concerning Terrorists...

Father, have mercy on the terrorists. I cry out for the souls lost in the decep-

*tion and allure of jihad. May those who would willingly sacrifice their lives to allah receive the sacrifice of Your dear Son for them. Put the holy fear of God in their hearts. And give them eyes to see You as the **Lord, Jehovah**, the personal, covenant-keeping God of love. Bring them up out the pit of miry clay that has them trapped and set their feet upon the rock* (see Psalm 40:2). *Deliver them from demonic power and from their prisons of hatred and destruction. O Mighty Deliverer, set the captives free* (see Luke 4:18) *and send laborers into the harvest fields!* (see Matthew 9:38).

Father, I pray that You would target every terrorist leader, and that, like Saul of Tarsus, You would knock them off their "high horses" of pride, delusion and deception. May the brilliance of Your glory surround them and bring them to their knees in surrender to You! (see Acts 9:1-6). *I push back the occult cover of darkness that conceals them. For it is written: "Their webs [of evil] will not become garments, nor will they cover themselves with their works." I declare, in Jesus' name, that their works will be exposed, and the perpetrators apprehended, for "their works are works of iniquity, and the act of violence is in their hands"* (Isaiah 59:6).

RESTORATION OF FAMILIES

As our nation has consistently slid off of her righteous foundation in recent years, there have been repercussions at every level of society. Many misled people have taken the freedoms that we cherish, and which our Constitution protects, and twisted them to support agendas that do not line up with the intentions of the Constitution writers. Notable examples are "Freedom of Speech" (the first amendment) and "separation of church and state," which is, in fact, nowhere in the Constitution. From the "right" to disseminate pornographic literature to the "right" to kill an unborn child, lawless perversions of justice have become the law of the land. These aberrations have not only weakened this Republic in general, but the institution of the family, specifically. The future of the biblical family model is seriously at risk, as *liberty* has become *license* to do whatever feels good. We need to heed the wise words of the late Reverend Peter Marshall, Chaplain of the United States Senate (1946-1947), who once said: *"Liberty is not the right to do as we please, but the **opportunity to please to do what is right**."*[3]

Between the "women's liberation" movement of the 1970's and the "gay rights" movement of the 1990's and continuing, the family unit has undergone drastic changes. Many families are fatherless, and more mothers are working outside the home than at any time in history. Children are largely left to fend for themselves, and with the lack of parental supervision, discipline and accountability, our schools have become battlefields where drugs, teen pregnancy and violence abound. God's intervention is needed desperately for the restoration of our families.

PRAYER FOR RESTORATION OF FAMILIES

Father, You have established the family unit as the backbone of society. I cry out for the restoration of our families to the biblical model. Lord, bring Your holy alignment into our fractured families…. Bring back the prodigal fathers to take their places as the priests of their homes. I pray that they would not provoke their children to anger, but bring them up in "the training and admonition of the Lord" (Ephesians 6:4). *And Father, I pray for mothers to adhere to their holy calling and forsake the lure of the marketplace and the business world. Let them hear the heart cries of their children and be the nurturers that their children need. Turn the hearts of the fathers — and mothers — to the children and the children to the fathers — and mothers* (Malachi 4:6*). May children honor and obey their parents according to Your Word in* Ephesians 6:1-2. *May husbands love and cherish their wives as Christ loves the Church, and wives honor and submit to their husbands as unto the Lord, according to Your Word in* Ephesians 5:22 and 25. *And may husbands and wives submit to one another in mutual compassion and humility* (see Ephesians 5:21 and 1 Peter 3:8). *I call men and women return to their natural affections* (see 1 Timothy 3:3), *and I rebuke the spirits of perversion that seek to redefine the American family. May the covenant of marriage be honored by all, and the marriage bed undefiled* (see Hebrews 13:4), *in Jesus' name!*

THE YOUTH

Many believe that this present generation will be the generation that takes the Gospel to the ends of the earth. One sure evidence of this likelihood is the increase in the attack of evil and violence against young people today. Between abortion and homosexual "unions" we have lost an entire generation of youth. And the ones who are still living are literally fighting for their lives — fighting drugs, peer pressure, sexual immorality, suicide, dysfunctional families and each other. But all is not lost — God has big plans for this generation, and He will fulfill them through the prayers of His intercessors!

DECLARATIONS TO MAKE OVER THE YOUTH

Almighty God and Father, may You bless our children indeed; may you en-large their territory, may Your hand be upon them to keep them from evil, that they would not cause harm (see 1 Chronicles 4:9-10), *but would be filled to overflowing with power from on high* (see Luke 24:49 and Acts 1:8) *to do mighty exploits* (see Daniel 11:32). *I pray and declare from Your Word...*

- *that those who are wayward in spirit will:*
  1. *gain understanding and accept instruction* (see Isaiah 29:24).
  2. *escape from the trap of the devil* (see 2 Timothy 2:26).
  3. *cleanse themselves from ignoble purposes so that they will be instru-ments for noble purposes, made holy, useful to the Master and pre-pared to do any good work* (see 2 Timothy 2:20-21).
  4. *flee sexual immorality and the evil desires of youth, and pursue righteousness, faith, love and peace, along with those who call on the Lord out of a pure heart.... Clothing themselves with the Lord Jesus Christ, they will not think about how to gratify the desires of the sinful nature* (see 1 Corinthians 6:18; 2 Timothy 2:22 and Romans 13:13-14).

- *that those who complain will accept instruction...and will keep God's name holy and acknowledge the Holy One* (see Isaiah 29:24 and 23).
- *that they are loosed from fear and intimidation, for You have not given them a spirit of fear, but of power, of love, and of a sound mind. I call them forth as victorious overcomers* (see 2 Timothy 1:7 and Revelation 3:21).
- *that they may become blameless and pure, children of God without fault in a crooked and depraved generation* (see Philippians 2:15-16).
- *that they are the "Jacob generation," blessed of God, who seek Your face with clean hands and pure hearts, with no idols and no deceit in their mouths* (see Psalm 24:4-6).
- *that they will be taught by the Lord, and great will be their peace. In righteousness they will be established. Terror and tyranny will be far re-moved from them* (see Isaiah 54:13-14).
- *that wisdom will enter their hearts, and knowledge will be pleasant to their souls. Discretion will protect them and understanding will guard*

them. Wisdom will save them from the ways of wicked men…and also from the adulteress (see Proverbs 2:10-12, 16).

- *that they would behave decently — not in orgies or drunkenness, not in sexual immorality and debauchery, not in dissension and jealousy, but rather that they might be filled with the knowledge of God's will in all wisdom and spiritual understanding. Father, help them to live a life worthy of You, pleasing You in every way, so they might bear fruit in every good work, and grow in the knowledge of God. Strengthen them with power by Your glorious might so that Christ may dwell in their hearts by faith* (see Ephesians 3:17), *and so they might have great endurance and patience. Lord, bless them that they will joyfully thank You, with joyful hearts. Thank You, Father for rescuing them from the dominion of darkness and filling them with Your light* (see Colossians 1:9-13).

- *that they, being rooted and established in love, may have power to grasp the full depth of the love of Christ, and to know this love that surpasses knowledge – that they may be filled to the measure of all the fullness of God* (see Ephesians 3:17-19, NIV).

LORD OF HOSTS — POSITION NOW THOSE WHOM YOU HAVE COMMISSIONED !!

[1] Dutch Sheets, "A Call to the Church for Emergency Prayer Regarding Supreme Court Justices," article posted on the *Elijah List* (www.elijahlist.com), June 10, 2003.

[2] Rick Ridings, *Succat Hallel* in Jerusalem, Internet letter (www.jerusalempraise.com), March 6, 2004.

[3] *The Senate Prayers of Peter Marshall* (Sandwich, MA: Chapman Billies, Inc., 1996), Preface p. XIII.

Chapter Eighteen

ISRAEL

"For the LORD has chosen Jacob for Himself, Israel for His special treasure."
Psalm 135:4

GOD WILL KEEP HIS COVENANT WITH HIS "CHOSEN"

We have already mentioned the significance of Israel in God's prophetic purposes. Because the Jews are God's covenant people, they have been targeted for extermination by the powers of darkness throughout history. Satan has used many people and nations to try to "cut them off from being a nation" (Psalm 83:4). But, of course, he will not succeed. God WILL keep His covenant word with Israel:

> *"And it shall be...that I will set up your [David's] seed after you...;*
> *and I will establish his kingdom.... I will establish his throne forever....*
> *I will not take My mercy away from him.... I will establish him in My*
> *house and in My kingdom* forever; *and his throne shall be established*
> forever." 1 Chronicles 17:11-14

Additionally, as we pointed out previously in chapter sixteen, God's covenant with Israel included her geographic heritage. This was a national land Covenant:

> *And I will establish My covenant between Me and you and your de-*
> *scendants after you in their generations, for an* everlasting covenant...
> *Also I will give to you and your descendants after you...*all the land of
> Canaan, as an everlasting possession; *and I will be their God."*
> Genesis 17:7-8

Knowing these truths gives foundation to our intercession. As we pray for Israel's destiny to be fulfilled, there are, first, some general principles and scriptures we can pray over the nation and its people.

KEY PRAYER POINTS RELATING TO
GOD'S COVENANT WITH ISRAEL
LORD, I lift up the 'apple of Your eye' and pray...

- *that the House of Israel will not be divided*, but will be established on firm biblical covenantal foundations, both naturally and spiritually. Father, expand Israel to its covenant borders (see Numbers 34:1-13), and may the covenant cities of Bethel, Shechem, Hebron and *Jerusalem* remain as the pillars of the whole house of Israel.
- *that the leaders of Israel will clearly hear God* and lead Israel according to His will: Loose the Knesset from the plans and wisdom of the flesh and bind them to God's Word and covenant for Israel's land, redemptive purpose and destiny.
- *that God would arise once again as Israel's Champion* and deliver her from her enemies. (See section on "Praying for Restoration.")

THE PEACE OF JERUSALEM

Since Jerusalem is so much on the heart and mind of God, and since He has commanded us to "pray for the peace of Jerusalem" (Psalm 122:6), we should give it special focus in our prayers. A sample decree follows.

PRAYER FOR THE PEACE OF JERUSALEM

O Jerusalem, may peace and prosperity be within your walls. For the sake of God's chosen ones, I say, Peace be within you (from Psalm 122). *Come, "Prince of Peace"* (Isaiah 9:6)*: establish peace for Israel* (see Isaiah 26:12) *and make Jerusalem a strong undivided city. Appoint salvation for walls and open the gates, that Israel may once again be that righteous and peaceful nation which keeps the truth, and "whose mind is stayed on You"* (Isaiah 26:1-3).

Lord, may You command Your blessing over Israel: May Your oil of peace and unity be poured out on that land like oil was upon the head of Aaron, refreshing as the dew of Hermon, descending upon the mountains of Zion (see Psalm 133). *May the Jewish and Arab descendents of Abraham live together in peace, love and justice on Your hallowed soil. Father, bring revival to the land of Israel and turn the hearts of the Jews and Arabs toward Messiah Yeshua, the God of Israel, and toward His Word and His purposes! O Jerusalem, because of the house of the Lord our God I seek your good. I pray for the peace of Jerusalem — and may all who love you prosper.*

TERRORISM

WHAT THE DEVIL MEANS FOR EVIL, GOD TURNS FOR GOOD

It is horrifying to watch the unfolding scenario of increasing violence and terrorism in Israel against God's covenant people. And as terrible as the violence and loss of life is, we must remember that the devil always over-plays his hand, and that our God is the Redeemer and Deliverer! For instance, satan thought he had won a victory when he manipulated men to crucify Jesus. But not only did he lose that battle when Jesus was raised from the dead, but Jesus was the One who triumphed over him from the cross: "Having disarmed principalities and powers, He made a public spectacle of them, triumphing over them in it [the cross]" (Colossians 2:15). Further, Jesus' shed Blood made the way for men to escape satan's evil clutches and come freely into God's Kingdom. So we see that the result of the devil's overplay is usually the exact opposite of what he has purposed. For what he means for evil, God turns for good and to the salvation of men (see Genesis 50:20).

A VEIL OVER THEIR HEARTS

As the Jewish people face increasing violence and aggression against themselves and their land, I believe that they will reach a point of such helpless desperation that their hearts will be softened as they cry out to God (see Psalm 60). The Bible tells us that since the time of Moses, there has been a veil over the hearts of the Jewish people in the reading of the Old Testament, so they cannot see the truth of the prophetic Messianic scriptures (see 2 Corinthians 3:14-16). I believe that God is setting the stage in His prophetic plan in this hour for such a desperate heart cry, and that as this cry rises up to Heaven, the veil will be removed from the hearts of His chosen ones, much like the veil was rent in two at the crucifixion. So that just as the cross gave us direct access to the throne room, this heart cry of His covenant people will rend the veil that has been covering their minds for centuries. Therefore, what the devil means for death and the destruc-

Praying With Authority and Power

tion of God's people, God will use to drive them into the very arms of their Messiah and Deliverer: "And so all Israel will be saved, as it is written: "the Deliverer will come out of Zion, and He will turn away ungodliness from Jacob; for this is My covenant with them, when I take away their sins" (Romans 11:26). In view of this, we can pray for the veil over their hearts to be taken away.

PRAYER FOR THE VEIL TO BE TAKEN AWAY

O Holy One of Israel (see Psalm 89:18), *I bring You in remembrance that your covenant with Israel through David was an everlasting covenant* (see 1 Chronicles 17:11-14). *I pray that the devil's strategies to bring terror and destruction to Israel will backfire, and that You will turn the evil perpetrated against Your chosen ones to good* (see Genesis 50:20). *Father, I pray that You will orchestrate the desperate heart cry that will cause the veil over their hearts* (see 2 Corinthians 3:16) *to be taken away and bring them into the presence of their Messiah, Yeshua. O Lord, "open their understanding that they might comprehend the Scriptures"* (Luke 24:45) *so that "in their affliction they will earnestly seek [God]"...and "acknowledge their offense" before Him* (Hosea 5:15). *"And so all Israel will be saved, as it is written: 'The Deliverer will come out of Zion, and He will turn away ungodliness from Jacob; for this is My covenant with them, when I take away their sins' "* (Romans 11:26).

ISRAEL'S PROPHETIC DESTINY

The following are model decrees to make concerning the nation of Israel and her prophetic destiny.

DECREES OVER ISRAEL
Concerning the establishment of Israel in her covenant land
(from Isaiah 22:22 and Psalm 24)

In the authority of Jesus Christ and in the power of His Name, I decree that Israel is the Lord's and all those who dwell therein.... I take the "key of the House of David" (Isaiah 22:22) *over the City of David, and I open it to the KING OF GLORY, declaring: "Be lifted up, you city gates of Jerusalem! And be lifted up, you ancient doors in Israel!...so that the KING OF GLORY may come in — the LORD OF HOSTS, THE LORD STRONG AND MIGHTY, THE LORD MIGHTY IN BATTLE — so that the ancient foundations of righteousness, justice, and truth, along with Israel's biblical boundaries, may be reestablished as decreed in covenant with Almighty God through Abraham, Isaac, and Jacob!"*

Concerning the Arab nations that seek Israel's annihilation

In the name and authority of Jesus Christ of Nazareth, who came in the flesh (see 1 John 4:3), I declare that satan is bound from mobilizing the forces of evil against Israel. I decree failure to these unholy coalition efforts, and failure to the enemy's efforts to escalate this conflict into WW III. I close the door in the spirit realm to keep other Arab nations from entering into this conflict. Lord, I thank You for sealing Israel's borders and airspace with a hedge of protection against all her enemies who would seek to destroy her. I decree that what is closed on earth is closed in heaven according to Your Word in Isaiah 22:22.

Concerning the unholy doctrines of men seeking to divide up Israel's covenant land
(The Oslo Accords, the Geneva Accords, the "Quartet's" Decrees: the Road Map to Peace)

I decree by the power and name of Jesus Christ of Nazareth that any plan to give away or divide up Israel's covenant land is null and void, and superseded by the blood covenant she has with Almighty God through His servant Abraham. I stand in agreement with the Word of God which states that the wicked shall "take counsel together and it shall come to nought; [they shall] speak the word, and it shall not stand" (Isaiah 8:10, KJV). *Then, having authority with God over all that opposes Him, I take the key of the house of David (according to* Isaiah 22:22) *and close the spiritual door of access used by any spiritual powers sent to divide and conquer Israel. And, finally, I seal it with the signet ring, the Blood of the Lamb, over the lintels and doorposts, declaring these spiritual powers of darkness may no longer enter. I decree that no weapon formed against the "apple of God's eye" shall prosper.*

AN EVIL SPIRITUAL "TRINITY"

Rick Ridings, reporting from his ministry base in Jerusalem (*Succat Hallel*: "Tabernacle of Praise"), has observed terrorist activity in Lebanon, just across Israel's northern border. He tells of training camps of what he calls "extreme terrorists" mobilizing forces against Israel. Additionally, he has observed troops from Iran and Syria training with the Lebanese army. This "evil trinity" aligned against Israel has ancient roots. Iran is located on the ancient land of Persia where, centuries ago, the Jewess Esther saved her people from annihilation. During the reign of King Ahasuerus (about 450 B.C.), while the Jews were in exile in Persia, a wicked man by the name of Haman devised a plan to have all the Jews massacred. While God disciplines His covenant people, He never abandons them. And so He raised up Esther "for such a time as this" (Esther 4:14) to intervene on the Jews' behalf, and He blessed her efforts to bring deliverance to her people. However, while Haman himself was executed, the spirit that incited him to such hatred and vengeance against God's covenant people is still at work in the land.

These ancient principalities over Persia were also evident two hundred years earlier during the period of the Jews' exile in Babylon, during the reign of King Nebuchadnezzar. We have talked about Daniel's visions he received while employed in Nebuchadnezzar's court. You will remember the angel telling Daniel during one of these visions that he was hindered from bringing the answer from God because "the *prince of the kingdom of Persia* withstood me twenty-one days; and behold, Michael, one of the chief princes, came to help me, for I had been left alone there with the *kings of Persia*" (Daniel 10:13). Clearly, these evil principalities and powers (see Ephesians 6:12) over Persia are still operating today. The following two decrees address the threat of this "evil trinity" of spiritual forces seeking to unite Lebanon, Syria and Iran against Israel.

Concerning Sidon, in southern Lebanon, as a staging ground for "extreme terrorism" threatening Israel from the north
(from Ezekiel 28:20-26, NIV)

I declare, Sidon, that you are strong no longer, for it is written that the Holy One of Israel has set His face against you. Almighty God of Israel, according to Your Word, I pray, strike down the stronghold of evil and murderous intent within Sidon. Show Yourself holy and glorious within her. Bring forth Your destruction within her gates so that they will know that You are the Sovereign Lord – the Holy One of Israel. I take the key to the house of David, according to the Word of the Lord in Isaiah 22:22, and close the doors in the spirit realm against violence coming across Israel's northern border. For it is written that the Sovereign Lord will show Himself holy among Israel, and she will live in safety when He inflicts punishment on all her neighbors who have maligned her.

Concerning spiritual forces uniting the evil trinity of Syria, Lebanon and Iran (Persia) against Israel

In the name and power of the Lord Jesus Christ of Nazareth, who came in the flesh (see 1 John 4:3), *I decree that the Blood of Jesus* (see Colossians 2:15) *has triumphed over, and prevails against, the entrenchment of demonic forces that are empowering the evil confederation of Lebanon, Iran (Persia) and Syria. I ask You, Almighty God, to send forth the archangel Michael and the hosts of Heaven to enforce this decree and to defeat the wicked kings over Persia according to the Word of the Lord in Daniel 10:13. And I decree that the wicked spirit of Haman who still seeks to destroy Israel was, and is, defeated according to the Word of God in Esther 8:7. I beseech You, Lord Jesus, the righteous Judge* (2 Timothy 4:8), *to bring Your holy judgments upon these wicked powers once and for all. I decree that all of these principalities and spiritual powers of darkness must bow to the name, authority and power of the Lord Jesus Christ, the Lord of Hosts. For it is written that every knee must bow and every tongue confess that Jesus Christ is Lord* (Philippians 2:10-11), *and "The kingdoms of this world [shall] become the kingdoms of our LORD and of His Christ, and He shall reign forever and ever!"* (Revelation 11:15). *Then, having authority with Almighty God over all that opposes Him, I take the key to the house of David (according to* Isaiah 22:22) *and close the spiritual door of access used by these powers of darkness, and I declare annulled all unholy alignments and covenants between Syria, Lebanon and Iran.*

Lord, I give You no rest until You make Jerusalem a praise in all the earth! (see Isaiah 62:7).

Thank You, Father, for fulfilling all Your covenant promises and plans for Israel!

PRAYING FOR RESTORATION

FOR GOD'S NAME'S SAKE

The Scriptures are replete with God's promises of the eventual restoration of Israel — its land, its people and its spiritual legacy. Additionally, God is personified as Israel's "Champion" through the many covenant names with which He has identified Himself to the Jewish people — names such as the *Mighty One of Israel* (Isaiah 1:24), the *Lion of Judah* (Revelation 5:5), the *Holy One of Israel* (Isaiah 12:6), the *Hope of Israel* (Jeremiah 17:13). The Lord God is very jealous for His name — that is, that His name not be profaned, but glorified and honored before all nations:

Sing to the LORD, all the earth.... Declare His glory among the nations.... For the LORD is great and greatly to be praised. He is also to be feared above all gods.... Honor and majesty are before Him.... Give to the LORD glory and strength. Give to the LORD the glory **due His name**.... *Tremble before Him, all the earth.... And let them say among the nations,* "The LORD reigns."

1 Chronicles 16:23-31, selected

Concerned for the integrity of His name, the Lord spoke to Israel through the prophet Isaiah these words:

"Hear this, O house of Jacob...who swear by the name of the LORD, and make mention of the God of Israel.... Because I knew that you were obstinate, and your neck was an iron sinew...and were called a transgressor from the womb.... For **My name's sake** I will defer My anger...*so that I do not cut you off.... I have tested you in the furnace of affliction. For My own sake,* for my own sake, *I will do it; for* how should **My name** be profaned? *And I will not give My glory to another."*

Isaiah 48:1, 4 and 8-11

The Lord was saying that He would not bring upon Israel the destruction she deserved, but would deliver her out of Egypt and into the land He had promised, because not fulfilling His Word would profane His name before the heathen:

"But I acted for **My name's sake**, that it should not be profaned *before the Gentiles among whom they were, in whose sight I had made Myself known to them, to bring them out of the land of Egypt.... Then you shall know that I am the LORD,* when I have dealt with you **for My name's sake**, *not according to your wicked ways nor according to your corrupt doings, O house of Israel, says the Lord GOD."*

Ezekiel 20:9 and 44

THE SIGNIFICANCE OF HIS NAME'S SAKE
...A blood covenant

The significance of God's name's sake goes back to the original blood Covenant that He made with Abram in Genesis 15. First of all, we need to understand that a covenant in Old Testament days was often made by cutting animal carcasses in two and having the two parties attesting to the covenant walk between the pieces to declare their commitment to it *to the death*. From this model we see that a covenant was a solemn oath, or word of honor, sealed, or ratified, through the shedding of blood. God's relationship with His people was (and is) a *covenantal relationship:* God chose the Jewish people, out of all the peoples on the earth, through which He would reveal Himself to the world. Then He made an *"everlasting covenant"* with them to place them in a land of His choosing, to be their God and they, His people (see Genesis 17:7-8). This Covenant he "cut" in blood with Abram:

> *So He* [God] *said to him* [Abram], *"Bring Me a three-year-old heifer, a three-year-old female goat, a three-year-old ram, a turtledove, and a young pigeon." Then he brought all these to Him and cut them in two, down the middle, and placed each piece opposite the other.... Now when the sun was going down, a deep sleep fell upon Abram.... And ...behold, there appeared a smoking oven* [pillar of cloud] *and a burning torch* [pillar of fire] *that passed between those pieces. On that same day the* LORD *made a covenant with Abram.*
>
> Genesis 15:9-10, 12, 17 and 18

(In Genesis 17:5, God gave Abram his *covenant* name of *Abraham*.) Notice in the previous passage that only God, in symbolic form like unto His wilderness appearances (see Exodus 13:21), passed between the pieces, thus binding Himself in a covenant relationship with men. God, understanding the human failings of men, knew that He *only* would be able to keep the Covenant:

> *For when God made His promise to Abraham, He swore by Himself, since He had no one greater by whom to swear.*   Hebrews 6:13

...A dispersed people

The Old Testament chronicles that, although God did bring Israel into the Promised Land, many years later the rebellious nation was stripped of that land and dispersed to the nations as judgment for their continual transgressions of the covenant law:

"So I scattered them among the nations, and they were dispersed through-out the countries; I judged them according to their ways and their deeds."

Ezekiel 36:19

...God's plan of restoration

However, even then God had a plan of restoration, *for the sake of His name*:

"But I had concern for **My holy name**, *which the house of Israel had profaned among the nations wherever they went. Therefore say to the house of Israel, 'Thus says the* LORD GOD: *"I do not do this for your sake, O house of Israel, but* for **My holy name's sake**, *which you have profaned among the nations.... And* I will sanctify **My great name**, *which has been profaned..., which you have profaned in their midst; and the nations shall know that I am the* LORD... *when I am hallowed in you before their eyes.* **For I will take you from among the nations, gather you out of all countries, and bring you into your own land."** *' "*

Ezekiel 36:21-24, selected

HOW TO PRAY

All of this gives the intercessor prayer strategy and power, as we pray God's Word back to Him, knowing that He stands behind it. *We bring Him into remembrance of His promises and pray* **for the sake of His glorious name**. For instance:

- **We can beseech the Lord to arise again as Israel's "Champion"** (as He is described in **Isaiah 51** and **Psalm 83**), and that through God's judgment upon her enemies, they might know "the Most High over all the earth":

  Awake, awake, put on strength, O arm of the LORD! *Awake as in the ancient days, in the generations of old.* Isaiah 51:9

  Do not keep silent, O God! Do not hold Your peace and do not be still, O God! For behold, Your enemies make a tumult; and those who hate You have lifted up their head. They have taken crafty counsel against Your people, and consulted together against Your sheltered ones. They have said, "Come, and let us cut them off *from being a nation, that the name of Israel may be remembered no more." For they have consulted together with one consent; they form a confederacy against You.... O my God, make them like the whirling dust, like the chaff before the wind! As the fire burns the woods, and as the flame sets the mountains on fire, so pursue them with Your tempest, and frighten them with Your storm. Fill their faces with shame, that they may seek **Your name, O LORD...,*** that they may know that You, **whose name alone is the LORD,** are the Most High over all the earth.

Psalm 83:1-5, 13-16, and 18

I don't pray verse 17 because that represents Old Testament thinking that all God's enemies should be destroyed, and doesn't take in the New Testament perspective of forgiveness and grace. Praying verse 18 directly following 16 is redemptive.

- **We can beseech the Lord, as the "righteous Judge," to take vengeance upon Israel's enemies** (again, we are thinking of spiritual enemies that manipulate people), as in **Psalm 94:1-2, 5, 7 and 21-22:**

  O LORD God, to whom vengeance belongs, shine forth! Rise up, O Judge of the earth; render punishment to the proud....They break in pieces Your people, *O LORD, and* afflict Your heritage..., Yet they say, "The LORD does not see..." They gather together against the life of the righteous, and condemn innocent blood.* But the LORD has been my defense, and my God the rock of my refuge.

- **We can also remind the Lord of some of His many words of restoration** that He has spoken over Israel. For instance, the prophetic message recorded in **Amos 9:11-15:**

  *"On that day I will raise up the tabernacle of David, which has fallen down,... and rebuild it as in the days of old".... "Behold, the days are coming," says the LORD, "when the plowman shall overtake the reaper, and the treader of grapes him who sows seed.... I will bring back the captives of My people Is*rael; they shall build

> *the waste cities and inhabit them.... I will plant them in their*
> *land, and no longer shall they be pulled up from the land I have*
> *given them," says the* LORD *your God.*

- **We can remind the Lord of His declared eternal Covenant with Israel** and the throne of David according to **Psalm 89:3-4 and 30-34**:

> *"I have made a covenant with My chosen. I have sworn to My*
> *servant David: 'Your seed I will establish forever'.... If his sons*
> *forsake My law..., then I will punish their transgression with the*
> *rod.... Nevertheless My lovingkindness I will not utterly take from*
> *him, nor allow My faithfulness to fail.* My covenant I will not
> break *nor alter the word that has gone out of My lips."*

Whichever Scriptures we use, putting the Lord in remembrance of His Word, and praying for the sake of His name, are powerful ways to pray.

Chapter Nineteen

THE NATIONS

"His name shall endure forever; His name shall continue as long as the sun. And men shall be blessed in Him; all nations shall call Him blessed."
Psalm 72:17

THE NATIONS ARE THE LORD'S

Psalm 67 is a declaration of God's sovereignty over the nations of the world:

God be merciful to us and bless us, and cause His face to shine upon us, that Your way may be known on earth, Your salvation among all nations. Let the peoples praise You, O God... Oh, let the nations be glad and sing for joy! For You shall judge the people righteously, and govern the nations on earth. Let all the peoples praise You. Then the earth shall yield her increase; God, our own God, shall bless us.... And all the ends of the earth shall fear Him.

God loves the nations; they are His creation, and His inheritance: "Arise O God, judge the earth; for *You shall inherit all nations*" (Psalm 82:8). And to Jesus He said: "You are My Son, today I have begotten You. Ask of Me, and I will give You *the nations for Your inheritance*" (Psalm 2:7-8). Psalm 67:6 above says that when the earth begins to praise God, then the Harvest will be brought in, that is, "the earth shall yield her increase." No matter what anti-God state the world is in today, God says that the nations will one day worship Him:

- *"All the ends of the world shall remember and turn to the LORD, and all the families of the nations shall worship before You. For the kingdom is the LORD's, and He rules over the nations."* (Psalm 22:27) and…

• *"The LORD brings the counsel of the nations to nothing; He makes the plans of the peoples of no effect. The counsel of the LORD stands forever, the plans of His heart to all generations."* (Psalm 33:10-12)

PRAYING FOR THE NATIONS

It is God's heart and plan that the nations come to Him, and so it should be our heart to pray for this to happen. Francis Frangipane said in his article, "The Father's Family of Nations," "The Spirit of God is doing something worldwide, and we should unite our hearts in faith and prayer for the Lord's amazing purpose. The Holy Spirit is being poured out upon the nations." [1]

The anointing and authority that the Lord gave to Jeremiah He gives to us as we pray over the nations:

"Behold, I have put My words in your mouth. See, I have this day set you over the nations and over the kingdoms, to root out and to pull down, to destroy and to throw down, to build and to plant."
Jeremiah 1:9-10

Jesus commissioned believers to "Go into all the world and preach the gospel to every creature" (Mark 16:15; see Matthew 28:19), and to *pray that His Kingdom would come* to the earth (Matthew 6:10). It is our calling and privilege through prayer to "root out and pull down, destroy and throw down" enemy strongholds that hold the Harvest captive, and to "build and plant" the Kingdom of God. Again: we pray, God works.

PRAYING FOR NATIONAL LEADERS

The Scriptures tell us that, ultimately, God is in control of the nations and their leaders:

• *"The king's heart is in the hand of the Lord, like the rivers of water; He turns it wherever He wishes."* (Proverbs 21:1)
• *"For exaltation comes neither from the east nor from the west nor from the south. But God is the Judge: He puts down one, and exalts another."* (Psalm 75:6-7)

- *"For there is no authority except from God, and the authorities that exist are appointed by God."* (Romans 13:1)

With these scriptures in mind, we can pray accordingly over the leaders of the nations:

PRAYER AND DECREE OVER NATIONAL LEADERS

Lord, Your Word says that the heart of the king is in Your hand and You turn it wherever You wish (Proverbs 21:1). *May Your hand be upon the hearts of these leaders to do Your will. And may salvation and truth dispel deception and corruption. (Name the leaders, if you know them.*) Sovereign Lord, exalt those whom You desire and put down the ones who stand against Your will and purposes* (Psalm 75:6-7) .

In the name of Jesus Christ of Nazareth, I decree to these leaders: "Now, therefore, be wise, O kings; be instructed, You judges of the earth. Serve the LORD with fear, and rejoice with trembling. Kiss the Son, lest He be angry, and you perish in the way, when His wrath is kindled but a little. Blessed are all those who put their trust in Him" (Psalm 2:10-12). *Come under the Lordship of Jesus Christ and obey Him, and He will prosper you in your land* (Deuteronomy 28:8).

(*Particularly significant in the world today are the Middle Eastern and Muslim nations, including Israel, Iraq, Iran, Jordan, Saudi Arabia, Lebanon, Pakistan, India (Hindu), Syria, Egypt, the United Arab Emirates, Oman, Qatar, Algeria, Morocco, Yemen, Kuwait, Turkey, Tunisia, Bahrain and Indonesia; and the Far Eastern nations of China, Korea and Japan.)

All the nations of the world need prayer, but for the sake of time and space, in this writing we will focus on a few model nations which have particular current, political or prophetic Kingdom significance.

ISLAM

NOT JUST A RELIGION

Though Islam is not a nation, a Muslim presence is evident in nearly every nation. Also, it is addressed here because of its prophetic and spiritual connection to Israel. First of all, it must be categorically stated that Islam is not a "peaceful" religion and allah is not the God of the Bible. Actually,

Islam is not just a religion, as many suppose, but is a controlling religious socio-political-economic system that enslaves people and nations. The Islamic culture of intolerance leaves no room for any other religious doctrine. According to Omar M. Ahmed, the chairman of the board of the Council on American-Islamic Relations: "Islam isn't in America to be equal to any other faith, but to become dominant. The Koran, the Muslim book of scripture, should be the highest authority in America, and *Islam the only accepted religion on earth*" [emphasis added].[2] The Muslim belief is that Muhammad gave them all the land of the earth, and therefore they have legal "right" to take the world for Islam. Additionally, Muslim theology holds that all people are born Muslim (even Jesus), and that all who deviate from this belief are therefore *infidels,* worthy of death.

A CULTURE OF HATE AND INTOLERANCE

Undoubtedly there are many followers of Muhammad who don't support violence and terrorism. But this does not negate the truth of the evil root of Islam, which, in its extremist form, is a culture of hate and intolerance "which turns its back on all humanity, suppresses freedom of thought, and condemns difference."[3] History shows that "the imperialism of the Islamic *jihad* [holy war against all *infidels*] has claimed millions of victims in three continents over more than a millennium, deported an incalculable number of slaves, annihilated entire peoples, destroying their history, their monuments, and their culture." [4] And, as has recently been exposed in Iraq and Afghanistan, Islam "not only seeks to terrorize the non-Muslim world and bring it into submission to Allah, it holds the souls of Muslims in the grip of terror as well. For instance, in most Muslim nations, conversion from Islam is a crime punishable by torture and death. This spirit of terror holds even moderate Islamic governments hostage, where leaders fear the violent reprisals of radical fundamentalists." [5]

ANCIENT ROOTS

So where did all of this hate and intolerance get its beginning? It had its roots in the book of Genesis and the establishment of the original Covenant with Abraham. We are told in Scripture that God visited Abram and told him that he would be the father of many nations (see Genesis 12:1-3). Because Abram and his wife, Sarai, were beyond their childbearing years, they developed a plan to "help" God fulfill His promise. The fruit of this plan was that a son, Ishmael, was born to Abram through Sarai's maidservant, Hagar (see Genesis 16). When Abram was ninety-nine years old, and Ishmael was thirteen, God appeared to him again and reinstated the Covenant:

> *"I am Almighty God; walk before Me and be blameless. And I will make My covenant between Me and you, and will multiply you exceedingly.... No longer shall you be called Abram, but your name shall be Abraham; for I have made you a father of many nations.... And I will establish My covenant between Me and you and your descendants after you in their generations, for an everlasting covenant, to be God to you and your descendants after you. Also I give to you and your descendants after you the land in which you are a stranger, all the land of Canaan, as an everlasting possession; and I will be their God."*
>
> Genesis 17:1-8, selected

...The Son of promise

We see from this passage that the Covenant was made with Abraham, and with his progeny, for an everlasting Covenant, and that the Covenant included a deed to the whole land of Canaan.

Later, God appeared to Abraham again and told him that *"Sarah your wife* shall have a son" (Genesis 18:10). So, in God's perfect timing, He miraculously gave Sarah a fruitful womb and she and Abraham had the "son of promise," Isaac. Isaac's son Jacob (later renamed *Israel*), became the patriarch of the entire Jewish race, as from him the twelve tribes of Israel descended. The apostle Paul wrote of the difference between the inheritance of Ishmael and that of Isaac in his letter to the Galatians:

> *For it is written that Abraham had two sons: the one by a bondwoman, the other by a freewoman. But he who was of the bondwoman was born according to the flesh, and he of the freewoman through* promise.... *What does the Scripture say? "Cast out the bondwoman and her son, for* the son of the bondwoman shall not be heir with the son of the freewoman."
>
> Galatians 4:22-23 and 30

...The son of the flesh

Since Ishmael was born through the flesh, and not by the Spirit and plan of God, he had no place in the Covenant. However, the Scriptures tell us that God had mercy on Hagar and her son, and had these words to say to her about Ishmael's posterity:

> *"I will multiply your descendants exceedingly, so that they shall not be counted for multitude... you shall bear a son. You shall call his name Ishmael ["God hears"], because the LORD has heard your affliction.* He shall be a wild man; his hand shall be against every man, and every man's hand against him. And he shall dwell in the presence of all his brethren."
> Genesis 16:10-12

...A warlike people

Notice that God said that Ishmael's descendants shall be a warlike people who will "dwell in the presence of all his brethren." The Arab peoples of the world today trace their lineage back to Abraham through Ishmael. And, though it is true that not all Arabs are Muslim, nor all Muslims Arab, the Arab/Muslim's proclivity for war can be seen today in the fact that twenty-eight of the approximately thirty wars that are currently being waged worldwide involve Muslims. Because Muslims believe that Ishmael is the covenant son of promise, and not Isaac, they believe that Israel is a usurper and a counterfeiter. And even though...

- the Koran does not make one mention of "Jerusalem" in its text and "Jerusalem" is mentioned over 800 times in the Bible
- and the Bible states that Ishmael's descendants shall "dwell *in the presence of* their brethren"

...the Muslims still claim that city — and the whole land of Canaan — as their own. And therein lies the Muslims' extreme hatred for the Jewish people (and for the Christians who support them).

...Blasphemy of the highest sort

Now, because the Jews are God's chosen people and because Israel is the "apple of His eye," he who comes against Israel comes against Almighty God. This puts Muslims in a very precarious position. And to compound the sin, the Muslims declare that *Almighty God* instructs them to kill the "infidel" Jews. This is blasphemy of the highest sort, which God will judge, for the sake of His holy name. Consider the words of the psalmist who cried out for God to stand behind His Covenant with Israel and against the railings of the blasphemers:

> Remember this, that the enemy has reproached, O LORD, and that a foolish people has blasphemed Your name. *Oh, do not deliver the life of Your turtledove* [term of endearment describing Israel] *to the wild beast!* [see "wild man" of Genesis 16:12]. *Do not forget the life of Your poor forever. Have respect to the covenant; for the dark places of the earth are full of the haunts of cruelty. Oh, do not let the oppressed return ashamed! Let the poor and needy praise Your name. Arise, O God, plead Your own cause; remember how the foolish man reproaches You daily.* Do not forget the voice of Your enemies; the tumult of those who rise up against You increases continually.
>
> Psalm 74:18-23

PRAYER FOCUS

As intercessors we need to pray not only for Israel's protection and deliverance from the "wild man," but also for the salvation of those who are blinded by deception and hatred. In most third-world countries, Muslim women wear a whole-body garment, covering even their faces and eyes, which is called a *burqa*. I believe that this is symbolic of the veil that is covering the "eyes of their understanding" (see Ephesians 1:18), and which keeps the Muslims in spiritual bondage. We need to pray that their eyes would be enlightened to see the truth.

PRAYER FOR REVELATION FOR THE ARAB/MUSLIM PEOPLES

O Great Jehovah (the personal, covenant-keeping God who manifests Himself to His people in grace and love), for Your name's sake, vindicate and glorify Your holy name before the heathen! (see Psalm 74:22). *Father, Your Word says that You "will destroy on this mountain the surface of the covering cast over all people, and the veil that is spread over all nations" (Isaiah 25:7). Most merciful Father, I beseech You to cause that veil over the Arab/Muslim peoples to be taken away so that those who are walking in darkness would see a great light, the light of Messiah Jesus!* (see Isaiah 9:2 and 6). *I pray that they would no longer walk in "the futility of their mind, having their understanding dark-*

185

ened, *[and] being alienated from the life of God, because of the ignorance that is in them, and because of the blindness of their heart"* (Ephesians 4:18). *O Lord, give them a "spirit of wisdom and revelation in the knowledge of [God]"* (Ephesians 1:17), *that "the eyes of [their] understanding [may be] enlightened"* (Ephesians 1:18) *to see the true God, the Mighty One of Israel, whose name alone is the Lord, the Most High over all the earth* (see Psalm 83:18). *I loose their minds from the bondage of law and "works." I loose them from spirits of fear and intimidation. I loose them from the deceiver and the Antichrist spirit* (see 2 John 7) — *the spirit of Islam. And I bind them to the Spirit of truth* (see John 14:6 and 17) *and to reconciliation with God* (2 Corinthians 5:20). *I pray that all of Abraham's children would live in peace and realize their destiny in God:*

> *Oh, that unto salvation Ishmael would come out of Islam!*
> *When the* Lord *brings back the captivity of His people,*
> *Let Ishmael rejoice and Israel be glad together!*
>
> Psalm 14:7, paraphrased

PRAYING AGAINST ISLAMIC STRONGHOLDS

Even as we pray for the deliverance of the Muslim people, we need to do warfare against the spiritual powers operating to keep them in deception and bondage. And though we know that our God reigns, the fact is that there is much evil power released through false worship. But the prayers of God's people can diminish and even reverse that power, says Emmanuel Kure, a Christian apostle from the Islamic stronghold of northern Nigeria: "Through prayer and spiritual warfare, we can reverse all the occult manipulations by the spirit of Islam and pray the thrust of the Kingdom of God over the lives of Islam's followers."[6]

I have a framed photograph hanging in my prayer room that I took when I was visiting Israel. I was standing inside the chapel *Dominus Flevit* ("The Lord Wept") near the Garden of Gethsemane on the Mount of Olives. The window over the altar overlooks the old city of Jerusalem, and in the distance is visible the golden Dome of the Rock, the Muslim mosque built on the Temple Mount. This mosque, along with the one in Mecca, is considered by Muslims to be the most holy place on the earth. I positioned myself so that in the photograph the crucifix on the altar of the chapel overlaid the golden dome of the mosque in the background. The Scripture caption on the photograph is from Revelation 11:15: "The kingdoms of this world have become the kingdoms of our Lord and of His Christ, and He shall reign forever and ever!" Although this verse speaks of a future time, it reminds us that the fate of the principalities and powers that we war against is already sealed through the Blood of the Lamb!

There is a hierarchy of kingdoms and powers over which the government of Almighty God reigns supreme. It is before that holy court that we offer our petitions and make our declarations. And just as Esther obtained favor before King Ahasuerus (see Esther 5:2), we have favor before the **KING OF KINGS.**

DECREE OVER THE SPIRITUAL STRONGHOLD OF ISLAM

I come before the court of the Almighty, who rules and judges with equity and truth, in the favor of Esther and make my decree which cannot be revoked (according to Esther 8:8*): I decree by the power and the name of Jesus Christ of Nazareth who came in the flesh* (see 1 John 4:3), *that the sword (Muslim symbol) of Islam is destroyed, including the entrenchment of all demonic powers coming out of this wicked stronghold. For the sword of the Spirit declares, "Your covenant with death is annulled and your agreement with hell shall not stand"* (Isaiah 28:18). *The Lord Jesus Christ has already disarmed your powers and authorities, by making a public spectacle of them, triumphing over them by the Blood of His cross* (see Colossians 2:15). *Therefore, I declare annulled this day the efficacy of every Islamic prayer and decree made from every minaret, mosque, and deceived mind. I bind up and cast out the spirits of superstition, fear, and intimidation which hold people in bondage. And I decree failure to the spiritual powers that would seek to draw people in by deception to their own destruction, and failure to all terrorist activity sponsored by this murdering jihad spirit. I decree: "Here your proud waves must stop!"* (Job 38:11). *I praise You, Lord, that the garment of Islam, and "the veil that is spread over all nations"* (Isaiah 25:7), *is being unraveled! Thank You, Mighty Deliverer, for setting the captives free from deception, oppression and destruction!*

Sovereign Lord, I implore You to topple this "throne of iniquity" (Psalm 94:20) *by bringing confusion and division into the enemy camp. For it is written: "Every kingdom divided against itself is brought to desolation"* (Matthew 12:25). *Then, having authority with Almighty God over all that opposes Him, I take the key of the house of David (according to* Isaiah 22:22*) and close the spiritual doors of access used by these wicked spirits to manipulate, deceive and oppress.*

And I declare annulled all unholy alignments and covenants. And finally, I seal these doors with the signet ring, the Blood of the Lamb, over the lintels and doorposts, declaring that these spirits of destruction may no longer enter and control or empower the sons of men.

— *"For by strength no man shall prevail. The adversaries of the LORD shall be broken in pieces; from heaven He will thunder against them. The LORD will judge the ends of the earth"* (1 Samuel 2:9-10).

— *I decree to these wicked powers and authorities: Your rule and influence have ended, for "He who sits in the heavens shall laugh; the Lord shall hold [you] in derision. Then He shall speak to [you] in His wrath, and distress [you] in His deep displeasure: 'Yet I have set MY King on My holy hill of Zion. [The King] will declare the decree: The LORD has said to Me, You are My Son, today I have begotten You. Ask of Me, and I will give You the nations for Your inheritance, and the ends of the earth for Your possession. You shall break them with a rod of iron; You shall dash them to pieces like a potter's vessel' "* (Psalm 2:4-9).

YOU… Almighty Sovereign God of the universe…the nations belong to You! And You dismantle principalities and powers of darkness and the strongholds of the enemies of God by Your Word, and make cease the wars that they incite. For it is written:

> *The nations raged, the kingdoms were moved;*
> *He uttered His voice, the earth melted….*
> *He makes wars cease to the end of the earth;*
> *He breaks the bow and cuts the spear in two*
> *He burns the chariot in the fire.* Psalm 46:6 and 9

O Lord, be glorified in the midst of Your enemies, and spread out Your hands to bring down their pride together with the trickery of their hands. May the fortress of the high fort of their walls be brought down, laid low, and brought to the ground, down to the dust (see Isaiah 25:11-12) — *in Jesus' name and to His glory!*

I declare that the dominion of allah is uprooted and cast out, and the dominion of the Lord Jesus Christ is established over our cities and over the nations. FOR IT IS WRITTEN: "The kingdoms of this world [shall] become the kingdoms of our Lord and of His Christ, and He shall reign forever and ever!" (Revelation 11:15).

AFGHANISTAN

As we mentioned in Chapter Eight, Afghanistan is in great turmoil culturally and politically, in the transition from Muslim Taliban rule to a democratic form of government. Women, particularly, are still struggling to get free of the constraints of the old, repressive regime. Because of this, the nation and people are in great need of prayer that God would intervene, order the reconstruction process, and set the captives free. This decree is a model for any nation that is in political and socioeconomic turmoil due to Islamic entrenchment and/or influence.

PRAYER DECREE OVER AFGHANISTAN

Almighty God, in the wake of war in Afghanistan, I pray that You would order the reconstruction process to bring economic, social and political stability to that nation. In the name and authority of Jesus Christ of Nazareth, who came in the flesh (see 1 John 4:3), *I decree failure to the spiritual powers seeking to incite and mobilize Taliban remnants and sympathizers, and exposure to all hidden terrorists. Exaltation comes from You alone, O God. You are the Judge: You put down one and exalt another* (see Psalm 75:6-7). *I pray You would fill the leadership void with righteous leaders, and bring a spirit of unity to the new government. The only wise God our Savior* (see Jude 25, KJV), *impart Your wisdom, and grant Your protection and salvation to all leaders. O God, the righteous Judge* (see 2 Timothy 4:8) *and Mighty Deliverer* (see Psalm 18:2), *bring order and restraint out of confusion and lawlessness, and deliver the people from the spiritual bondage of Islam. Father of mercy, protect the innocent and those with no voice. Restore women to their rightful and proper positions of dignity and respect. Protect the young girls and cut off the evil forces seeking to prevent their equal access to education. Use Your mighty arm and strong hand to establish Your throne over Afghanistan so that righteousness, justice, and peace may rule in that land* (see Psalm 89:13-14) — *in the name of Jesus and to His glory!*

IRAQ

ANCIENT BABYLONIAN INFLUENCES

Iraq has recently come through a devastating war that set the nation free from a tyrannical regime, but did nothing about its spiritual bondage. In fact, in the vacuum of political control, a state of lawlessness, terror and violence continues to rage for the souls and lives of men. Desperate and deceived people are pawns of the spiritual powers still seeking dominion in this part of the world. Iraq is on the ancient land of the wicked and powerful Babylonian Empire, whose roots go back to the earliest recorded history in Genesis. This is the place where Nimrod built the infamous Tower of Babel, "whose top is in the heavens" so the people could "make a name for ourselves" (Genesis 11:4). It is recorded in verses 6 and 7 that the Lord intervened in their plan:

> *"Come, let Us go down and there confuse their language.... So the* Lord *scattered them abroad from there over all the face of the earth, and they ceased building the city. Therefore its name is called Babel ("confusion"), because there the* Lord *confused the language of all the earth... and scattered them abroad."*

The same principalities and powers active during the time of ancient Babylonian rule and conquest are still active in the land today. As we mentioned earlier, deposed Iraqi despot Saddam Hussein has even likened himself to the pagan Babylonian king, Nebuchadnezzar, who ruled during the lifetime of Daniel the prophet.

Recently, while in prayer for Iraq, I had a picture of a ferocious spiritual battle in the heavenlies over this war torn land. But I sensed that it was not so much a battle between good and evil as it was between EVIL and EVIL. I believe that the prayers of God's people are activating such intense warfare in the spirit realm that the rival demonic strongholds are in a last all out epic battle for control in this ancient of all battlegrounds. We see this playing out in the natural in the contention and power grabbing between the rival muslim sects in various locations around Iraq. It would appear that the demonic dominion over this area is in its death throes. For we know that Jesus said," Every kingdom divided against itself is brought to desolation...and if satan cast out satan he is divided against himself; how then shall his kingdom stand?" (Matthew 12:25-26). Additionally, as we consider this battle for supremacy between the rival demonic principalities and powers, the Scriptures tell us Who really is supreme:

> *He [Jesus] is the image of the invisible God, the firstborn over all creation, for by Him all things were created...* whether thrones or powers

or rulers or authorities; all things were created by Him and for Him...*so that in everything HE might have the SUPREMACY.*
Colossians 2:15, 16 and 19

As intercessors, we need to come against this demonic stronghold over Iraq with the authority, Word and Blood of Jesus, and petition God to set the captives free.

DECREE OVER IRAQ (Biblical Babylon)

"The LORD is righteous; He has cut in pieces the cords of the wicked" (Psalm 129:4). *I praise You, Almighty God, for destroying the government of evil in Iraq, and for bringing down the reign of terror of Saddam Hussein! Sovereign Lord, I ask You to bring order and restraint out of lawlessness and ethnic and religious divisions. I bind up and cancel the influence of those muslin clerics seeking to sow division, terror, murder and violence. And to the rival demonic powers manipulating these people, I declare that IT IS WRITTEN: "Every kingdom divided against itself is brought to desolation"* (Matthew 12:25-26). *O Lord, direct the reconstruction process to bring economic, social, and political stability to this nation. I pray that a democratic government will be raised up, free from the bondages of Islam. I take the key of the house of David (according to* Isaiah 22:22) *and I close the door in the spirit realm to the radical Islamic insurgence coming from Iran, Syria, Turkey,, Saudi Arabia and Jordan.*

In the name and power of the Lord Jesus Christ of Nazareth who came in the flesh (1 John 4:3), *I decree that the Blood of the Lamb of God stands against the entrenchment of all demonic forces still seeking dominion in Iraq, and that Jesus Christ reigns supreme over all. For it is written that Jesus "is the image of the invisible God"...and that all "thrones, powers, rulers and authorities" were created by Him "so that in everything HE might have the supremacy"* (Colossians 2:15, 16 and 19). *I decree that the spiritual kingdom of Babylon and the stronghold of Islam must bow to the* **name, Kingdom** *and* **authority** *of the* **Lord Jesus Christ.** *FOR IT IS WRITTEN:*

- *"God has also highly exalted [Jesus] and given Him the* **name** *which is above every name, that at the name of Jesus every knee should bow... and every tongue should confess that Jesus Christ is Lord."* (Philippians 2:10-11) *and*

- *"The kingdoms of this world [shall] become the **kingdoms** of our Lord and of His Christ, and He shall reign forever."* (Revelation 11:15)
- *"And the **government** will be upon His shoulder."* (Isaiah 9:6) *"For the LORD is our Judge, the LORD is our Lawgiver, the LORD is our King."* (Isaiah 33:22)

Then, having authority with Almighty God over all that opposes Him (see Luke 10:19), *I take the key of the house of David (according to Isaiah 22:22) and close the spiritual door of access used by these powers of darkness, and I declare annulled all unholy alignments and covenants against the land and people. I call the people out of the reign of darkness and death and into the Kingdom of light and truth — out of the bondage of Islam and into the lordship of Jesus Christ. I loose the people from the spirit of "jihad" that seeks to incite hatred. murder and revenge. I call the lost sheep into the fold, declaring, "Their Redeemer is strong; the LORD of hosts is His name. He will thoroughly plead their case, that He may give rest to the land.... [He] will punish Bel [Babylonian god] in Babylon, and…bring out of his mouth what he has swallowed…[He] will give rest from your sorrow, and from your fear and the hard bondage in which you were made to serve"* (Jeremiah 50:34 and 51:44; Isaiah 14:3).

Over the Church in Iraq, I bind religious tradition and orthodox control, and I loose love and unity: one mind, one Body, one Spirit. I call forth the release of Christ's victorious Apostolic Church (see 1 Corinthians 15:57). *I call forth a mighty army of intercessors to arise in the power and anointing of the Holy Spirit. O Lord, You are "the saving refuge of [Your] anointed. Save Your people and bless Your inheritance; shepherd them also, and bear them up forever"* (Psalm 28:8-9). *I declare God's sovereign protection over the Christians and the wells of revival. I say, "Spring up, O well, and flood the land with the glory of God so that with joy the people may draw water from the wells of salvation!"* (see Numbers 21:17 and Isaiah 12:3).

*I declare a NEW DAY in Iraq: May the dawn of redemption break over this land, and may the **Son of Righteousness** arise with healing in His wings!* (Psalm 37:6, KJV and Malachi 4:2)

And, finally, I decree the Word of the Lord from Psalm 24 over Iraq, saying: "Iraq is the LORD's, and all its fullness,…and all those who dwell therein." I command the gates of the cities to be lifted up, saying: "Be lifted up, you city gates and ancient doors in Iraq, so the KING OF GLORY may come in — the

LORD OF HOSTS, the LORD STRONG AND MIGHTY, the LORD MIGHTY IN BATTLE."*I declare the dominion of allah is uprooted and cast out of Iraq and the dominion of the Lord Jesus Christ is established!* (see Revelation 11:15). *For the Lion of Judah has triumphed and prevails!* (Revelation 5:5)

I call forth warrior angels to enforce this decree (Hebrews 1:14) *and to fight this battle in the heavenlies!* (see Daniel 10:13).

SUDAN

A LAND RAVAGED BY CIVIL WAR

Much of northern Africa is fraught with the devastation of civil war or, at best, political instability. Famine, poverty, persecution and the deadly scourge of AIDS are taking their toll daily in many African nations. Sudan, a notable example, is the largest country on the continent, located just south of Egypt and divided by the Nile River. Sudan is situated near the ancient biblical land of Cush. We know that the Gospel spread to this area very early. Acts 8 documents the story of Philip's encounter with a eunuch of "great authority" from "the court of Candace, the queen of Ethiopia" (see Acts 8:26-38). Professing faith in Jesus Christ, he no doubt carried the Good News back to Cush, where it has survived to this very day. However, since the resurgence of Islam in recent times, Christians presently make up only about five percent of the total population, while Muslims account for seventy percent.

The devil has made every effort to cut off Sudan's godly spiritual heritage. The people of Sudan have suffered for several decades under a violent and repressive Muslim regime which has persecuted, enslaved, maimed and murdered millions of Sudanese Christians.

A JEWISH REMNANT

There is an interesting historical fact that brings a special importance to Sudan from a biblical/prophetic perspective. There is a group of people in Sudan who trace their lineage to Israel. They are remnants of an ancient tribe that has kept alive their Jewish religious practices. Called *Falashas,* they are Ethiopian Jews who have immigrated to Sudan as refugees. Various attempts have been made to repatriate these Jews to their homeland, but some still remain, having been absorbed into the population of the refugee camps. Man may not know exactly where they are, but God does. He does not lose track of His chosen ones.

Sudan is a land of great suffering, and the desperate cries of God's people do not go unheeded. But warfare intercession will help topple the evil strongholds and move the hand of the Mighty Deliverer.

PRAYING THE WORD OVER SUDAN
To set the captives free

O Mighty Deliverer, establish Your righteousness in the midst of Sudan and bring Your justice to light in that dark place (see Zephaniah 3:5). Destroy the "throne of iniquity" over this land which condemns innocent blood (see Psalm 94:20-21). "Cut in pieces the cords of the wicked" that have the Sudanese people bound (Psalm 129:4). Preserve Sudan from evil men and from violent men, who plan evil things in their hearts, and continually gather together for war (see Psalm 140:1-2). O Lord, maintain the cause of the afflicted, and justice for the poor (Psalm 140:12). — Arise over Sudan and let Your enemies be scattered!...that those who hate You may flee before You.... Be a father to the fatherless, and a defender of the widows; and bring out those who are bound into prosperity (see Psalm 68:1,5, and 6). O God, be awesome to them!...Intervene and return their captives (Zephaniah 2:11 and 7). Thank You, Lord, for delivering Your Jewish remnant in Sudan and restoring them to their homeland!

Prophetic decree of hope

Sing, O Sudan, and shout, O broken one! The Lord is in your midst! You shall see disaster no more.... The Mighty One will save you. He will rejoice over you with gladness.... He will rejoice over you with singing. He will gather those who sorrow.... He will deal with all who afflict you, save the lame, and gather those who were driven out.... He will return your captives before your eyes! (See Zephaniah 3:14,15 and 17-20, selected.)

IRELAND

A LAND OF DIVISION AND STRIFE FOR CENTURIES

Ireland has been the backdrop for intense spiritual and natural warfare for many years. Political unrest began in the sixteenth century when Henry

VIII of England declared himself king over Ireland and tried to introduce Protestantism into this Catholic religious stronghold. Then in 1919, when Ireland attempted to declare its independence from British rule, violent fighting broke out between the Irish rebels and British forces. As a result of this, Ireland was eventually divided into two separate countries: *Northern Ireland* and the *Irish Free State* (eventually the *Republic of Ireland*) in the south. This arrangement didn't please anyone, as both the Catholics and Protestants feared domination by the other. Unable to resolve their differences, and plagued continually by rioting, terrorism and political unrest, the British government stepped in and resumed direct rule of Northern Ireland in 1972.

SIGNIFICANT FACT: THIS CONFLICT IS WITHIN THE CHURCH

Unfortunately this still hasn't solved the problem of political unrest, and Catholics and Protestants are still at war: Families are divided; hatred, murder and retribution are rampant; and innocent people are being caught in the crossfire. The fact that all of this violence is coming from *within* the Church of Jesus Christ is an abomination to God and blasphemes His name in the earth. So, *for the sake of God's holy name*, as well as for the souls and lives involved, we must pray for Ireland to be restored in love and unity to be a glorious witness of Him before the nations. Additionally, spiritual strongholds are deeply entrenched, and must be challenged before real and positive change can come.

DECREEING THE WORD OVER IRELAND

O Ireland, you island of firey passions, I decree that you shall be passionate for Jesus! I loose you from the spirit of religion and bind you to the Spirit of truth and love (see Matthew 16:19). In the authority of Jesus Christ of Nazareth, I take the key of the house of David (according to Isaiah 22:22) and close the spiritual door over Ireland to the prince of darkness and death and open it to the Prince of life and Peace (see Acts 3:15 and Isaiah 9:6).

Spirit of the Sovereign Lord, for the sake of Your holy name, establish the dominion of Your throne over Ireland, and destroy the strongholds of hate and retribution. "For it is written, 'Vengeance is Mine, I will repay,' says the Lord" (Romans 12:19). I declare that the Blood of Jesus has triumphed over, and prevails against, the wicked spirits of murder and rage. Jehovah Raphe, bring healing and restoration to those who have suffered from the hand of violence. O King of the nations, glorify Your name in Ireland once again. Send Your holy, refining fire to heal Your Church of her carnal divisions and strife (see 1 Corinthians 3:3), *and restore her to love and the unity of the Spirit so that the Church in Ireland might be one as You and the Father are one* (see John 17:21-23). *As a witness to the world of Your great love, help those who call themselves "Christians" to walk as Christ did* (see 1 John 2:6). *FOR IT IS WRITTEN:*

> **God did not appoint us to wrath**, *but to obtain salvation through our Lord Jesus Christ.... Therefore comfort each other and edify one another.... Recognize those who labor among you, and...* **esteem them very highly in love....** **Be at peace among yourselves....** **Warn those who are unruly**, *comfort the fainthearted, uphold the weak, be patient with all.* **See that no one renders evil for evil to anyone**, *but always pursue what is good both for yourselves and for all. Rejoice always, pray without ceasing, in everything give thanks; for this is the will of God in Christ Jesus for you. Do not quench the Spirit. Do not despise prophecies. Test all things; hold fast what is good.* **Abstain from every form of evil.** *HE WHO CALLS YOU IS FAITHFUL, WHO ALSO WILL DO IT.*   1 Thessalonians 5:9-24, selected

Jehovah Nissi, may You set Your banner of love over Ireland (see Song of Solomon 2:4). *Make Your face shine on her. Bless her and keep her and be gracious unto her. Lift up Your countenance upon her and give her Your peace* (see Numbers 6:24-26 and John 14:27).

Thank You, Mighty God, King of the universe, for hearing my prayer to establish your divine order in, and to fulfill all Your Kingdom plans for Ireland! May Ireland be a glorious light shining for You to the nations! (see Matthew 5:16).

THE HARVEST

THE "WHEAT AND THE TARES"

The term "the Harvest" refers to the reaping of *souls* from the nations of the world that God will do at the end of the age in order to build His Kingdom. Scripture gives us several pictures of this scenario. For instance, in Matthew 13:24-30, is the parable of *the wheat and the tares*:

> *"The kingdom of heaven is like a man who sowed good seed in his field;*

but while men slept, his enemy came and sowed tares among the wheat.... But when the grain had sprouted and produced a crop, then the tares also appeared. So the servants of the owner came and said to him, 'Sir, did you not sow good seed in your field? How then does it have tares?' He said to them, 'An enemy has done this.' The servants said to him, 'Do you want us then to go and gather them up?' But he said, 'No, lest while you gather up the tares you also uproot the wheat with them. Let both grow together until the harvest, and at the time of harvest I will say to the reapers, "First gather together the tares and bind them in bundles to burn them, but gather the wheat into my barn." ' "

As Jesus explained this parable to His disciples (in verses 37-43), this pictures an "end-time" scenario, i.e., the *final* Harvest:

"He who sows the good seed is the Son of Man. The field is the world, the good seeds are the sons of the kingdom, but the tares are the sons of the wicked one. The enemy who sowed them is the devil, the harvest is the end of the age, and the reapers are the angels...and they will gather out of His kingdom all things that offend...and will cast them into the furnace of fire.... Then the righteous will shine forth as the sun in the kingdom of their Father."

So we see that there are two groups of people who inhabit the earth: those described as *wheat* (good grain which the Lord desires to harvest and put into His barn), and *tares* (a weed that resembles wheat while it is growing, but does not produce grain). One represents the Christians and those who are "ripe" for salvation ("sons of the kingdom"). The other represents those who are hardened and resistant to the Gospel, with no potential for fruit-bearing ("sons of the wicked one"). These will end up being burned in the fire, while the true wheat will be gathered into God's Kingdom.

RAIN FOR THE FALLOW GROUND

The prophet Hosea paints a beautiful picture of the importance of softened, repentant hearts in bringing in the Harvest:

Come, and let us return to the LORD; for He has torn, but He will heal us; He has stricken, but He will bind us up. On the third day He will raise us up, that we may live in His sight.... Let us pursue the knowledge of the LORD.... He will come to us like the rain, like the latter and former rain to the earth.... Break up your fallow ground, for it is time to seek the LORD, till He comes and rains righteousness on you. Hosea 6:1-3 and 10:12

Our "fallow ground" represents hearts that have grown hard and nonarable. The Lord is saying that if we seek the Lord and pursue the knowledge of God, He will come and rain upon us, softening the ground of the heart so the seeds can germinate and bring forth the crop — the Harvest of the nations!

THE "LORD OF THE HARVEST"

There is another dimension to this picture which is described in Matthew 9:37-38 and Luke 10:2-3:

"The harvest truly is great, but the laborers are few; therefore **pray** *the* Lord *of the harvest to send out laborers into His harvest.* **Go** *your way; behold, I send you out."*

First of all, Jesus said: *"Pray."* Never forget that as we pray, God works. The shafts of wheat must be threshed in order to sift out the kernels of grain. The prophet, Haggai, speaks of a great shaking that is coming that "will shake heaven and earth, the sea and dry land." " 'I will *shake all nations*, and they shall come to the *Desire of All Nations*, and I will fill this temple (also a prophetic picture of the Church) with glory,' says the LORD of hosts... 'The glory of this latter temple shall be greater than the former' " (Haggai 2:6,7 and 9). So, in this prophetic picture, as the Lord shakes (threshes) the nations, they will come to Him ("the *Desire of All Nations*") and He will build His Church into a glorious temple!

Then Jesus also said, in Luke 10:3: *"Go."* There is something for each of us to do. Paul instructed the Corinthian church that as they *go* and labor in the harvests fields, there are some who *plant* (sow seeds of truth through witnessing and preaching), some who *water* (nurture the seed to come to fruition), and those who *reap* the harvest (lead souls into salvation). But, so that no one can boast, it is *God* who gives the increase (see 1 Corinthians 3:5-9).

We need a vision for the vastness of the Harvest. It is as close as our next-door neighbor and as far away as China. It includes souls from every tribe, tongue, people and *nation* (see Revelation 5:9).

God's heart is for the nations, as we saw at the beginning of this chapter. In Psalm 67, which was quoted earlier, it states that, as God's glory is released upon the earth and the nations rise up and praise Him, the earth will then "yield her increase" (verse 6). This is a picture of the Harvest coming forth, with the result that "all the ends of the earth will fear Him" (verse 7). Praise the Lord!

So it is an urgent hour in which we must call upon the God of mercy to release His glory in the earth for the sake of the Harvest, because His prophetic clock is ticking, and the final reaping is at hand:

> *"The Son of Man will send out His angels, and they will gather out of His kingdom all things that offend, and those who practice lawlessness, and will cast them into the furnace of fire. There will be wailing and gnashing of teeth. Then the righteous will shine forth as the sun in the kingdom of their Father. He who has ears to hear, let him hear!"*
>
> Matthew 13:41-43

PROPHETIC CALL TO BRING IN THE HARVEST

O Lord of the Harvest, send out Your laborers into Your harvest fields (Luke 10:2). *Give Your people vision to see the fields that are ripe. Propel us out of our lives of complacency and apathy and "into the streets and lanes of the city, [to] bring in…the poor and the maimed and the lame and the blind"* (Luke 14:21). *Take us out of our comfort zones and burden us with Your heart for the lost. Anoint us to go "into the highways and hedges and compel them to come in, that [Your] house may be filled!"* (Luke 14:23).

O Lord of the Increase (see 1 Corinthians 3:7), *may the seeds You have scattered over the earth bring forth a hundred-fold Harvest for Your kingdom!* (see Matthew 13:8). *Bring forth a spirit of repentance so that Your former and latter rain of righteousness will come and soften the soil of our hearts, so that we might break up the fallow ground and seek the knowledge of the Lord and His mercy!* (Hosea 6:1-3 and 10:12).

O Desire of All Nations, shake the nations so that they will come and fill Your glorious temple (see Haggai 2:6-7). *Let the earth be filled with Your glory and Your praises so that the earth may yield her increase* (Psalm 67:6). *I call in the increase from the north, south, east and west — COME! — so the Lord's barns may be filled* with wheat (Matthew 13:30), *and "the righteous will shine forth as the sun in the kingdom of their Father"* (Matthew 13:43).

WORLD PEACE

WE HAVE SLID OFF OF OUR MORAL COMPASS

Many nations and people are crying out for peace. For centuries, and as recently as the Middle East "Road Map," men have attempted to negotiate peace. But the truth is, we cannot have genuine peace without the **God of the Bible**: *the Prince of Peace*. And we cannot have genuine peace without a **moral compass**: *the Word of God.*

Part of the problem is that even the Church has slid off of this compass and into the ways of the world. Moses instructed the children of Israel to diligently teach their children and grandchildren the laws of God so that they would be passed down through the generations:

> *"And what great nation is there that has such statutes and righteous judgments as are in all this law which I set before you this day? Only take heed to yourself, and* diligently keep yourself, lest you forget *the things your eyes have seen, and lest they depart from your heart.... And* teach them to your children *and your grandchildren."*
>
> Deuteronomy 4:8-9

A PARABLE IN NATURE

Recent generations have failed to do this. God demonstrates this principle in nature through the migrating birds. Some birds travel thousands of miles from their summer to their winter homes, making the trip twice a year at the change of seasons. Instinct may tell them when to leave, but research shows that the path through the sky is a result of *learned* behavior: The adult birds must *teach* the young ones the way to go. If the young birds are not taught, they lose their way and motivation to travel. An example of this can be seen in the Canada geese that live in the cove behind my house. These magnificent birds should spend the winters in my harbor and the summers up north in Canada. But at some point there was a breakdown in the generational teaching, and these birds are now year-round residents.

Similarly, the present generation of youth has lost its way in the modern immoral sea of humanity. They are without a compass and a rudder and have drifted way off course. Unless they are taught, they, too, will be helplessly lost and so will the generations that follow. As Jesus said, we need to "discern the signs of the times" (Matthew 16:3). and take action before we have lost an entire generation. We need to return to righteousness and teach our children to do the same.

WE ARE REAPING THE CONSEQUENCES OF OUR GODLESS LIVING

The world does not have peace because men have turned from God and His commands. In this state, one cannot stand before a holy God or enjoy the benefits of His blessing. The nations are reaping the consequences of following after the ways of the world. The Bible teaches that war is inevitable as God brings judgment upon these unrighteous nations. Jesus said that there will be "wars and rumors of wars" as this age draws to a close (Matthew 24:6). And Revelation 6 depicts devastation coming that will take the lives of one quarter of the world's population (see verses 1-8). But Jesus also taught that there is a peace that is not of this world:

> *"Peace I leave with you, My peace I give to you; not as the world gives, do I give to you. Let not your heart be troubled, neither let it be afraid."*
> John 14:27

ONLY ONE WAY TO PEACE

There is only one way to live in peace, and that way is called *righteousness*. And that way can only be lived through the indwelling Holy Spirit of God. So while the world may be at war, there is a safe (peaceful) place for the people of God. Consider the words of the Lord through the prophet Isaiah:

> The work of righteousness will be peace, *and the effect of righteousness, quietness and assurance forever. My people will dwell in a peaceful habitation, in secure dwellings, and in quiet resting places, though hail comes down on the forest, and the city is brought low in humiliation.*
> Isaiah 32:17-19

Yes, war may be raging around us, but His peace is guaranteed us as we rest in Him and in the promise of His Word:

> *The LORD will give strength to His people; the LORD will bless His peo-*
> *ple with peace.* Psalm 29:11

In the glorious temple of Haggai's vision, the Lord of hosts said, "In this place I will give *peace*" (Haggai 2:9). This place is the place where His glory dwells among His people.

The promise of peace is for HIS people — those who walk in righteousness. We need to call the world to God and His righteousness, and those who hear His voice will come....

A PROPHETIC CALL FOR PEACE

O God of Peace, come and crush Satan under our feet! (see Romans 16:20). *Bring down the evil structures of this world that hold your Harvest captive. Scatter the peoples who delight in war* (see Psalm 68:30). *Banish the reproach of our sin so that righteousness may exalt the nations* (see Proverbs 14:34). *May judgment return to righteousness and all the upright in heart follow it* (see Psalm 94:15). *And may righteousness and salvation go forth in the earth as a blazing torch* (see Isaiah 62:1, NIV). *O God, open the blinded eyes to see the Lord and walk in His light* (see Isaiah 2:5). *O righteous Judge, may You hasten the day when people will "beat their swords into plowshares, and their spears into pruning hooks, [so that] nation shall not lift up sword against nation, neither shall they learn war anymore"* (see Isaiah 2:4). *Prince of Peace* (see Isaiah 9:6), *come and establish Your throne upon this earth that Your Kingdom will come and Your will be done as it is in Heaven!* (see Matthew 6:10).

---

[1] Francis Frangipane, "The Father's Family of Nations," Internet article: www.inChristsimage.org, May 19, 2003.

[2] Omar M. Ahmed, quoted from Haywood, CA, *Daily Review*, Saturday, July 4, 1998.

[3] Ibid.

[4] Ibid.

[5] Francis Frangipane, "The Muslim World Shall Hear the Gospel," www.inChristsimage.org, Arrow Publications, December 14, 2001.

[6] Reprinted from Internet article by Chuck Pierce: C. Peter Wagner and Joseph Thompson, general editors, *Out of Africa* (Ventury, CA: Regal Books, 2003).

PART FOUR

❖ ❖ ❖

PERSONAL SCRIPTURAL PRAYERS

Creating scriptural prayers for personal intercession.

Chapter Twenty

BUILDING FAITH

"But without faith it is impossible to please [God]."
Hebrews 11:6

WHAT IS FAITH?

Because of the vital importance of faith to victorious living and in breakthrough intercession, this chapter will expand on what we said about faith back in Chapters Two and Four.

There are over 240 references to *"faith"* in the Bible. According to the Scriptures, faith is essential, not an option. The writer to the Hebrews said, very succinctly, that without faith it is impossible to please God. Why? Because everyone who wants to approach God must believe both that He exists and that He cares enough to respond to those who seek Him (see Hebrews 11:6). Additionally, all the promises of Scripture and benefits of the Covenant are accessed by faith. Simply put, it is by faith that we come to God and it is by faith that we receive all that He has to offer us.

So what, exactly, is faith? Hebrews 11:1 tells us that "faith is the substance of things hoped for, the evidence of things not seen." Does this mean that faith is "blind," believing in things it can't see? Far from it! Faith's evidence is the very visible written Word of God. It is the historical account of thousands of years of men interacting with their God according to His recorded laws, promises and decrees. According to Dr. R.C. Sproul, Hebrews 11:1 can be interpreted as "trusting God for the future based on our faith in what He has accomplished in the past." He goes on to say: "There is every reason to believe that God will be as faithful to His promises in the future as He has been in the past. [Therefore] there is a substantive reason for the hope that is within us."[1]

TRUSTING GOD

It is important to understand that precisely because of the importance of faith, the enemy of our souls is constantly working to tear down and undermine it. A common strategy he uses is fear, which is the opposite of faith. Fear causes us to doubt God and His promises, and thus takes the power out of our prayers and victory out of our life. The devil can't snatch us out of God's hand, but he can cause us to live in defeat and intimidation. We need to *trust* God at His word and receive His promises for us *personally.* To trust God does not mean to have a "positive attitude" or "wishful thinking." Trust involves an active conviction of the heart that, based on God's unchangeable character and His irrevocable promises, He brings into the lives of His children everything pertaining to their ultimate good and godliness. The words of Jeremiah 17:7-8 express the blessings of trusting God:

"Blessed is the man who trusts in the LORD, and whose hope is in the LORD. For he shall be like a tree planted by the waters, which spreads out its roots by the river, and will not fear when heat comes; but its leaf will be green, and will not be anxious in the year of drought, nor will cease from yielding fruit."

Fear saps the strength out of our spirit man along with the productivity and fruit that glorifies God (see John 15:4-8). We all experience fear and uncertainty from time to time, but we must not *live* there. Some wise person once said that *courage is fear that **prays.*** We must always turn our fears over to God in prayer and trust Him with the outcome. Indeed, "to believe God, to trust Him for our very life, is the *essence* of the Christian faith." [2]

FAITH AND HEAVEN

So faith helps us to live life on the earth, but it also determines our place in Heaven. We are challenged in Scripture to press into faith to the point of *overcoming:* that is, overcoming every temptation and pitfall that is arrayed against us by the enemy of our souls and by the weaknesses of our flesh. The Lord tells us in 1 John 5:4 that "whatever is born of God overcomes the world. And *this is the victory that has overcome the world — our **faith.*** *Overcoming* is in our spiritual DNA: As Jesus totally overcame the devil in our behalf, our victory is complete through Him. The challenge is to live this way, triumphantly, in faith. Just as Jesus overcame the devil, so can we. Revelation 3:21 tells us that as *overcomers* we will have a place of honor in Heaven:

> "To him who overcomes I will grant to sit with Me on My throne, *as I also overcame and sat down with My Father on His throne."*

BUILDING OURSELVES UP ON OUR "MOST HOLY FAITH"

Without faith, all of the promises and truths of God's Word would be meaningless and empty. But *with* faith, all things are possible (see Mark 9:23), and with God there is nothing that is impossible (Luke 1:37). That makes a pretty powerful combination! So it behooves us to do all we can to build ourselves up on our most holy faith (see Jude 20). "Building ourselves up in faith" suggests a continuing process. Faith involves making a conscious, progressive decision to believe God at His word regardless of circumstances. Faith is not stagnant, but should be continually growing. So how does faith grow? James said that faith without works is dead, or empty (see James 2:17). To put it another way, faith without exercise is weak. Like bodybuilding, our faith "muscle" requires working against resistance to make it grow. A.B. Simpson once said, "Power (faith) is developed by resistance…and so we shall find someday that even satan has been one of God's agencies of blessings." Jesus told Peter that He allowed satan to "sift him as wheat" because He knew that it would strengthen his faith (see Luke 22:31-32). Scripture teaches that adversity strengthens and refines our faith, bringing it into the full bloom of maturity:

> *Count it all joy when you fall into various trials, knowing that the testing of your faith produces patience. But let patience have its perfect work, that you may be perfect and complete, lacking nothing.*
>
> James 1:2-4

WHAT DOES FAITH BELIEVE ABOUT GOD?

The following statements are facts about God that our faith needs to grab hold of:

God wants to reveal Himself to us... even live with us...
- *"If anyone loves Me, he will keep My word; and My Father will love him, and We will come to him and make Our home with him."* John 14:23
- *"I am the vine, you are the branches. He who abides in Me, and I in him, bears much fruit."* John 15:5

God wants to have fellowship with us...
- *"The LORD is near to all who call upon Him."* Psalm 145:18
- *"Behold, I stand at the door and knock. If anyone hears My voice and opens the door, I will come in to him and dine with him, and he with Me."* Revelation 3:20

God wants to bring us into His Kingdom...
- *"For the Son of man has come to seek and to save that which was lost."* Luke 19:10
- *"For God so loved the world that He gave His only begotten Son, that whoever believes in Him should not perish but have everlasting life."* John 3:16

God wants to bless us...
- *"These things I have spoken to you, that My joy may remain in you, and that your joy may be full."* John 15:11
- *"Eye has not seen, nor ear heard, nor have entered into the heart of man the things which God has prepared for those who love Him."* 1 Corinthians 2:9
- *"Blessed be the Lord, who daily loads us with benefits."* Psalm 68:19

God wants to fill us with Himself...
- *"Do you not know that your body is the temple of the Holy Spirit who is in you, whom you have from God?"* 1 Corinthians 6:19
- *"I have been crucified with Christ; it is no longer I who live, but Christ lives in me."* Galatians 2:20

God wants to equip us...
- *"His divine power has given to us all things that pertain to life and godliness,...by which have been given to us exceedingly great and pre-*

cious promises, that through these you may be partakers of the divine nature." 2 Peter 1:3-4

- *"Put on the whole armor of God, that you may be able to stand against the wiles of the devil."* Ephesians 6:11
- *"Blessed be the LORD my Rock, who trains my hands for war, and my fingers for battle."* Psalm 144:1
- *"I will instruct you and teach you in the way you should go; I will guide you with My eye."* Psalm 32:8

God wants to provide for us according to His covenant promises...

- All needs: *"And my God shall supply all your need according to His riches in glory by Christ Jesus."* Philippians 4:19
- Healing of mind, body and spirit: *"He was wounded for our transgressions [spiritual],...the chastisement for our peace was upon Him [emotional/mental], and by His stripes we are healed [physical]."* Isaiah 53:5

God wants to protect us...

- *"The angel of the LORD encamps all around those who fear Him, and delivers them."* Psalm 34:7
- *"The name of the LORD is a strong tower; the righteous run to it and are safe."* Proverbs 18:10

DECLARING THE WORD BUILDS FAITH

God stretches us in many ways to build our faith, as we read earlier in James 1:2-4. As we submit to these dealings of the Holy Spirit and also to His teaching and commandments in the Word, we advance into *overcoming* faith. A good way to build our faith as we study the Word is to *say it out loud.* For Romans 10:17 tells us that faith comes by *hearing* the Word of God. Now this could mean to listen to preachers and teachers, and this is important. But there is power in *declaring* the Word in an audible voice. When the enemy comes at us with fear, doubt, sickness, confusion, and the like, we need to resist him by standing on and declaring the Word, and he will have to flee (see James 4:7). Read and declare the following scriptures aloud, and as the Word goes forth you will see faith rise up! Many of the Psalms are actually prayers and songs of deliverance and victory. Make them your own! Here are some "Faith Builders" to get you started:

FAITH BUILDERS

- *"The LORD is on my side; I will not fear. What can man do to me?"* Psalm 118:6
- *"Fear not, for I am with you; be not dismayed, for I am your God. I will strengthen you, yes, I will help you, I will uphold you with My righteous right hand."* Isaiah 41:10
- *"For the LORD your God is He who goes with you, to fight for you against your enemies, to save you."* Deuteronomy 20:4
- *"Be strong and of good courage, and do it; do not fear nor be dismayed, for the LORD God...will be with you."* 1 Chronicles 28:20
- *"Whoever trusts in the LORD shall be safe."* Proverbs 29:25b
- *"Fear not, for I have redeemed you; I have called you by your name; you are Mine."* Isaiah 43:1
- *"The LORD is my light and my salvation; whom shall I fear? The LORD is the strength of my life; of whom shall I be afraid?"* Psalm 27:1
- *"Be strong and of good courage, do not fear nor be afraid of them; for the LORD your God, He is the One who goes with you. He will not leave you nor forsake you."* Deuteronomy 31:6
- *"For God has not given us a spirit of fear, but of power and of love and a sound mind."* 2 Timothy 1:7
- *"I [Jehovah-Shammah — The Lord Our Protection] will never leave you nor forsake you."* Hebrews 13:5
- *"The LORD is your keeper [protector].... [He] shall preserve you from all evil; He shall preserve your soul."* Psalm 121:5 and 7
- *"But no weapon that is formed against you shall prosper....This [peace, righteousness, security, triumph over opposition] is the heritage of the servants of the Lord."* Isaiah 54:17, TAB
- *"[And indeed] the Lord will certainly deliver and draw me to Himself from every assault of evil. He will preserve and bring me safe unto His heavenly kingdom."* 2 Timothy 4:18, TAB
- *"In the day when I called, You answered me; and you strengthened me with strength (might and inflexibility to temptation) in my inner self.... Though I walk in the midst of trouble, You will revive me; You will stretch forth Your hand against the wrath of my enemies, and Your right hand will save me."* Psalm 138:3, TAB
- *"For the Lord God is a Sun and a Shield; the Lord bestows [present] grace and favor and [future] glory (honor, splendor, and heavenly bliss)!*

No good thing will He withhold from those who walk uprightly." Psalm 84:11, TAB

- *"You are my hiding place and my shield; I hope in Your word."* Psalm 119:114, TAB

- *"He preserves the lives of His saints (the children of God), He delivers them out of the hand of the wicked."* Psalm 97:10, TAB

[1] R.C. Sproul, *Essential Truths of the Christian Faith* (Wheaton, IL: Tyndale House Publishers, Inc., 1992), p.184.

[2] Ibid.

Chapter Twenty-one

PERSONAL PRAYERS

"Therefore I say to you, whatever things you ask when you pray, believe that you receive them, and you will have them." Mark 11:24

PRAYER LIFE IS ESSENTIAL

There are many things that compete for our personal prayer and devotional time with God. But the fact remains that prayer is essential to our spiritual life and growth. Leonard Ravenhill goes one step further and makes the statement that *"No Christian is greater than his prayer life."* He further remarks…

The church has many organizers, but few agonizers; many who pay, but few who pray; many resters, but few wrestlers; many who are enterprising, but few who are interceding. People who are not praying are playing. Two prerequisites of dynamic Christian living are vision and passion, and both of these are generated in the prayer closet. The ministry of preaching is open to a few. The ministry of praying is open to every child of God. Don't mistake action for unction, commotion for creation, and rallies for revivals. The secret of praying is praying in secret. A worldly Christian will stop praying and a praying Christian will stop worldliness. When you pray, God listens to your heartbeat. Hannah's "lips moved, but her voice was not heard" (1Samuel 1:12 and 13). When we pray in the spirit, there are groanings which cannot be uttered. Tithes may build a church, but tears will give it life. That is the difference between the modern church and the early church. Our emphasis is on paying; theirs was on praying. When we have paid, the place is taken. When they prayed, the place was shaken (Acts 4:31). In the matter of effective praying, never have so many left so much to so few. Brethren, let us pray!

PRAYING THE PSALMS

The Psalms give us excellent models of prayer, both for intercession and for devotion. These poetic words were written to be sung during worship thousands of years ago, and they are still powerful prayers to pray/sing today. "Praying the Psalms" is an effective way to pray prayers that will touch the heart of God. Turning the pages through the book of Psalms, you can pick up on selected verses that express the thoughts of your heart as you read. In this way, many Psalms can become personal expressions of your own supplications, such as:

PRAYERS IN THE MIDST OF TRIALS:
- *"Be merciful to me, O God, be merciful to me! For my soul trusts in you; and in the shadow of Your wings I will make my refuge, until these calamities have passed by. I will cry out to God Most High, to God who performs all things for me. He shall send from heaven and save me; He reproaches the one who would swallow me up. God shall send forth His mercy and His truth."* Psalm 57:1-3
- *"Hear my cry, O God; attend to my prayer. From the end of the earth I will cry to You, when my heart is overwhelmed; lead me to the rock that is higher than I. For You have been a shelter for me, a strong tower from the enemy. I will abide in Your tabernacle forever; I will trust in the shelter of Your wings."* Psalm 61:1-4
- *"Have mercy on me, O LORD, for I am in trouble; my eye wastes away with grief. I am like a broken vessel. Fear is on every side. But as for me, I trust in You, O LORD; I say, 'You are my God.' My times are in Your hand; deliver me from the hand of my enemies, and from those who persecute me. Make Your face shine upon Your servant, save me for Your mercies' sake. Do not let me be ashamed, O LORD, for I have called upon You… Oh, how great is Your goodness, which You have laid up for those who fear You, which You have prepared for those who trust in You in the presence of the sons of men! Oh, love the LORD, all you His saints! For the LORD preserves the faithful. Be of good courage, and He shall strengthen your heart, all you who hope in the LORD."* Psalm 31:9,12-17,19,23 and 24

- *"Give ear, O LORD, to my prayer; and attend to the voice of my supplications. In the day of my trouble I will call upon You, for You will answer me.... Teach me Your way, O LORD; I will walk in Your truth; unite my heart to fear Your name. I will praise You, O Lord my God, with all my heart, and I will glorify Your name forevermore. For great is Your mercy toward me."* Psalm 86:6-7 and 11-13

- *"I am troubled, I am bowed down greatly. I groan because of the turmoil of my heart. Do not forsake me, O LORD; O my God, be not far from me! Make haste to help me, O LORD, my salvation!"* Psalm 38:6,8,and 21-22

PRAYERS FOR STRENGTH AND ENCOURAGEMENT:

- *"Uphold my steps in Your paths, that my footsteps may not slip. I have called upon You, for You will hear me, O God; incline Your ear to me, and hear my speech. Show Your marvelous lovingkindness by Your right hand, O You who save those who trust in You from those who rise up against them. Keep me as the apple of Your eye; Hide me under the shadow of Your wings."* Psalm 17:5-8

- *"Whom have I in heaven but You? And there is none upon the earth that I desire besides You. My flesh and my heart fail; but God is the strength of my heart and my portion forever.... It is good for me to draw near to God; I have put my trust in the LORD God, that I may declare all Your works."* Psalm 73:25-26 and 28

- *"My soul melts from heaviness; strengthen me according to Your word.... Teach me, O LORD, the way of Your statutes, and I shall keep it to the end. Give me understanding, and I shall keep Your law.... Make me walk in the path of Your commandments, for I delight in it. Incline my heart to Your testimonies, and not to covetousness. Turn away my eyes from looking at worthless things, and revive me in Your way."* Psalm 119: 28 and 33-37

PRAYERS OF REPENTANCE:

- *"Have mercy upon me, O God, according to Your lovingkindness; according to the multitude of Your tender mercies.... Wash me thoroughly from my iniquity, and cleanse me from my sin. For I acknowledge my transgressions, and my sin is always before me.... Purge me with hyssop, and I shall be clean; wash me, and I shall be whiter than snow.... Cre-*

ate in me a clean heart, O God, and renew a steadfast spirit within
me.... Restore to me the joy of Your salvation, and uphold me by Your
generous Spirit." Psalm 51:1-3,7,10 and 12

- "Show me Your ways, O LORD; teach me Your paths. Lead me in Your
truth and teach me, for You are the God of my salvation.... For Your
name's sake, O LORD, pardon my iniquity, for it is great.... Turn Yourself
to me, and have mercy on me, for I am desolate and afflicted. The troubles
of my heart have enlarged; bring me out of my distresses! Look on my
affliction and my pain, and forgive all my sins.... Let integrity and upright-
ness preserve me, for I wait for You." Psalm 25:4-5,11, 16-18 and 21
- "I acknowledged my sin to You, and my iniquity I have not hidden. I
said, 'I will confess my transgressions to the LORD,' and You forgave the
iniquity of my sin.... Blessed is he whose transgression is forgiven, whose
sin is covered. Blessed is the man to whom the LORD does not impute
iniquity, and in whose spirit there is no deceit." Psalm 32:5 and 1-2

FAITH DECLARATIONS OF AN "OVERCOMER"

In Chapter Twenty we talked about the importance of having overcoming faith in order to live a victorious and holy life that pleases God. The
following declarations of truth from the Word of God speak to that end.

DAILY CONFESSIONS OF AN *"OVERCOMER"*

- God is quickening me today to fulfill all that He has for me. I have a
sure future because all His plans for me are for good, and He orders
my steps according to His perfect will. (See 1 Timothy 6:13, KJV;
Jeremiah 29:11 and Psalm 37:23.)
- I am filled with power from on high and enabled to do exceedingly
abundantly more than I could imagine, for He has prepared me to
walk in the riches of His glory and He surrounds me with His favor.
(See Ephesians 3:20; Romans 9:23; and Psalm 5:12.)
- God chooses to bless and prosper me and my finances in every way
so that I can bless His children and fulfill my calling. (See Philippians
4:19 and 1 Chronicles 4:9-10.)
- I am more than a conqueror today through Jesus. His Blood and my
testimony cause me to triumph! (See Romans 8:37 and Revelation

12:11.)

- I have the mind of Christ and so all I think and do is in agreement with His will. I have direction and focus because I hear His voice. I have no fear, for God has given me a sound mind, power and love. And perfect love casts out all fear. (See 1 Corinthians 2:16; John 10:4; 1Timothy 1:7 and 1 John 4:18.)
- I can rest in my work because I have confidence that He will work through me – and I do not have to strive. (See Hebrews 4:9.)
- I am seated above circumstances with Christ in a place of protection and authority. There is no weapon formed against me that will prosper; because I am in covenant with Almighty God. (See Ephesians 3:20; Luke 10:19; Isaiah 54:1 and 1 Corinthians11:25.)

Influences to weaken our faith come basically from two fronts: those from **without** (satan and his demons) and those from **within** (the flesh and the "self" life). The following is a simple declaration from the Word of God against these two enemies of our faith:

DAILY FAITH DECLARATIONS

To the enemy without: satan and his demons...

I declare that all the plans and schemes of the devil that are arrayed against me today are null and void according to the Blood covenant I have with Almighty God.

For it is written:

> *"No weapon formed against [me] shall prosper, and every tongue that rises against [me] in judgment [I] shall condemn."* Isaiah 54:17

To the enemy *within*: the "flesh" (self) life...

I declare my allegiance to the work and power of the Holy Spirit within me, and I deny all the passions, works and influences of the flesh.

For it is written:

> *"I have been crucified with Christ; it is no longer I who live, but Christ lives in me; and the life which I now live in the flesh I live by faith in the Son of God, who loved me and gave Himself for me."*
>
> Galatians 2:20

A powerful general confession concerning safety and protection is Psalm

91. The following version is a paraphrased (modernized) and annotated adaptation which can also be prayed over families, nations or armies, etc. Filled with promises of God's sovereign protection, I call it God's "Life Assurance Policy."

PERSONAL CONFESSION OF FAITH
FOR SAFETY AND PROTECTION

Because I (we) dwell in the secret place of the Most High, I (we) abide under the shadow of the Almighty. I (we) declare of the Lord, "He is my (our) refuge and my (our) fortress; my (our) God, in Him I (we) will trust." For surely He shall deliver me (us) from the traps of the enemy and from the perils of chemical and biological weapons. He shall cover me (us) with His protection, and under His sovereign care I (we) shall take refuge. His truth shall be my (our) shield and defense, and His Word my (our) sword (see Ephesians 6:17).

I (we) shall not be afraid of the terror by night, nor of the missile that flies by day, nor of biological or nuclear warfare. I (we) have no fear because God has given me (us) a spirit of power, of love and of a sound mind (see 2 Timothy 1:7). *A thousand may fall at my (our) side, and ten thousand at my (our) right hand; but it shall not come near me (us). For no weapon formed against me (us) shall prosper* (see Isaiah 54:17). *The wicked will only* appear *to be winning.*

Because I (we) have made the Lord, who is my (our) refuge, even the Most High, my (our) dwelling place, no evil shall befall me (us), nor shall any plague come near my (our) dwelling. For He shall give His angels charge over me (us), to keep me (us) in all my (our) ways. In their hands they shall bear me (us) up, lest I (we) stumble and fall. I (we) have authority to render ineffective all the strategies of destruction of the enemy. For God has given me (us) authority over ALL his power (See Luke 10:19).

Because I (we) have set my (our) love on Him, therefore He will deliver me (us); He will set me (us) on high because I (we) have known Him personally. He honors His Blood Covenant with me (us) (see 1 Corinthians 11:25*). I (we) shall call upon Him, and He will answer me (us); He will be with me (us) in trouble; He will deliver me (us) and honor me (us). His plans for me (us) are for good, to give me (us) hope and a sure future* (see Jeremiah 29:11*). With long life He will satisfy me (us) and show me (us) His salvation.*

BINDING AND LOOSING

In Chapter Nine we talked about "Binding and Loosing." This is a very powerful way to pray for yourself and for others. Using this strategy, I first loose the person from *deception* and all demonic and fleshly influences, and then I bind him to the *truth* and the will and purposes of God. Following is a personal prayer of binding and loosing:

I LOOSE myself from:
All deception and demonic hindrance or influence over my body mind and spirit everything that exalts itself against the knowledge of God (see 2 Corinthians 10:5), lack, defeat and infirmity
All works, influences, passions of the flesh: pride, confusion, control, doubt, fear, competition, jealousy, offense, etc.

I BIND:
My mind, will and emotions to the **will and purposes of God**, bringing every thought captive to the obedience of Christ (see 2 Corinthians 10:5).
My heart to His heart of love and compassion, mercy and forgiveness.
My feet to the paths of righteousness.
My ears to hearing the word/voice of the Spirit.
My eyes to seeing in the spirit.

Also, I BIND myself to:
The Truth: the divine nature and all the fruit of the Spirit; knowledge, wisdom and discernment and all the gifts of the Spirit the work of the *cross* and the *Blood of the covenant;* the work of the *resurrection* with its overcoming faith, abundant life and health, prosperity and victory; a passion for Jesus; righteousness and purity; humility and obedience to God's Word.

SECURE IN GOD'S LOVE

GOD'S CROWNING WORK

We will never experience the full victory of the life of faith if we don't appreciate the immensity and sincerity of God's love for us. In the vastness of the universe, God fashioned a tiny little planet to be the home of His crowning work, mankind, created in His own image. The universe itself is a miraculous creation, according to physicist, Lambert Dolphin: "From the submicroscopic realm of the atom to the expanding reaches of the galaxies, our universe runs like intricate and well-oiled clockwork according to great physical laws and principles which never change nor falter."[1] But that wasn't enough for God. He wanted someone to lavish His love upon. And so He created man to inhabit earth, as the object of His love. *The Living Bible* paraphrase says it this way:

> *Long ago, even before he made the world, God chose us to be his very own, through what Christ would do for us; he decided then to make us holy in his eyes, without a single fault — we who stand before him **covered with his love**. His unchanging plan has always been to adopt us into his own family by sending Jesus Christ to die for us. And he did this because he wanted to!"* Ephesians 1:4-5

HIS LOVE IS UNCONDITIONAL, UNCHANGING AND ETERNAL

God's love is so resolute toward you that there is nothing that you can do to make Him love you any more or any less than He already does. The Bible says that His love is unconditional, unchanging, and eternal. God, the Father, so loved the world that He *gave* His only Son (see John 3:16). And Jesus, the Son, so loved the world that He *willingly came* and offered his life as a ransom for many (see Mark 10:45). The following little dialogue reminds us of this great, incomprehensible love:

Father God, How Much Do You Love Me?

My child,
I love you so much that I sent My only begotten Son, Jesus, to die in your place, so that you might live forever with Me.
(John 3:16; Romans 10:13; 2 Corinthians 5:21; 1 John 3:1 and 4:10)

I love you just as you are, and yet I love you too much to leave you there.
So I continuously draw you by My love to a higher place.
(Song of Solomon 1:4; Romans 5:8; Philippians 3:12-14; 1 John 3:1-2; Revelation 3:20)

You are wrapped in My holy Covenant...
(Jeremiah 31:31-33; 1 Corinthians 11:25; ; Hebrews 9:12-15)

...and showered with My promises...
(Acts 1:4-5; 2 Corinthians 1:20; 2 Peter 1:3-4)

...and gifts.
(Romans 6:23; Ephesians 2:8; 1 Corinthians 7:7 and 12:4-10)

I provide for your every need.
(Psalm 23:1 and Psalm 103:2-6; Philippians 4:19)

And I call you "Beloved."
(Colossians 3:12; 1 John 4:7)

Thank You, Father. Forgive me for ever doubting Your love.

For this reason I bow my knees to the Father of our Lord Jesus Christ,...that you, being rooted and grounded in love, may be able to comprehend...what is the width and length and depth and height – to know the love of Christ which passes knowledge."
Ephesians 3:14 and 17-19

STANDING ON THE TRUTH: RESISTING THE ENEMY

When we do experience a spiritual or physical attack, we must remember the admonition from Scripture: "Resist the devil and he will flee from you" (James 4:7). One powerful way to resist the enemy of our souls is to remind him of his defeat and destiny in hell and of our place of victory in God (Remember, we *overcome the devil* by the blood of the Lamb and the *word of our testimony*! Revelation 12:11), with such scriptures as:

- *"I [Jesus] saw satan fall like lightning from heaven. Now shall the prince of this world be cast out."* Luke 10:18 and John 12:31,KJV
- *"Having disarmed principalities and powers, He made a public spectacle of them, triumphing over them in it* [the cross].*"* Colossians 2:15
- *"And the devil that deceived them was cast into the lake of fire and brimstone...and shall be tormented day and night for ever and ever."* Revelation 20:10, KJV
- *"Behold, I* [Jesus] *give you authority...over all the power of the enemy, and nothing shall by any means hurt you."* Luke 10:19
- *"If God is for us, who can be against us?"* Romans 8:31
- *"Thanks be to God, who gives us the victory through our Lord Jesus Christ."* 1 Corinthians 15:57

UNDERSTANDING OUR COVENANT PROMISES

TOTAL HEALTH THROUGH THE ATONEMENT

We must understand what is provided for us as covenant children of Almighty God in order to stand on it and declare it in faith. For instance, according to Isaiah 53:4-5, total wellness is ours through the Atonement, and thus health and healing are our covenant privilege:

> *"Surely He has borne our* griefs [identified in Matthew 8:17 as "sicknesses"] *and carried our sorrows* [physical healing]... *He was wounded for our* transgressions, *He was bruised for our* iniquities [spiritual healing], *the chastisement of our* peace *was upon Him* [mental/emotional healing], *and by His stripes* we are healed [totally].*"*

"We are healed" — it is a "done deal" from God's perspective. This is how we stand before Him: totally vindicated, totally cleansed and healed from *every vestige* of sin. Scripture teaches that sickness is a curse of the law brought on by sin (see Deuteronomy 28:15 and 58-61). However, the covenant promise of Galatians 3:13 is that "Christ has redeemed us from the curse of the law, having become a curse for us." Since healing is a covenant promise purchased and guaranteed by the precious Blood of the Lamb, it is ours to walk in.

APPROPRIATED BY FAITH

So how do we appropriate this in our lives? Jesus said often as He healed people, "According to your *faith*, be it unto you." *All of the covenant prom-*

*ises of God are appropriated by **faith**. They are ours judicially (legally), being purchased by the Blood of Christ, but they are not automatic.* They become a reality in our lives as we "walk by faith, not by sight" (2 Corinthians 5:7). In other words, we must walk by faith according to what we *have* in the Kingdom of God (covenant promises), and not by sight according to what we *see* in the kingdom of this world (circumstances).

Indeed, we are citizens of a higher Kingdom and are subject to its rules and principles. It is a common assumption, for instance, that we must all die of something. This is a worldly perspective. *Christians do not have to get sick to die.* May people have passed on to Heaven in perfect health. Consider Moses, who died at the ripe old age of one hundred and twenty years: "His eyes were not dim nor his natural vigor diminished (Deuteronomy 34:7). Psalm 92:12-14 has this to say about the aging of God's people:

The righteous shall flourish like a palm tree,
He shall grow like a cedar in Lebanon.
Those who are planted in the house of the LORD
Shall flourish in the courts of our God.
They shall still bear fruit in old age;
They shall be fresh and flourishing.

IN ALL THINGS GOD IS SOVEREIGN

Having said all of this, we must understand that in all things God is sovereign. We can see the balance between satan and the fallen world order (from which sickness and disease come) and the sovereignty of God as we look at the life of Job. Satan could only oppress Job *with God's permission*, and only to *the limits that God set* (see Job 1:6-12 and 2:1-6). While God has made the way for us to enjoy wholeness in mind, body and spirit, He does not promise that we will never suffer or get sick. There are many reasons why we experience these things, but they usually fall into one or more of several categories:

- To reveal God's glory (see John 11:4 and 1 Peter 4:12-13).
- As an opportunity for us to exercise, and grow in, faith (see James 1:2-4.)
- As a result of sin and disobedience (see Psalms 32:1-5 and 102:17-18).
- To share in Christ's sufferings (see Philippians 1:29 and 3:10).

- To grow in humility and dependence on God (see 2 Corinthians 12:7-10).
- To grow in Christ-likeness (see 2 Corinthians 4:7-11).
- Because we abuse our bodies with harmful habits or weaken them through lack of proper hygiene, diet, exercise or sleep (see Galatians 6:7).

Ultimately, it is God's sovereign privilege to grant His blessings as He chooses. But it is our right and privilege to pray His kingdom/covenant blessings into people's lives. David summarized these covenant benefits in Psalm 103:2-5.

"Bless the LORD, O my soul, and forget not *all His benefits*:
- Who *forgives* ALL your iniquities,
- Who *heals* ALL your diseases,
- Who *redeems* your life from destruction,
- Who *crowns* you with lovingkindness and tender mercies,
- Who *satisfies* your mouth with good things, so that your youth is renewed like the eagle's."

Psalm 103 goes on to say: *"The mercy of the LORD is from everlasting to everlasting on those who fear Him,... to such as keep His covenant, and to those who remember His commandments to do them"* (verses 17-18). Following a period of repentance, the Lord *"sent His word* and healed" the Israelites *"and delivered them from their destructions"* (Psalm 107:20). We should likewise counter an attack from a spirit of infirmity or sickness with repentance and the **Word of truth**. Following are scriptures and personal confessions of faith concerning healing, safety and protection.

BUILDING FAITH FOR HEALTH AND HEALING
...Truth from Scripture
- *"Blessed is the man who fears the LORD, who finds great delight in His commands....* He will have no fear of bad news; his heart is steadfast, trusting in the LORD." Psalm 112:1 and 7, NIV
- " *'I know the plans I have for you,' says the LORD, 'plans to prosper you and not to harm you, plans to give you hope and a future.' "* Jeremiah 29:11, NIV
- "No weapon formed against [me] shall prosper." Isaiah 54:17
- *"Christ has redeemed [me] from the curse of the law."* (According to Deuteronomy 21:23, sickness is a curse of the law.)

- "By His stripes [I was] healed." Isaiah 53:5 and 1 Peter 2:24
- *"He drove out the spirits with a word and* healed all the sick. *This was to fulfill what was spoken through the prophet Isaiah: 'He took up our infirmities and carried our diseases'* (Isaiah 53:5)." Matthew 8:16-17
- *"Jesus went about all the cities and villages,…* healing every sickness and every disease *among the people."* — *"Jesus Christ is the same yesterday, and today, and forever."* Matthew 9:35 and Hebrews 13:8
- "Then they cried out to the LORD *in their trouble, and He saved them out of their distresses. He sent His word and healed them."* Psalm 107:19 and 20
- "I am the LORD *who heals you…. If you listen, and do all that I say,…* I will take away sickness from among you…. I will give you a full life span." Exodus 15:26 and 23:22-26, NIV
- *"Bless the* LORD, *O my soul, and forget not all His benefits…who* heals all your diseases." Psalm 103:2-3
- *"No evil shall befall you,* nor shall any plague *come near your dwelling…. With* long life *I will satisfy him, and show him My salvation."* Psalm 91:10 and 16

…Personal confession of faith for health and healing [2]

Father, in the name of Jesus, I confess Your Word concerning healing…. I am the body of Christ. I am redeemed from the curse of the law, because Jesus bore my sicknesses and carried my diseases in His own body. By His stripes I am healed. I forbid any sickness or disease to operate in my body. Every organ, every tissue of my body functions in the perfection in which God created it to function. I honor God and bring glory to Him with my body.

Now, Father, because I reverence and worship You, I have the assurance of Your Word that the angel of the LORD encamps around me and delivers me from every evil work. No evil shall befall me; no plague or calamity shall come near my dwelling. I confess the Word of God abides in me and delivers to me perfect soundness of mind and wholeness of body and spirit from the deepest parts of my nature in my immortal spirit even to the joints and marrow of my bones. That Word is medication and life to my flesh, for the law of the spirit of life operates in me and makes me free from the law of sin and death.

I have on the whole armor of God, and the shield of faith protects me from all the fiery darts of the wicked one. Jesus is the High Priest of my confession, and I hold fast to my confession of faith in Your Word. I stand immovable and fixed in full assurance that I have health and healing now, according to Your covenant promises to me as a Bloodbought child of Almighty God. I declare that no weapon formed against me can prosper.

Satan, I speak to you in the name of Jesus and say that your principalities and powers, your spirits who rule the present darkness, and your spiritual wickedness in heavenly places are bound from operating against me in any way. I am the property of Almighty God, and I give you no place in me. I dwell in the secret place of the Most High God. I abide, remain stable and fixed, under the shadow of the Almighty, *whose power no foe can withstand.*

(Scripture references: Psalms 34:7, 91:1-16 and 112:7; Proverbs 4:22; Isaiah 53:5 and 54:17; Matthew 8:17; Luke 10:19; Romans 8:2; 1 Corinthians 6:20; 2 Corinthians 10:4; Galatians 3:23; Ephesians 6:10-18; 2 Timothy 1:7; Hebrews 12:14; and 1 Peter 2:24)

OTHER COVENANT PROMISES AND BENEFITS

All of the promises listed in the New Testament are part of the "New Covenant," being purchased by the Blood of the Atonement: Christ's sacrifice for our salvation. Other covenant promises and benefits (besides those relating to health) that can serve as an anchor in intercession guarantee:

1. *Our assurance of God's **provision:***
   • "And my God shall supply all your need according to His riches in glory by Christ Jesus." Philippians 4:19
   • "He who did not spare His own Son,…how shall He not with Him also freely give us all things?" Romans 8:32
2. *Our **forgiveness** and cleansing from sin:*
   "If we walk in the light as He is in the light,…the blood of Jesus Christ His Son cleanses us from all sin. …If we confess our sins, He is faithful and just to forgive us our sins and to cleanse us from all unrighteousness." 1 John 1:7 and 9
3. *Our **inheritance** in Christ:*
   "The Spirit Himself bears witness with our spirit that we are children of God, and if children, then heirs — heirs of God and joint heirs with Christ, if indeed we suffer with Him, that we may also

be glorified together. For…the sufferings of this present time are not worthy to be compared with the glory which shall be revealed in us." Romans 8:16-18

4. *Our **victory** over the world:*

"His divine power has given to us all things that pertain to life and godliness,…by which have been given to us exceedingly great and precious promises, that through these you may be partakers of the divine nature, having escaped the corruption that is in the world through lust." 2 Peter 1:3-4

…over the flesh:

- "But if the Spirit of Him who raised Jesus from the dead dwells in you, He who raised Christ from the dead will also give life to your mortal bodies through His Spirit who dwells in you….. For if you live according to the flesh you will die; but if by the Spirit you put to death the deeds of the body, you will live. For as many as are led by the Spirit of God, these are sons of God." Romans 8:11, and 13 -14

- "I have been crucified with Christ; it is no longer I who live, but Christ lives in me; and the life which I now live in the flesh I live by faith in the Son of God, who loved me and gave Himself for me." Galatians 2:20

…and over the devil:

"And they overcame him [the devil] by the blood of the Lamb and the word of their testimony." Revelation 12:11

5. *Our **freedom** from condemnation:*

"There is therefore now no condemnation to those who are in Christ Jesus, who…walk…according to the Spirit… For…neither death nor life, nor angels nor principalities nor powers, nor things present nor things to come, nor height nor depth, nor any other created thing, shall be able to separate us from the love of God which is in Christ Jesus our Lord." Romans 8:1and 38-39

…and from fear:

- "For you did not receive the spirit of bondage again to fear, but you received the Spirit of adoption by whom we cry out, 'Abba, Father.' " Romans 8:15

- "For God has not given us a spirit of fear, but of power and of love and of a sound mind." 2 Timothy 1:7

STRENGTHENING OUR ARMOR

In Chapter Two we talked about the "Armor of God" as essential "attire" for spiritual warfare. This is especially strategic and important for someone who is an intercessor or a leader on the front lines of battle. The following scriptures (featuring a different piece of armor to pray for each day of the week) are powerful declarations to make to strengthen spiritual armor, to protect us from enemy attacks, and to equip us for battle.

PRAYING THE ARMOR OF GOD: Ephesians 6:10-18
"Be strong in the Lord and in His mighty power. Put on the whole armor of God so that you can *take your stand* against the devil's schemes" (vv 10 and 11).

DAY ONE: Helmet of Salvation: (importance of saving knowledge over the mind)

1. *Protecting* our minds
   - "Therefore, prepare your minds for action; be self-controlled; set your hope fully on the grace to be given you when Jesus Christ is revealed. As obedient children, do not conform to the evil desires you had when you lived in ignorance." (1 Peter 1:13-14,NIV) — *That my mind might be prepared for action, depending on His grace, obedient to His will.*
   - "You will keep him in perfect peace, whose mind is stayed on You, because he trusts in You. Trust in the LORD forever, for in Yah, the LORD, is everlasting strength." (Isaiah 26:3-4) — *That as my mind stays focused on Him, in Him I will find sustaining strength and perfect peace.*

2. Having the mind of Christ (*humility*)
   - "Let this mind be in you, which was also in Christ Jesus: who...made himself of no reputation...and being found in fashion as a man, he humbled himself, and became obedient unto death." (Philippians 2:5- 8,KJV) — *That I would have the mind of Christ: pure humility and obedience: I have been crucified with Christ, and I no longer live, but Christ lives in me. (Galatians 2:20)*
   - "Take my yoke upon you, and learn of me; for I am meek and lowly in heart: and ye shall find rest unto your souls." (Matthew 11:29, KJV) — *That I would learn to rest in Him, casting all my care upon Him, trusting in Him only, in humility and submission.*

- "Clothe yourselves with humility toward one another, because, 'God opposes the proud but gives grace to the humble.' Humble yourselves, therefore, under God's mighty hand, that he may lift you up in due time." (1 Peter 5:5-6, NIV) — *That I may always interact with others in complete humility before God.*

3. *Transforming* of the mind by revelation knowledge
   - "Do not conform any longer to the pattern of this world, but be transformed by the renewing of your mind. Then you will be able to test and approve what God's will is." (Romans 12:2, NIV) — *That my mind might be renewed by His Truth so that I might demonstrate the will of God.*
   - "You were taught...to be made new in the attitude of your minds; and to put on the new self, created to be like God in true righteousness and holiness." (Ephesians 4:22-24, NIV) — *That the new attitude of my mind would successfully resist the old nature so that I would increasingly take on the righteousness and holiness of God.*

DAY TWO: Breastplate of Righteousness:

1. Putting on the *righteousness of Christ*
   - "God made him who had no sin to be sin for us, so that in him we might become the righteousness of God." (2 Corinthians 5:21, NIV) — *That I might take on the righteousness appropriated to me.*
   - "This is my prayer: that you... may... be filled with the fruit of righteousness that comes through Jesus Christ — to the glory and praise of God." (Philippians 1:9-11, NIV) — *That my life may richly produce the fruit of righteousness, bringing glory and praise to God.*
   - "You were taught...to be made new in the attitude of your minds; and to put on the new self, created to be like God in true righteousness and holiness." (Ephesians 4:22-24, NIV) — *That I may increasingly know Christ and be thus renewed in my mind so that my character might take on His holiness and righteousness.*

2. Walking in *holiness*
   - "But just as he who called you is holy, so be holy in all you do; for it is written: 'Be holy, because I am holy.' " (1 Peter 1:15-16, NIV) — *That my life would increasingly demonstrate the charactistics of holiness.*

- "Our fathers disciplined us for a little while as they thought best; but God disciplines us for our good, that we may share in his holiness." (Hebrews 12:10-11, NIV) — *That God would be severe in His chastening of me now so that it might produce a harvest of righteousness and peace.* (v.11)

DAY THREE: Girdle of Truth:

1. Being *established* in the Truth

   "So then, just as you received Christ Jesus as Lord, continue to live in him, rooted and built up in him, strengthened in the faith as you were taught, and overflowing with thankfulness." (Colossians 2:6-7, NIV) — *That I would be settled on the firm foundation of Jesus, strengthened in faith, and manifesting a lifestyle of praise.*

2. Being *sanctified* by the Truth

   "My prayer is not that you take them out of the world but that you protect them from the evil one.... Sanctify them by the truth; your word is truth. As you have sent me into the world, I have sent them into the world." (John 17:15 and17-18,NIV) — *That as the Word becomes a part of me, I would be sanctified and strengthened against the weaknesses of the flesh.*

3. *Rightly dividing* the word of Truth

   "Do your best to present yourself to God as one approved, a workman who does not need to be ashamed and who correctly handles the word of truth. Avoid godless chatter, because those who indulge in it will become more and more ungodly." (2 Timothy 2:15-16, NIV) — *That I would be so transformed by the renewing of my mind in His Word of Truth that all my speech would bring only blessing to others, honor to God, and godliness to my character.*

4. *Being set free* in the Truth

   "If you hold to my teaching, you are really my disciples. Then you will know the truth, and the truth will set you free." (John 8:31-32, NIV) — *That I would be so grounded in the Truth that I would be set free from any hindrance in spirit or flesh that would prevent the free flow of the Holy Spirit through my life.*

DAY FOUR: Shoes of Gospel of Peace:

1. *Being firmly established*

   "And having shod your feet in preparation [to face the enemy with the firm-footed stability, the promptness, and the readiness produced by the good news] of the Gospel of peace." (Ephesians 6:15, TAB) — *That I would be so firmly established in the Gospel of peace that I would face the enemy with great confidence in the truth of that Word.*

2. *Walking* in peace

    "Do not repay anyone evil for evil. Be careful to do what is right in the eyes of everybody. If it is possible, as far as it depends on you, live at peace with everyone. Do not take revenge." (Romans 12:17-19, NIV) — *That I would not only walk in peace, repaying good for evil, but would be a peace facilitator.*

3. *Speaking* peace

    • "How beautiful upon the mountains are the feet of him that bringeth good tidings, that publisheth peace." (Isaiah 52:7, KJV) — *That I might be one who proclaims the good news of the Gospel of peace.*

    • "Do not let any unwholesome talk come out of your mouths, but only what is helpful for building others up according to their needs, that it may benefit those who listen." (Ephesians 4:29, NIV) — *That my speech would nurture reconciliation, healing, and blessing in the lives of all whom God brings across my path.*

DAY FIVE: Sword of the Spirit:

1. *Purifying our* minds

    • "For the word of God is living and active. Sharper than any double-edged sword, it penetrates even to dividing soul and spirit, joints and marrow; it judges the thoughts and attitudes of the heart." (Hebrews 4:12, NIV) — *That I would be so sensitive to the Word of Truth that it would continually sanctify my thoughts and purify the motivations of my heart.*

    • "With my whole heart have I sought thee: O let me not wander from thy commandments.... Open thou mine eyes that I may behold wondrous things out of thy law." (Psalm 119:10 and 18, NIV) — *That the LORD would, as I learn to seek Him on new levels, so kindle my love for, and understanding of, His Word that I would never stray from His commandments.*

2. Using a mighty weapon of spiritual *warfare*

    "Take ...the sword of the Spirit, which is the word of God. And pray in the Spirit on all occasions with all kinds of prayers and requests." (Ephesians 6:17-18, NIV) — *That as I learn to pray the Word of God boldly in supplication and intercession, the Lord will move mightily by His Spirit.*

DAY SIX: Shield of Faith:

1. Being *well-covered* by and *grounded* in faith:
    • "Be wellbalanced,... be vigilant and cautious at all times; for that enemy of yours, the devil, roams around like a lion roaring [in fierce hunger], seeking someone to seize upon and devour. Withstand him: be firm in faith against his onset — rooted, established, strong, immovable, and determined." (1 Peter 5:8-9, TAB) *That I would be confident of the protection and power of the Blood of Christ who dwells in my heart through faith.*
    • "Continue in the faith grounded and settled, and be not moved away from the hope of the gospel." (Colossians 1:23, KJV) — *That my faith shield would be impenetrable and immovable, firmly grounded in the Truth of God.*
2. Being unwavering:
    "Let us hold fast the profession of our faith without wavering; for he is faithful that promised." (Hebrews 10:23, KJV) — *That I would be unwavering in my faith, trusting in all that God has promised.*

DAY SEVEN: Pray Psalm 91 for the family.

[1] Lambert Dolphin, Jr., *My Search for "The Ultimate"* (Kansas City, MO: StonecroftBookCenter), pp. 7-8.

[2] Adapted from Word Ministries, Inc., *Prayers That Avail Much* (Tulsa, OK: Harrison House, 1989), pp. 23, and 67 - 68.

Chapter Twenty-two

PRAYING FOR OTHERS

"Therefore take up the whole armor of God,...praying always with all prayer and supplication in the Spirit,...with all perseverance... for all the saints." Ephesians 6:13 and 18

FAITH—SPRINGBOARD FOR PRAYER

Faith, as we have said, is the basis of our relationship with God and the basis upon which we receive all of His Covenant promises into our lives. Faith also is the springboard from which we minister in prayer to others. As intercessors, we pray because we believe that God cares about us and is able to help us. Therefore, we "come boldly to the throne of grace, that we may obtain mercy and find grace to help in time of need" (Hebrews 4:16). We pray His Word because that is how we pray His will, and we have faith that He will do what He says:

> *"Now this is the* confidence *that we have in Him, that if we ask any-thing according to His will, He hears us. And we have the petitions that we have asked of Him."* 1 John 5:14

JESUS' MODEL FOR INTERCESSION

Jesus gave us a model of intercession, recorded in John 17, the night before His crucifixion. In verses 1-5 of this chapter, Jesus prayed for Himself, that both He and His Father would be glorified through Calvary and in the events that would follow. Then, in verses 6-19, we see our Lord passionately interceding for His disciples. And in verses 20-26, He prayed for all believers throughout the generations. This is our model: first we pray for our own needs, secondly for our "inner circle" of family and friends, and thirdly for the wider Church — and the Harvest (the nations) from which the Church will come. Chapters Fifteen through Eighteen of this book covered praying for the nations. Chapter Twenty focused on prayer for personal needs. This chapter will look at praying for those in our own circle of friends and acquaintances.

THE HARDEST MISSION FIELD

Sometimes those who are closest to us are the hardest "mission field" to impact. The Bible tells us that even Jesus' ministry was not accepted in His own hometown:

> "*When He had come to* His own country, *He taught them in their synagogue, so that they were astonished and said, 'Where did this man get this wisdom and these mighty works? Is this not the carpenter's son?'...* So they were offended at Him... *But Jesus said to them, 'A prophet is not without honor except in his own country, among his own relatives, and in his own house.' Now He could do no mighty work there...because of their unbelief."*
>
> Matthew 13:54-5 and Mark 6:4-6

It is amazing that, because of their unbelief, the Son of God was hindered from doing many mighty works there (see Matthew 13:58). So don't be surprised if your unsaved (or "carnal" Christian — see 1 Corinthians 3:1-3) family members don't appreciate your efforts to witness or to share spiritual matters. In praying for family and loved ones, some of the hardest cases may be those who resist the Gospel. But since the Word says it is God's will for them to be saved, we can pray with great faith. Peter tells us that the Lord is actually delaying His return so that none should be lost but that all would have the opportunity to repent and be saved. (2 Peter 3:8-9) This "all" includes our family, the Church, and the nations. God is waiting for His Harvest to be brought into the storehouse:

> "*And this gospel of the Kingdom will be preached in all the world as a witness to all the nations, and then the end will come."*
>
> Matthew 24:14

I have a reminder on my refrigerator that says, "When we work, we work; but when we pray, GOD works!" Even when nothing short of a miracle is needed, there is always hope through prayer. I have a friend whose husband had a problem with pornography. Her efforts to confront him were futile. But some time after turning it over to God in prayer, he gave up the bad habit on his own, admitting to her that it was wrong, and getting rid of all the offensive materials. Prayer is powerful because "**with God nothing [is] impossible**" (Luke 1:37).

THE POWER OF THE BLESSING

A Practice That Appears Throughout the Bible

Jacob, the son of Isaac, understood the power of the blessing. He wrestled with the angel of God all night and then said, "I will not let You go unless You *bless* me!" (Genesis 32:26). "Blessing" is a practice that appears throughout the Bible. In the Garden of Eden, God blessed His creation, saying, "Be fruitful and multiply" (Genesis 1:22 and 28). Later on, God told Abraham that He would bless him (make him a father of many nations) so that he could in turn *be* a blessing (his progeny could be a witness of God to the heathen). This is the Covenant blessing, still being fulfilled, that still belongs to Israel today.

Model Blessings

A model blessing is found in Numbers 6:24-27, where the Lord instructed Moses to tell Aaron and the other priests to bless the children of Israel, saying:

> " '*The* LORD *bless you and keep you; the* LORD *make His face shine upon you, and be gracious to you; the* LORD *lift up His countenance upon you, and give you peace.'* **So shall they put My name on the children of Israel, and I will bless them.**"

The Lord said that when the priests invoked this blessing upon the children of Israel, they were putting God's name on them, imparting His presence: "make His face shine" and "lift up His countenance." The principle is that *with the blessing comes the enabling — God's life and power — to accomplish it*. Just as this blessing enabled the twelve tribes of Israel to fulfill their destiny to conquer and settle the Promised Land, blessings which parents speak over their children today can direct and fulfill God's purposes for them. Following the example of the Aaronic priesthood, Scripture records that all of the patriarchs blessed their children. Jacob's blessing of his grandsons, Ephraim and Manasseh (see Genesis 48), is the model of the father's blessing that is still observed by the Jews today.

WORDS OF LIFE

Blessing can be simply speaking words of life and prosperity over someone (as opposed to criticism, which acts like a curse to keep people in bondage or hinder their development). Jesus told His disciples (Matthew 5:13 - 14): "You are the salt of the earth" and "You are the light of the world," while they were still unregenerate men struggling with fears, jealousy and anger. Yet He looked beyond their weaknesses and character flaws to see what they could be with God's love and power working in their lives. He spoke over them what He saw in the Spirit. And *what He said is what they became. The blessing imparts God's presence and activity into a life, bringing His healing, restorative, life-giving power.*

Just as Jesus looked beyond the weakness of the people in the Matthew 13 passage, we have to have similar vision when praying for children that have special needs and challenges. We need to look beyond the problems, disabilities and wounds and see the possibilities of what they can be with God's love and power working in their lives. For when we pray blessings on them, God's favor, life and power are released to fulfill the blessing. For instance, a blessing over a child struggling with a poor self-image might be something like: "Lord, bless (this child) with the assurance of Your love for her. Help her to know how special she is to You. Bless her with confidence in social settings, and bring a special friend into her life." There have been testimonies of barren wombs opening, wounded and abused children healed, and dysfunctional families restored as a result of God working through imparted blessings.

PRAYING FOR CHILDREN

There is a wonderful scriptural promise that we can claim for our children in Isaiah 44:3: "I will pour My Spirit on your descendants, and *My blessing* on your offspring."

There are many scriptures that we can pray over our children to bless them. The following list I accumulated over a twenty-year period of praying for our children.

SCRIPTURAL BLESSINGS TO PRAY OVER CHILDREN
Father, I invoke Your blessing upon my child according to Your Word:

- **To be strengthened with might by Your Spirit in his inner man**, that Christ may dwell in his heart through faith; that he may have power to grasp and know the immeasurable depth of the love of Christ; that he may be filled with wisdom and spiritual understanding to know the will of God...that he may live a life worthy of the Lord and may please Him in every way, bearing fruit in every good work, and growing in the knowledge of God. May he be strengthened with all power according to God's glorious might, so that he may have great endurance and patience, with a thankful heart (see Ephesians 3:16-19 and Colossians 1:9-12). Lord, complete the good work that You have begun in him (see Philippians 1:6).

- **With the desire and ability to do your will and walk in Your ways.** (Philippians 2:13) Father, may he hide Your Word in his heart that he might not sin against You (Psalm 119:11). Lead him into godliness, truth and the abundant (see John 10:10) and Spirit-filled (see Romans 12:11) life. And when the time comes, may he be equally yoked together with the helpmate of Your choice (see 2 Corinthians 6:14). May he walk in the courage of his convictions which are molded by Your will, and may his convictions become commitment and not compromise.

- **To walk in victory** in the power and protection of the Holy Spirit in all wisdom, diligence, godliness, kindness, humility, compassion and forgiveness (see Colossians 3:12-16). And may he walk in the Spirit, manifesting "love, joy, peace, longsuffering, gentleness, goodness, faith, meekness, [and self-control]" (see Galatians 5:22-25), KJV. May there be a release of supernatural ministry gifts and power by the Holy Spirit.

- **That You would guide him**, inclining his heart to You, to walk in all Your ways, and to keep Your commandments...that his heart (and body) may be perfect (and pure) with the Lord (see 1 Kings 8:57- 5 and 61)...and that You, Lord, would quicken his heart after righteousness, that he may be transformed by the renewing of his mind in Your Word (see Romans 12:1 and 2). Thank You that You will order his steps (see Psalm 37:23), and that he will hear only the voice of the Shepherd and not follow the voice of a stranger (see John 10:4 and 5).

- **That You would protect him**...that Your truth may be his shield and buckler (see Psalm 91:4). Thank You that You are his refuge and strength (see Psalm 91:2). Father, protect him from error and violence; the world and the flesh and the devil; accident, injury, and illness. Lord, strengthen him from falling to temptation and deliver him from the influence of the evil one (see Matthew 6:13). Thank you, Lord, that he abides under the shadow of the Almighty and that you give your angels charge over him to keep him in all his ways (Psalm 91:1 and 11).

- **That You would prosper him**...Thank You that he will be as a tree planted by streams of water, which yields its fruit in season, and whose leaves shall not wither, and whatever he does shall prosper (see Psalm1:3). Father, stir in him a hunger for truth and righteousness and fellowship with You, that he may both desire and know the presence of God. Bless him to grow up in the grace and knowledge of the Lord (2 Peter 3:18) and that he would always seek the Lord's will over his own (see Matthew 6:10). Father, may he pursue holiness and peace with all men (see Hebrews 12:14). May he be a doer of the Word, and not a hearer only (see James 1:22). May he love the Lord with all his heart, soul, mind and strength (see Matthew 22:37). seeking first the kingdom of God and His righteousness (Matthew 6:33). Whatever he does, may he work at it with all his heart, as for the Lord and not men (see Colossians 3:23). And may he continue to increase in wisdom and in favor with God and men (see Luke 2:52).

_____, "The Lord bless you and keep you. The Lord make His face to shine upon you and be gracious unto you. The Lord lift up His countenance upon you, and give you peace." Thank You, Father, for putting Your name on him, and releasing Your power into his life, as I bless him (see Numbers 6:24-27).

Thank You, Lord, that You will not let anything touch him today which is outside of Your perfect will!

IMPARTATION THROUGH THE LAYING ON OF HANDS

...New Job Blessing

The above blessing is to be spoken during prayer time. But laying your hands on and blessing your children with a few sentences as they go off to face the world each day is a good habit to develop. Reading scripture over them is a powerful way to invoke a blessing, especially for special occasions. After our son graduated from college, I prayed the blessings of Deuteronomy 28:2-8 and 13 (paraphrased) over him before he left for work on his first day at his new job:

> *"And all these blessings shall come upon you and overtake you, because you obey the voice of the LORD your God: Blessed shall you be wherever you go; blessed shall be all that belongs to you; blessed shall be your provision. Blessed shall you be when you come in, and blessed shall you be when you go out. The LORD will cause your enemies who rise against you to be defeated before your face; they shall come out against you one way and flee before you seven ways. The LORD will command the blessing on you in your storehouses and in all to which you set your hand, and He will bless you in the land which the LORD your God is giving you... And the LORD will make you the head and not the tail; you shall be above only, and not beneath, if you heed the commandments of the LORD your God."*

...Marriage Blessing

When our daughter got married, my husband blessed her and her husband (instead of offering the traditional "toast") during the reception following the ceremony. He placed his hand over their joined hands as he invoked the following blessing.

THE MARRIAGE BLESSING
- *Unconditional love reigns supreme in your life because the love of God is shed abroad in your hearts by the Holy Spirit (see Romans 5:5, KJV).*
- *Your love is patient and kind; it does not envy or boast. It is not rude, or self-seeking, or easily angered. It does not delight in evil, but rejoices in the truth. It will always protect, always trust, always hope and always persevere. Your love will never fail (see 1 Corinthians 13:4-8, NIV).*

- *You will be imitators of God, living a life of love, in humility, each esteeming the other as better than yourself* (see Ephesians 5:1 and Philippians 2:3).
- *You will submit to one another out of reverence to Christ* (see Ephesians 5:21) *(wife) will submit to and honor (husband) as unto the Lord. (husband) will love (wife) as Christ loved the church and gave Himself for her* (Ephesians 5:22 and 25).
- *You are together united with Christ, like-minded, having the same love, being one in spirit and purpose* (see Philippians 2:2).
- *What God has joined together, man will not separate* (see Mark 10:8).

PRAYING FOR UNSAVED LOVED ONES

BINDING AND LOOSING

In my daily prayers I often use the binding and loosing prayer strategy over my unsaved loved ones. First I remind the Lord of His Word that says that God "desires all men to be saved and to come to the knowledge of the truth" (1 Timothy 2:4); and further that He is "not willing that any should perish but that all should come to repentance (2 Peter 3:9)." I ask the Lord to bring my loved ones into life-changing encounters with the Living God, and for Him to establish the dominion of His throne — His sovereignty — in their lives. Then I bind them to a spirit of wisdom and revelation in the knowledge of God…that the eyes of their understanding may be enlightened to understand the hope to which He has called them and the riches of His glorious inheritance (see Ephesians 1:17-18). I loose them from anything that "exalts itself against the knowledge of God" (2 Corinthians 10:5), including religious spirits, pride, self-righteousness, self-sufficiency, deception of all kinds and fear.

Sometimes there are strongholds blocking salvation that require spiritual warfare, or more in-depth and targeted praying. At such times declaring the Word of Truth over them can bring powerful results. Following are some scriptures to pray:

SCRIPTURAL PRAYERS FOR SALVATION
- *I thank You, Lord, that You desire (___) to be saved and come to the knowledge of the truth* (see 1 Timothy 2:4).

- *I thank You, Lord, that You do not want (___) to perish, but that he/she may come to repentance* (see 2 Peter 3:9).
- *I thank You that wisdom and discretion will save him/her from the ways of wicked men* (see Proverbs 2:10-12, NIV).
- *I thank You that Your plans for (___) are for good and not for evil, to give him/her a future and a hope* (see Jeremiah 29:11).
- *I thank You that You will deliver and draw (___) to Yourself from every assault of evil. You will preserve and bring him/her safely into Your heavenly kingdom* (see 2 Timothy 4:18).
- *Father, thank you that (___) will be as a tree planted by the rivers of water that brings forth fruit in season, whose leaves shall not wither, and whatever he/she does shall proper* (see Psalm 1:3).
- *"I pray that out of God's glorious riches He may strengthen (___) with power through His Spirit in his/her inner being, so that Christ may dwell in (his/her) heart through faith. And I pray that (___), being rooted and established in love, may have power...to grasp how wide and long and high and deep is the love of Christ, and to know this love that surpasses knowledge — that (___) may be filled to the measure of all the fullness of God* (see Ephesians 3:16-19, NIV).
- *I ask You, Lord, to fill (___) with the knowledge of Your will through all spiritual wisdom and understanding. I pray that he/she may live a life worthy of the Lord, pleasing Him in every way, bearing fruit in every good work, growing in the knowledge of God, and being strengthened with all power through His glorious might so that he/she might have endurance and patience....Father, please rescue (___) from the dominion of darkness and bring him/her into the kingdom of the Son Your love, in whom she he/has redemption, the forgiveness of sins* (see Colossians 1:9-14, NIV).
- *I pray that (___) will come to his/her senses and escape from the trap of the devil, who has taken him/her captive to do his will* (see 2 Timothy 2:26, NIV).
- *Lord, strengthen (___) from falling to temptation and deliver him/her from the influence of the evil one* (see Matthew 6:13).
- *Thank you, Lord, for giving your angels charge over (___) to keep him/her in all her ways* (see Psalm 91:11).

PRAYING FOR DELIVERANCE — OVER PEOPLE

The following declarations are particularly effective as prayed over someone caught up in a cult or false religion, or any such deception.

BINDING AND LOOSING TO SET THE CAPTIVE FREE
Loose him/her from DECEPTION

Loose his/her mind, will and emotions from every fleshly and demonic influence, including...

- Loose him/her from a darkened mind, alienated from the life of God (see Ephesians 4:18).
- Loose him/her from the works of the flesh (see Galatians 5:19-21).
- Loose him/her from the "old man" which grows corrupt according to deceitful lusts (see Ephesians 4:22).
- Loose him/her from the deceiver and the anti-Christ spirit – the spirit of Islam, Mormonism, etc. (see 2 John 7).
- Loose him/her from the voice of the stranger (see John 10:5).
- Cut asunder the cords of the wicked that keep him/her bound (see Psalm 129:4, KJV).
- Loose him/her from the trap of the devil (see 2 Timothy 2:26, NIV).
- Loose him/her from the works and kingdom of darkness (see Romans 13:12).
- Loose him/her from every argument and pretension that sets itself up against the knowledge of God (see 2 Corinthians 10:5, NIV).

Bind him/her to TRUTH

Bind his/her mind, will and emotions to the will and purposes of God, including...

- Take captive every thought and make it obedient to Christ (see 2 Corinthians 10:5, NIV).
- Bind his/her mind to the mind of Christ (see 1 Corinthians 2:16).
- Bind him/her to a hunger and thirst after truth and righteousness (see John 14:6 and Matthew 5:6).
- Bind him/her to true faith and sound doctrine (see 1 Timothy 4:6).
- Bind him/her to spiritual transformation by the renewing of her mind (see Romans 12:2).
- Bind him/her to the "new man created according to God in true righteousness and holiness" (Ephesians 4:24).

- Bind him/her to the fruit of the Spirit (see Galatians 5:22-23).
- Bind him/her to the Truth and to the Spirit of Truth (see John 14:6 and 17).
- Bind him/her to hearing God's words and Word (see John 10:4 and 8:47).
- Bind him/her to abundant life in God (see John 10:10).
- Bind him/her to wisdom, knowledge, discretion and understanding (see Proverbs 2:1-12 and 16).
- Bind him/her to the Kingdom of God: righteousness, peace and joy in the Holy Spirit (see Romans 14:17).
- Bind him/her to reconciliation with God (see 2 Corinthians 5:20).
- Bind him/her to a pure heart, a good conscience, and sincere faith (see 1 Timothy 1:5).
- Bind him/her to belief in the name of the Lord Jesus Christ (see 1 John 3:23).
- Bind him/her to the spirit of wisdom and revelation in the knowledge of God, that the eyes of his/her understanding may be enlightened with truth (see Ephesians 1:17-18 and Colossians 1:9).

I call him/her forth as a child of God and into the place in His Kingdom that He has prepared for him/her.

PRAYING FOR DELIVERANCE — OVER TERRITORY

DEFILEMENT OF LAND

Sometimes the deliverance needed is larger scale than merely over a person. Land itself can become defiled and bring curses upon those who inhabit it. For example, the Lord God spoke to the nation of Israel concerning the defilement of the land brought on by the sexual sins of other wicked nations:

> *"Do not defile yourselves with any of these things; for by all these the nations are defiled, which I am casting out before you.* For the land is defiled; therefore I visit the punishment of its iniquity upon it, *and the land vomits out its inhabitants."*   Leviticus 18:24-25

As people groups throughout history surrender to such sinful lifestyles, it can have the effect of opening spiritual doors over nations which bring demonic activity and generational curses upon later inhabitants. We saw this principle demonstrated back in Chapters Eighteen and Nineteen when talking about the ancient demonic strongholds over Iran and Iraq.

CLEANSING THE LAND

This same principle of defilement is applicable on a smaller scale, such as over properties and buildings. In a discussion of "cleansing the land" as such, we need to first reestablish (from Chapter Seven) the authority of the Blood of the Atonement.

...The power of the Blood

Some key Scriptures, which we have already talked about previously, but we need to review, are:

- **Revelation 12:11**: *"And they* [Believers] *overcame him* [satan] *and by the BLOOD OF THE LAMB and the WORD of their testimony."*
- **Colossians 2:15**: *"having disarmed principalities and powers, He made a public spectacle of them, TRIUMPHING OVER THEM in it [the cross]."*

Jesus triumphed over satan with the Blood of His sacrifice, and that Blood continues to avail for that same victory for the Believer. In the Revelation scripture above, the "word of their testimony" is our declaration of faith in the victory of the cross. Our overcoming authority over the devil comes not from our own righteousness, but from the righteousness of Christ imparted to us (see 2 Corinthians 5:21) and through the power of His *cleansing Blood*:

- *"If we walk in the light as He is in the light, we have fellowship with one another, and the blood of Jesus Christ His Son* cleanses *us from all sin."* 1 John 1:7
- Jesus *"loved us and* washed *us from our sins in His own blood."* Revelation 1:5

Further Scriptures tell us that we have victory through the Blood of Jesus over all the power of sin and death:

- Christ *"is the Mediator of the new covenant...He has appeared to put away sin by the sacrifice of Himself.* With His own blood *He entered*

the Most Holy Place once for all, having obtained eternal redemption."
Hebrews 9:15, 26, and 12
- *"The sting of death is sin, and the strength of sin is the law. But thanks be to God, who gives us the victory through our Lord Jesus Christ."* 1 Corinthians 15:56-57

This Blood of the Covenant represents for us both a covering of protection, which demons cannot cross, and a mantle of authority. For through the Blood we are brought into God's family and share in the inheritance of Christ:

- *"For as many as are led by the Spirit of God, these are sons of God...and if children, then heirs — heirs of God and joint heirs with Christ."* Romans 8:14 and 17

What this means for us, practically, is that all that Jesus has and does belongs to, and is available to, us — not by virtue of our goodness or righteousness, but through His Blood Covenant with us. And so to His followers He has delegated His authority:

- *"Behold,* I give you the authority...*over all the power of the enemy, and nothing shall by any means hurt you."* Luke 10:19
- *"Most assuredly, I say to you, he who believes in Me, the* works that I do he will do also; *and greater works than these he will do..."* John 14:12

In light of all of this, we can declare with certainty that the Blood of the Lamb stands against all the power of the enemy, and against whatever plans he may be bringing against us or the person/situation we are praying for.

...Strategic operations

In cases where the land has become defiled (like in the opening Scripture from Leviticus 18) through generational and historical sins and iniquity, additional warfare is needed. In this scenario, I have found the following strategy to be powerful in cleansing defilement from land and property (buildings). In this strategy there are three distinct operations to perform: *Confront - Depose - Occupy.*

Confront: First we confront the demonic stronghold with the "Blood scriptures" above and declare the enemy's defeat according to Colossians 2:15 (above), and John 12:31, in which Jesus states: "Now is the judgment of this world; now the ruler of this world will be cast out." And again in Luke 10:18-19: "I saw Satan fall like lightning from heaven."

Depose: Then, we need to cancel any curses with the declaration of the word of our testimony (according to Revelation 12:11)

- **God turns curses into blessings:** *"but* the LORD your God turned the curse into a blessing for you, *because the* LORD *your God loves you."* Deuteronomy 23:5
- **God has laid the sure foundation, and any other will not stand:** *"Behold, I lay in Zion, a stone for a foundation, a tried stone, a precious cornerstone,* a sure foundation. Your covenant with death will be annulled, *and your agreement with Sheol will not stand."* Isaiah 28:16 and 18
- **Jesus is the Redeemer and Deliverer:**
  - *"Christ has* redeemed us from the curse *of the law, having become a curse for us."* Galatians 3:13
  - *"The Spirit of the* LORD *is upon Me...*to set at liberty those who are oppressed." Luke 4:18

Occupy: The words that the Lord told Joshua are ours today: *"Every place that the sole of your foot will tread upon I have given to you.*Have I not commanded you? Be strong and of good courage; do not be afraid, nor be dismayed, for the LORD your God is with you wherever you go (Joshua 1:3 and 9) Additionally, Jesus told His disciples to "Occupy till I come (Luke 19:13, KJV). Another powerful warfare "occupation" passage is Isaiah 14:22-27. Here the prophet speaks of God's judgment against Babylon and Assyria, which shared Babylonian culture and gods. In Scripture, "Babylon" prophetically represents the kingdom of this world, or the kingdom of darkness. It embodies the systems, powers and forces set up to thwart the Kingdom of God in the earth. In this passage, God declares judgment and destruction over these entrenched forces:

- Verse 22: **God will utterly annihilate the enemy:** " *'I will rise up...and cut off from Babylon the name and remnant, and offspring and posterity,' says the Lord."*
- Verse 23: **God will cleanse the land:** *"I will sweep it* [clean] *with the broom of destruction."*

- Verse 25: **God will deliver the people:** *"His yoke shall be removed from them, and his burden removed from their shoulders."*
- Verse 26: **God will destroy evil strongholds and deliver the people everywhere in the earth:** *"This is the purpose that is purposed against the whole earth, and this is the hand that is stretched out over all the nations."*
- Verses 24 and 27: **Because the Lord of Hosts has decreed it, it shall happen:** *"Surely...it shall come to pass, and as I have purposed, so it shall stand.... For the* LORD *of hosts has purposed, and who will annul it? His hand is stretched out, and who will turn it back?"*

...Summary

As we **occupy** the land, we can employ these and many other such passages that declare that the devil's failure is sure and complete. In summary, we can then:

1. CONFRONT satan with the Blood of the Lamb and the word of our testimony.
2. DEPOSE the enemy in the authority of that Blood and His name as we declare the curses broken, the covenants with Babylon annulled, the land cleansed from every defilement, and the people set free.
3. OCCUPY according to the commandment and Word of God, taking back the land and its occupants for the Kingdom of God.

REPENTANCE IS THE KEY

Considering land defilement from a national perspective, Scripture identifies at least three main examples of iniquity that are involved: sexual sins (as seen previously in Leviticus 18 passage), the shedding of innocent blood (such as Genesis 4:10), and broken covenants. In the United States, the sexual sins (especially in the Church) of homosexuality and pornography have brought defilement upon our land. Additionally, the innocent blood of aborted babies and African and Native Americans cries out to God for vindication from the land upon which it was spilled. Compounded by the

372 covenants made with Native American tribes and broken by our federal government, these iniquities continue to bring defilement upon our land and curses upon our people.

1 John 1:9 assures us that if we confess our sins before God, He is faithful and just to forgive us and to cleanse us from all unrighteousness. This applies nationally as well as personally. *The first step to cleanse iniquity off of land is REPENTANCE.* Since most of the actions that defile land have historical roots, the repentance in this case is "identificational." In other words, the intercessor *identifies* with those who were or are responsible for the defilement and stands in repentance FOR them. If representatives of the opposing parties are available, it is strategically important for them to reconcile through mutual repentance and forgiveness. For instance, our federal government is presently engaged in formulating an official "Resolution of Apology" to the Native American peoples of our land for the atrocities that we have committed as a nation to these rightfully "*First* Nations" peoples. What a powerful stream of restoration and healing such a resolution will release when it comes forth! And what a strategic focus for prayer in the meantime!

In conclusion, as we consider the positive spiritual influence of cleansing the land through *identificational repentance* and the previously mentioned strategic warfare operations, we see that all aspects of society can be affected. For example:

- Setting the captives free from the spiritual strongholds over the land and releasing them to hear and receive the Gospel.
- Creating a spiritual atmosphere where the government of God will influence the minds and the government of men.
- Creating a spiritual atmosphere influencing the educational system to come into alignment with God's purposes for our youth.
- Setting the stage for REVIVAL! (see 2 Chronicles 7:14)

Let us use the spiritual weapons and strategies God has given us to cleanse our land and usher in Revival!

Epilogue

WHAT DOES THE FUTURE HOLD?

A PROPHETIC PICTURE FROM THE PAST

Ezekiel 37 records the prophet Ezekiel's vision of the valley of dry bones. This is a prophetic picture of Israel being restored as a nation through which God will then glorify Himself before all the nations of the earth. In the vision, the Lord asked Ezekiel, "Can these bones live?" He then commanded Ezekiel to prophesy over the bones to bring life into them. "So I prophesied as He commanded me, and breath came into them, and they lived, and stood upon their feet, an exceedingly great army" (verse 10).

There is an army that the Lord is calling forth out of the Church today. By all appearances, the Church seems to be filled more with dry bones than mighty warriors. But the Lord of hosts (see Psalm 24:8-10) is assembling His troops. The roar of the Lion of Judah will be heard out of Zion (see Joel 3:16). The bones are coming together — and they WILL live! And they will go into battle, breaking up the fallow ground, sowing righteousness (see Hosea 10:12) and reaping the Harvest. The darkness will be eclipsed by the light as God's people arise and shine with the glory of the Lord upon them (see Isaiah 60:1-2). This prophetic picture is powerfully illustrated in a song recorded by Glory of Zion International Ministries, Inc., entitled, "Can These Dry Bones Live?"[1]:

I hear a roar out of Zion.
I hear a cry saying, "Send Judah forth!"
I see dark clouds, but I see a light.
I see an army of warriors — hope deferred within.
I hear a voice saying, "Can these dry bones live?" ... YES, they can!...

Though the grave has pursued them —
Though the enemy has robbed and destroyed —
And they have walked through the valley of the shadow of death...
Judah roars like a lion — Judah plows where the ground won't give.
And THE LORD WILL ACCOMPLISH ALL THAT HE HAS SAID.
You say, "Four more months and then comes the harvest."
I say, "Lift up your eyes, the Harvest is HERE!"
THIS is the Day - THIS is the Hour - NOW is the time - And WE are the people!

THE CALL TO INTERCESSION

The prophet Isaiah spoke of a time when God's people were in desperate need and there was no intercessor. Lying, hatred, murder and all kinds of violence, perversity and oppression were rampant. Justice and righteousness were "afar off," and truth had "fallen in the street." There was no light in the darkness. The iniquity of the people had separated them from God (see Isaiah 59:1-15). "The LORD saw it, and it displeased Him that there was no justice. He saw that there was no man, and wondered that there was no intercessor" (verses 15-16). The world is in a similar state today. And the Lord is still looking for intercessors to stand against the forces of evil and to pray His purposes into the earth. He has given us our marching orders:

"Lift up your eyes, the Harvest is HERE!" (see John 4:35).

THIS is the Day - THIS is the Hour - NOW is the time - And **YOU** are the people!

GOD IS WAITING

The Lord has further instructed us, in Jeremiah 33:3:

"Call to Me, and I will answer you, and show you great and mighty things which you do not know."

God is waiting to demonstrate His mighty power and to fulfill His prophetic Word and will in the destinies of men and nations:

"For as the rain comes down, and the snow from heaven,
And do not return there,
But water the earth,
And make it bring forth and bud,
That is may give seed to the sower
And bread to the eater,
So shall My word be that goes forth from My mouth;
It shall not return to Me void,
But it shall accomplish what I please,
And it shall prosper in the thing for which I sent it."

Isaiah 55:10-11

In this prophetic picture, the "seed" represents the *promise* of God. The "bud" represents the *promise in process* of being fulfilled. Like the flower that has the full bloom in the seed and the bud, the Word of God carries in it the "full bloom" of the promise — the fulfillment of the Word. But in order for the seed to grow and the bud to blossom and bring forth fruit, it must be watered. The rain and snow represent the **intercession** of the saints to activate the Holy Spirit to "water" the "seed" and bring it to fruition. The "bread" then represents the promise *received* ("eaten") — the fulfillment of God's Word in the earth: His Kingdom come and His will done.

As we said previously, God is waiting to demonstrate His mighty power. And He is looking for intercessors who will partner with Him to bring His Kingdom into the earth and accomplish His will in the lives of men and nations. The question He is asking today is:

Will you be one of them?

---

[1] John Dickson, LeAnn Squier and Dr. Chuck D. Pierce, "Can These Dry Bones Live?" (Glory of Zion International Ministries, Inc., c2002).

For further information regarding Barbara's ministry,
you may contact her at:

BLpotts@comcast.net

Why are humans given chance after chance to be redeemed but angels chose wrong once and are condemned forever? Is it because we're different and they can't be saved? Or is there a history we don't know?   4/8/13